China's Communist Party

China's Communist Party

Atrophy and Adaptation

David Shambaugh

Woodrow Wilson Center Press
Washington, D.C.

University of California Press
Berkeley   Los Angeles   London

EDITORIAL OFFICES

Woodrow Wilson Center Press
Woodrow Wilson International Center for Scholars
One Woodrow Wilson Plaza
1300 Pennsylvania Avenue, N.W.
Washington, D.C. 20004-3027
Telephone: 202-691-4010
www.wilsoncenter.org

ORDER FROM

University of California Press
California/Princeton Fulfillment Services
1445 Lower Ferry Road
Ewing, N.J. 06818-1424
Telephone: 1-800-822-6657
www.ucpress.edu

2 4 6 8 9 7 5 3

ISBN 978-0-520-26007-8

Library of Congress Cataloging-in-Publication Data

Shambaugh, David L.
   China's Communist party : atrophy and adaptation / David Shambaugh.
      p. cm.
   Includes bibliographical references and index.
   ISBN-13: 978-0-520-26007-8 (paper)
   1. Zhongguo gong chan dang. 2. Communism—China. 3. China—Politics and government—
2002– I. Title.
   JQ1519.A5S44   2007
   324.251′075—dc22

2007046834

To my professors

Contents

Tables and Figures   x

Acknowledgments   xi

1   Introduction: The Chinese Communist Party
after Communism   1

2   The Western Discourse on Communist Party-States   11

3   The Western Discourse on the Chinese Communist
Party-State   23

4   The Chinese Discourse on Communist Party-States   41

5   The Chinese Discourse on Noncommunist Party-States   87

6   Rebuilding the Party: The Ideological Dimension   103

7   Rebuilding the Party: The Organizational Dimension   128

8   Staying Alive: Can the Chinese Communist Party Survive?   161

Notes   183

Index   221

Tables and Figures

Tables

2.1 Western Assessments of Factors and Causes in the
Collapse of Communist Power   18

4.1 Chinese Assessments of Factors Contributing to the
Collapse of the Soviet Union   62

7.1 Central Committee Turnover Rates at Party Congresses   153

8.1 Factors in the Collapse of Communist Power: China
in Comparison   162

Figures

4.1 Chinese Analysis of Soviet Reforms and Collapse   55

7.1 County-Level Cadre Postsecondary Education   147

Acknowledgments

This study has grown out of a long-standing interest I have had in the evolution of communist-type political systems. These (neo-)Leninist political systems contain many elements in common, although each evolves in its own distinct political culture. I have long been convinced that to adequately explain the political evolution of the People's Republic of China, one must understand and appreciate how communist-type political systems operate, the rather predictable stages through which they pass, their bureaucratic institutions, and their instruments of rule—all of which set them apart from other types of political systems.

My interest in communist party-states grew out of my university education. It was initially ignited by a fiery Marxist professor (John Ehrenberg) at the University of New Mexico, but it mushroomed in the fertile environment of the Institute of Sino-Soviet Studies at George Washington University, where I completed my undergraduate studies. The Sino-Soviet Institute was singularly devoted to the comparative and individual analysis of communist systems (one of the few of its kind in the world), and there was a nexus of professors under whom I trained and who stimulated my interest in the subject: Charles Elliott, Andrew Gyorgy, Harold Hinton, William Johnson, Carl Linden, Franz Michael, Vladimir Petrov, Gaston Sigur, Richard Thornton, and others. Professors Hinton, Michael, and Johnson also grounded me in the scholarly study of China, while Sigur, Hinton, and Michael triggered my study of the international politics of Asia. Their monthly Sino-Soviet Colloquium offered invaluable exposure to several leading international scholars in the field of comparative communism: Seweryn Bialer, Jurgen Domes, Jerry Hough, Chalmers Johnson, Richard Lowenthal, Richard (Dixie) Walker, and others.

Subsequently, at the Paul H. Nitze School of Advanced International Studies at Johns Hopkins University, where I did my M.A. studies in international affairs, George Liska, Robert Lystad, Bruce Parrott, Gareth Porter, and James Reardon-Anderson taught seminars and directed independent studies on individual and comparative communist party-states that offered further case studies and perspectives. It was here, for example, that I was introduced to the study of interest groups and different professional sectors (e.g., scientists) in communist societies.

Subsequently, at the University of Michigan, where I went for doctoral training in political science, I was again the beneficiary of a unique set of professors knowledgeable in comparative communist systems. Alfred G. Meyer, one of the true doyens of the field, taught a stimulating first-semester field seminar and later directed both an independent study and served on my Ph.D. dissertation committee. Al Meyer was one of those rare professors who would give a curious student seemingly endless hours of his time, patiently explaining the lacunae of Marxist-Leninist theory while sparking curiosities and linkages into related areas of political philosophy and comparative political systems. Al Simkus and Martin King Whyte, both sociologists, taught a stimulating research seminar on comparative socialist societies. Robert Dernberger taught a course on comparative command economies. William Zimmerman, a specialist in Soviet politics and foreign policy, taught a course on comparative communist foreign policies and directed an independent study on change in communist leaderships. My choice of dissertation topic, China's America watchers' perceptions of the United States, was stimulated by Zimmerman's classic book *Soviet Perspectives on International Relations, 1956–1967* (Princeton University Press, 1969). Zvi Gitelman opened my eyes to East European communist systems. Ron Inglehart, a world renowned expert on political elites, explained the various theories and modalities of elite circulation in communist and noncommunist systems. Larry Mohr helped me understand organization theory and bureaucratic politics, and my adviser—the late Michel Oksenberg—encouraged me to apply them to communist and authoritarian systems. It was Mike who told me pointedly my first day on campus, as I was trying to work out my course schedule, "If you want to understand China, you have to understand bureaucracy. If you want to understand communist systems, you have to understand bureaucracy." Off I dove into the pathologies of large hierarchical organizations. Finally, one could not have asked for more knowledgeable specialists in Chinese politics than I had at Michigan, who themselves were equally interested in comparative communist systems: Michel Oksenberg, Kenneth Lieberthal, and Allen Whiting. All three brought comparative communist perspectives into their teaching about China, and each had their own unique impact on my intellectual development and life.

To all these former professors, I owe an enormous and lasting intellectual debt. One could not have asked for better teachers and mentors.

Although the field of comparative communist studies collapsed overnight along with the Soviet Union and East European party-states in the period 1989–91, the field's theoretical and empirical findings from before that time continue, I believe, to offer many valuable insights for analysts of the four remaining communist party-states on earth: China, Cuba, North Korea, and Vietnam. China specialists are, I believe, well advised to study and understand the continuing evolution of the Chinese political system through this prism.

I have also benefited greatly from discussions and interactions with, and reading the writings of, contemporary colleagues who work on Asian, Chinese, Russian, and Central European politics. I wish to single out these colleagues for having a particularly influential impact on my thinking: Richard Baum, Thomas Bernstein, Kjeld Erik Brødsgaard, Zbigniew Brzezinski, Cheng Li, Bruce Dickson, Joseph Fewsmith, Michael McFaul, Alice Lyman Miller, Andrew Nathan, Gilbert Rozman, Susan Shirk, and Andrew Walder. Each one has been a major contributor to the study of communist party-states, and I am honored to have had the opportunity to interact with and learn from them over the years. Professors Brødsgaard, Dickson, Rozman, and Walder were also kind enough to read and offer many useful comments on the manuscript of this book.

This study also benefited from the help of a variety of institutions, bookstores, and libraries in China, Hong Kong, and the United States. In China, the International Department of the Chinese Communist Party and the Institute of Central European and Central Asian Studies (formerly the Institute of Soviet and East European Studies) of the Chinese Academy of Social Sciences were particularly helpful. In Hong Kong, the unmatched library resources of the Universities Service Center at the Chinese University of Hong Kong offered many valuable materials and a conducive research environment on several visits. In the United States, I was able to test out some draft chapters at the Modern China Seminar of Columbia University's East Asian Institute. But I particularly owe an enormous debt of gratitude to the Woodrow Wilson International Center for Scholars, where I was fortunate to spend a sabbatical year as a fellow in residence during the period 2002–3. The Woodrow Wilson Center offered a wonderful intellectual and collegial atmosphere, where I did much reading and thinking and began writing this book.

Although I got a good start on the book at the Woodrow Wilson Center, the available time there did not afford completion. Following my year's fellowship there, my return to full-time teaching and administration at George Washington University inevitably slowed down the book's completion. Fortunately, the Smith Richardson Foundation came to the rescue with another fellowship that made possible academic leave during the years 2005–6 and enabled me to complete the book. I am most grateful to the Smith Richardson Foundation; to its International Security Program officer, Alan Song; and to its board and several project evaluators for not only awarding me the grant but also helping me think through and sharpen the scope of the study.

In addition to the Woodrow Wilson Center and the Smith Richardson Foundation, I am indebted to George Washington University's Academic Excellence Initiative and the Sigur Center for Asian Studies for other research and travel grants. Without this support, the project never would have been completed.

I also could not have completed this study without the assistance of a series of fine student research assistants at George Washington and the Woodrow Wilson Center: Rosalie Chen was my full-time research assistant for two years, and she became a model against whom I will judge all future research assistants. Han Enze, Wang Liang, Laura Paler, Liang Sun, Tseng Yisuo, and Li Yuan and all served as research assistants for different periods of time, and I am truly appreciative to all of them for their time and valuable assistance.

Finally, I owe a special debt to my family. This includes our faithful golden retriever Sandi, who literally stayed by my side throughout the writing of the book. I also thank my wife of twenty-five years, Ingrid, and our two fine sons, Christopher and Alexander. Chris and Alex frequently showed interest in what Daddy was writing—I only wish that I could have explained more cogently to them what this book is about. Perhaps as they grow older, they can read it for themselves and better understand what I was trying to explain.

Washington, D.C.
July 2007

China's Communist Party

1

Introduction: The Chinese Communist Party after Communism

Few, if any, issues affect the future of China—and hence all the nations that interact with it—more than the nature of its ruling party and government. Since 1949, that has been the Chinese Communist Party (CCP).[1] This study assesses the strengths and weaknesses, durability and adaptability, and potential longevity of the CCP as the ruling party in China. Its focus is on the party as an *institution* rather than on the political system writ large (which would necessarily include the State Council, National People's Congress, provincial and local governments and congresses, and other nonparty actors). This is an important distinction for readers to grasp at the outset, lest they wonder why a whole range of factors—ranging from ethnic minorities and the economy to Taiwan and foreign relations—are not considered as issues affecting CCP rule. Of course, ultimately, *everything* that occurs within China and involves it externally affects the CCP. However, the scope of this study is much narrower, because it concentrates on the party as an institution.

The Party's Period of Introspection— Toward Lessons for Longevity

Why has the CCP survived in power when so many other communist parties have fallen from power? What lessons has the CCP learned from the collapse of these communist party-states and other ruling party systems (surviving communist states, single-party authoritarian states, multiparty systems, and social democratic systems)? How has the CCP analyzed its own condition, and how has this analysis been fused with the study of other systems? How have these lessons been applied in China since 1989? Will

1

the CCP endure as the ruling party in China? These are the central questions that animate this book.

The study argues and demonstrates that, after a period of catharsis in the early 1990s, following the cataclysmic events of 1989 in China and the subsequent collapse of communist ruling parties in the Soviet Union and Eastern Europe, the CCP undertook very systematic assessments of the causes of collapse of these other ruling parties, as well as analyzing the range of internal and external challenges to itself. This process of understanding the reasons and precipitating causes for the collapse of these other party-states was protracted (resulting in more than a decade of introspection and debate), but it was also infused with a sense of immediacy and urgency: What lessons should the CCP learn from the implosion and demise of these other regimes that might help it avoid a similar fate?

Thus, this internal CCP assessment was not an idle exercise in academic research among some Marxist theoreticians—the research spanned a number of institutions and had very practical implications for both the CCP's "general line" (*Zhongyang luxian*) and its longevity. The internal Chinese analyses of the causes of collapse of the USSR produced debates and differing emphases over time. But there was broad agreement that a range of factors contributed to the overthrow of Mikhail Gorbachev, the Communist Party of the Soviet Union, and the Soviet Union itself. Unlike many Western analyses—which tended toward a singular emphasis on Gorbachev's individual actions and failings—Chinese analysts took a much broader and historical view and offered a more systemic analysis of the multiple reasons for collapse.

These assessments in turn have triggered a range of intraparty reforms, as well as reforms affecting other sectors of the state, society, and economy. While *reacting* to the events in former communist party-states, the CCP has been very *proactive* in instituting reforms within itself and within China. The reforms have been sweeping in scope and have collectively been intended to strengthen the party's ruling capacity.

The totality and efficacy of these reforms belies the prevailing general image among scholars and journalists in the West (including those based in China) that there has not been any political reform in China and that the Chinese political system remains an ossified Leninist state that will eventually succumb to the inevitable march of democracy.[2] Western analysts tend to not pay much attention to these reforms because they are incremental and hard to track, and because they take place within a single-party system and are aimed at strengthening—rather than replacing—that system.

Many Western analysts seem to believe that if reforms are not protodemocratic, they are not valid. Yet the CCP has zero interest in transitioning to a Western, or even an Asian, democratic system of competitive parties. Its principal goal is to strengthen its rule and remain in power as a single ruling party.

The political reforms also belie the other accepted image in the West that the CCP only sustains its rule on the twin pillars of economic growth and nationalism. To be sure, these are two key sources of its legitimacy—but they are far from sufficient explanations for its sustained ruling capacity. Nor is coercion sufficient for it to maintain control over time. Even one-party states need to periodically relegitimate themselves by addressing the needs of different constituencies within the nation.

The political reforms also belie a third prevalent image in the Western media—that China is chronically beset by multiple socioeconomic weaknesses and tensions that could ignite at any time.[3] This combustible environment, it is argued, is both the result of the political system and a threat to it. This study argues that while such structural weaknesses and tensions exist, they are not so acute as to threaten the CCP's continued rule.

One thing is certain: The CCP is definitely *not* awaiting the inevitable collapse of its power. Though it is keenly aware that implosion *is* one possibility, its leaders and cadres are also betting that such a terminal fate can be avoided through such introspection, adaptation, and implementation of preemptive reforms and policies.

The Party's Simultaneous Atrophy and Adaptation

Along with elucidating the CCP's efforts to adapt and reform, the other principal argument of the study is that the CCP has been in a progressive state of *atrophy* for many years. Some would date this declining condition to 1958 and the Great Leap Forward, some to 1966 and the Cultural Revolution, some to the post-1978 reforms, and others to 1989 and the Tiananmen Square suppression. Whatever starting date one selects, it is evident from a wide variety of indicators that the CCP, *as an institution,* has been in a state of progressive decline in terms of its control over various aspects of the intellectual, social, economic, and political life of the nation. The CCP's traditional instruments of control—propaganda, coercion, and organization—have all atrophied and eroded considerably over time, although they remain effective tools of party control. Globalization and China's multifaceted interactions with the outside world have further undermined the party's control over society. The CCP today also currently faces pressing challenges of increasing social stratification and inequality, widespread corruption, pervasive unemployment, rising crime, and rural unrest.

Thus, the subtitle of this study—*atrophy and adaptation*—captures twin, simultaneous processes that the CCP has been experiencing for a number of years. Whether the reforms that the CCP has undertaken will prove sufficient to indefinitely sustain itself in power is, of course, the proverbial $64,000 question. Thus far, however, they have been sufficient to keep it in power (and even to strengthen its grip), and this study concludes that the reforms' continued implementation will help it further consolidate its power. Yet the party finds itself coping with a constant cycle of reform-readjust-reform-readjust . . . , whereby each set of reforms triggers certain consequences (some expected, others unexpected) that in turn cause readjustments and further reforms. It is an inexorable dynamic in which the party is simultaneously proactive and reactive, and is only partially in control of its own fate. Thus, for the party, there is a premium placed on being adaptable and flexible. This is probably *the* single most important conclusion the CCP reached in its postmortem of the USSR's collapse: that a certain recipe for collapse is an ossified party-state that has a dogmatic ideology, entrenched elites, dormant party organizations, and a stagnant economy and that is isolated from the international community.

We should certainly not take for granted that the CCP will remain in power perpetually, just because it has been the ruling party in China since 1949. To do so would be naive in the extreme and would ignore the principal lesson of the collapse of the Soviet Union and other communist party-states from 1989 to 1992, as well as a number of authoritarian one-party states across the world. The Soviet and East European experiences are particularly salutary. As chapter 2 makes clear, virtually no Western specialists (except Zbigniew Brzezinski) predicted or accurately forecast the implosion of those regimes. Though there may have been a good deal of political *hope* in the West that they would collapse (and the containment and "peaceful evolution" policies of the Cold War era were designed in large part to produce just that outcome), the actual dénouements of those regimes were neither foreseen nor forecast. It was an operative assumption of most Sovietologists that, despite occasional challenges, the power of those regimes was not really threatened and that, in any event, they possessed a number of coercive and other instruments that would enable them to maintain power. These assumptions were obviously wrong—or, at least, the coercive instruments were insufficient to the task.

Thus, to adopt the same analytic logic to the CCP today would be seriously remiss. Just because a party has ruled for a long period of time does not, ipso facto, mean that it will do so indefinitely. This is *not,* however, to predict that all such parties will eventually implode and lose power. There is no such iron law of governments—communist or otherwise. One-party states can indeed remain in power for long periods of time, and they possess a variety of tools and tactics to do so. The "end of history" is not inevitable.[4] Nor do all such states inevitably "transition" and morph into democracies, as much of the literature on "transitology" and comparative democracy suggests. Some party-states' strategies and tactics are reactive and defensive, whereas others' are proactive and offensive. The latter tend to offer better chances for survival than the former, but a combination is usually advisable. Doing nothing or simply strengthening the coercive powers of the state are insufficient. If they are wise, single ruling parties will constantly try to adapt themselves and their government to new circumstances—yet this is a treadmill and balancing act difficult to manage and maintain.

Adaptation is the key concept here. Political parties, even communist ones, are like plants. If they do not receive sufficient nutrients and sunlight, they will ossify and die; yet if they receive such stimuli, they can continue to grow in a dynamic way. Indeed, the danger of ossification and death can be just such a spur to adaptation and growth. Moreover, ossification *and* adaptation are not necessarily mutually exclusive; they often exist and proceed in tandem.

This is what has been occurring in China. The CCP has exhibited many classic symptoms of an atrophying and decaying Leninist party—but, at the same time, it is also showing itself capable of significant adaptation and reform in a number of key areas. Whether or not this adaptation will be sufficient to forestall or reverse the decay and save the regime in the long run remains an open question and a matter of great debate among China watchers. Some predict collapse, others see retrenchment, some envision lengthy stagnation, and a few see signs of meaningful reform, while many think the party-state and nation can "muddle through" without significant alteration of the political status quo.

Whatever the ultimate outcome, it is a question with monumental implications not only for the people of China but also the nations of Asia and the world. Whether the CCP can survive is no idle academic question—it is as central a practical policy issue as exists in international affairs today. If it does survive, the CCP will accomplish something that no other communist party-state has been able to do: adapting and transforming itself from a classic Leninist party into a new kind of hybrid party. And it must be remembered that this new hybrid is growing in the large garden (to continue the metaphor) of Chinese political culture and history. China had a government and a political culture long before it encountered Leninism and the CCP— although, as Lucian Pye has reminded us, the indigenous Confucian political culture was very conducive to embracing Leninism.[5] This cultural and historical reservoir feeds the soil in which this new hybrid is growing.

What this means in practice is that the CCP today is engaged in a historically unprecedented political experiment. For more than a century, since the "Self-Strengthening Movement" of the 1870s, China has been a "borrowing" culture—scanning the globe for appropriate models and ideas that could be imported and grafted onto indigenous roots—creating, as I have argued elsewhere, an "eclectic state."[6]

The political hybrid that the CCP is attempting to become today is born out of its study of the reasons that the Soviet and East European regimes collapsed but is also very much informed by its study of other modernizing and newly industrialized states, particularly in East Asia, Western Europe, and Latin America. In other words, the CCP is learning not only negative lessons from the former communist party-states but also positive lessons from noncommunist political systems. This is quite natural, because China is now reaching the stage of development that many Asian, European, and Latin countries have already entered, and there are numerous lessons to be learned.

One of the principal lessons China can learn from these other countries is that after societies reach this stage of industrializing development— where wealth is created and poverty is alleviated, the populace reaches a modest standard of living and possesses most basic consumer durables, and a middle class begins to emerge—is that the task of government increasingly is to provide a range of core public goods—health care, safety, education, environmental protection, social welfare, and so on—to the population. Consequently, the nature and challenges of *governance* become different than for either a developing country or a socialist society.

Thus the policy instruments, and the very nature of politics itself, must adapt to such new circumstances. In some respects, Leninist systems are well positioned to address many of these governance challenges, because they often require a "strong state" (capacity) to do so. In other respects, however, Leninist systems are not well equipped to respond to the changing demands and needs of society—precisely because they are intrinsically top-down "mobilization" regimes rather than regimes that possess the feedback mechanisms to hear and respond to aggregated social needs and demands. Democracies are obviously far better prepared to receive and respond to such societal feedback, given their electoral politics, civil society, legislatures, open media, interest groups, and other mechanisms for aggregating disparate demands. Thus a Leninist system can be both an asset and a liability as a nation grapples with the new demands of modernization.

This initial phase of industrialization and modernization also often results in various social inequities. Coastal areas grow faster than interior areas; prosperous inner city cores are ringed by poor peripheries; income disparities and social stratification quickly become pronounced; rent seeking and exploitation by the owner classes become widespread; corruption flourishes, and the local state (if not the national state) is infected, resulting in predatory practices; and so on. The phenomenon of "Latin Americanization" arises. Some believe that this is China's future—even present.[7]

This is the stage—the transition from being a developing country to a newly industrialized one—that much of China has now entered. As a result, the challenges the CCP faces in maintaining its power and legitimacy increasingly involve governance and providing public goods. This is a new kind of revolution for a Leninist party: the revolution of rising expectations. Thus, it is not enough for the CCP to identify what went wrong in the Soviet Union and Eastern Europe, and to try and correct those same maladies that exist in China—the CCP must also *simultaneously* effectively address the increasing pressures for good governance and public goods. These are not simply issues on the government's agenda but are more and more the expectations of the mass populace. If they are not met effectively, the CCP's legitimacy will be further undermined.

Even communist and authoritarian single party-states require popular legitimacy to sustain their rule. Control and coercion can sustain despots and dictators in power for some time, but ultimately they need to ground their claim to power in some kind of popular support. Beyond individual leaders, ruling parties in such states need to adapt to changing circumstances to renew and strengthen their power. Ossified party organizations, which only exercise top-down methods of control without offering bottom-up channels of societal input, are a sure indicator of atrophy and a disintegrating state. Such moribund regimes may be able to hang onto power for a period of time, but they are in fact infected with a deeply corrosive cancer.

Today, the CCP faces a variety of very profound challenges, many of them systemic and fundamental to its rule. This study examines many of these challenges, discusses steps being taken by the party to tackle them, and assesses the efficacy of these efforts.

Although the CCP today confronts many problems, each has its own origins and consequences. Some of the challenges the CCP faces are intrinsic to single party-states—such as leadership succession. Some (as noted above) are the result of the broad processes associated with socioeconomic modernization—such as sharpened social stratification, the demand for public goods, rising corruption, and growing pressures for an enfranchised civil society. Some are of the party's own making—such as widespread alienation and cynicism in society about politics in general and the party's leadership in particular (both of which have contributed to the legitimacy and identity crises the CCP experiences today). Some are the result of the declining efficacy of the coercive tools of an authoritarian or (formerly) totalitarian state—such as rising crime, dissent, and intellectual diversity. Some are the product of the growth of a market economy—such as the party's inability to monopolize the distribution of goods and services (hence breaking "neotraditional" networks of those formerly dependent on such resources). Some—such as corruption—are the result of an insufficient rule of law, political checks and balances, and transparency. Some are the product of organizational atrophy within party cells and committees, particularly in the countryside—or the absence of party organs in newly emergent commercial enterprises. Though many of these phenomena have indigenous origins, no doubt many problems confronted by the CCP are also stimulated by China's "opening to the outside world" and the attendant manifestations of globalization and interdependence that buffet the country on a daily and increasing basis.

All these phenomena (and others) are apparent in present-day China. They cumulatively add up to a comprehensive set of challenges for the CCP. Taken together, they pose the problem of how the party can remain relevant in the extremely complex environment of contemporary China. If it fails to remain relevant, it is valid to wonder whether it can endure as a ruling party.

If the CCP is to remain in power without having to resort to force and coercion, it must effectively develop sufficient responses to the aforementioned challenges. To be sure, the CCP seems aware of a number of these problems and challenges (although it may not define them in the same way), and the party and state leadership are attempting to address them. As a political institution, the party itself is also attempting to adapt to new challenges and circumstances by attempting to broaden its membership base, promoting a new generation of leaders, reformulating its ideological content, appealing to nationalist impulses in society, strengthening its organizational apparatus throughout the country, and opening the channels of discourse within the party and between the party-state and society. Yet one wonders if these efforts are not too little, too late.

This study explores these questions and argues that, thus far, it has *not* been too little, too late. Other knowledgeable China watchers disagree and argue that the party-state is in a kind of free-fall owing to a variety of systemic maladies.[8] The central conclusion of this study, however, is that the CCP is adapting fairly (but not entirely) effectively to meet many of these challenges, has learned the negative lessons of other failed communist party-states, and is proactively attempting to reform and rebuild itself institutionally—thereby sustaining its political legitimacy and power. Whether the CCP can continue to make the necessary adaptations and enact the necessary reforms is, of course, an open question. So far, so good—but this is no guarantee of continued success.

Organization of the Book

Chapters 2, 3, and 4 sequentially develop the argument outlined above. Because this study intentionally and explicitly seeks to view the CCP through a comparative lens, chapter 2 summarizes the assessments made by Western experts of the generic issues that confronted the communist party-states in the Soviet Union and Eastern Europe and that led to their downfall. Chapter 3 assesses how foreign China scholars see the evolution and current state of the CCP. Chapter 4 then turns the analysis to the CCP's own internal assessments of the reasons for the collapse of the Soviet and Eastern European party-states, and what lessons should be learned by the CCP, as well as those communist party-states that have survived.

Chapter 5 briefly considers the CCP's assessments of other party-states in Asia, the Middle East, Europe, and Latin America. This comparative background provides the necessary context for explaining the origins and nature of CCP reforms since the early 1990s. Chapter 6 then examines the CCP's internal discourse and new initiatives in the ideological realm, which have served as the theoretical rationale for various party reforms. Chapter 7 analyzes a number of these reforms in the organizational (*zuzhi*) realm, the CCP's self-assessment of its own shortcomings and challenges, and its program of action for dealing with them and improving its "governing capacity" (*zhizheng nengli*). The study then concludes in chapter 8 with a net assessment of the CCP's current situation and potential longevity.

2

The Western Discourse on
Communist Party-States

There is no shortage of theorizing by social scientists and policy analysts about the evolution of communist parties and party-states. Before the collapse of the party-states in Eastern Europe and the former Soviet Union, and throughout the prolonged period of the Cold War, the study of "comparative communism" was a bona fide subfield within comparative politics and comparative sociology.[1] During the Cold War, a whole generation of students and scholars cut their teeth and came of professional age studying these parties and party-states. A large number of books were published, and prestigious journals such as *Problems of Communism, Studies in Comparative Communism, China Quarterly, Slavic Review* became staples for the field.[2] American philanthropic foundations—such as Ford, Luce, Rockefeller, Scaife, and Smith Richardson—played major roles in establishing and underwriting programs at leading American universities on the Soviet Union, East European and Slavic states, the People's Republic of China, other Asian communist states and insurgencies, and Cuba and Latin American Marxist communist movements. Thousands of American students benefited from the National Defense Foreign Language Act to fund the costs of their graduate training, including in the languages of the communist world. To be sure, the U.S. government was proactively involved in supporting and recruiting students into government service and intelligence analysis. Through government-funded research institutions, such as the RAND Corporation, a large number of studies of the communist world were supported. Through bona fide institutions, such as the German Marshall Fund of the United States, or via front organs covertly funded by the Central Intelligence Agency (CIA), such as the Congress on Cultural Freedom, the analytical (and propaganda) effort was also pursued overseas.[3]

Just as the postwar rise of communist states stimulated the development of the field in the West, so too did their collapse during 1989–91 cause considerable introspection in this scholarly community. The successive demise of communist party-states in the former Soviet bloc induced a collective gestalt and produced a veritable cottage industry of such scholarship and postmortem analyses.[4] Inside the U.S. government, similar fingers were being pointed—as the shivering accusation "intelligence failure" rang through the corridors of Congress and the CIA. In fact, a declassified set of the CIA's intelligence estimates from the period 1989–91 shows that its record was quite good.[5] Though it did not predict the collapse of these regimes per se, its analyses did a very good job of identifying the indicators and the severity of the strains that afflicted the former Soviet Union and its client states in Eastern Europe. Two other sets of declassified CIA intelligence analyses, released in 2004 and 2007, respectively, shed light on the CIA's assessments of China from 1948 to 1976, including Sino-Soviet relations.[6]

Following the implosion of the Soviet bloc, a political triumphalism unfortunately infected the American government and political class, with pronouncements that the United States had "won" the Cold War—and therefore the "end of history" had arrived with the total "victory" of liberalism and capitalism over communism.[7] Fortunately, the scholarly community was not seized with such self-congratulation. Rather, scholars wrestled with the perplexing and empirical questions "How could this happen?" and "Why didn't we predict it?"[8] As a whole, the academic community was also criticized for failing to predict the political earthquake. To my knowledge, the only analyst to actually predict the implosion of the Soviet state was Zbigniew Brzezinski.[9]

Although it did not have the same political hue as the "Who lost China?" recriminations fifty years earlier, the dynamic was similar. As both a political act of self-defense and an empirical exercise, the field of Soviet and East European studies undertook an introspective review of its analytical record and the assumptions that underlay previous scholarship. Leading journals such as *Problems of Communism* sponsored large symposia and dedicated whole issues to trying to explain both the reasons for the collapse and the failure of the scholarly community to anticipate them.[10]

If this retrospective postcollapse literature has a central thread, it is that there is no singular path to "extinction" for communist party-states.[11] Though there are commonalities and pathologies apparent in the Soviet and East European cases, there was no singular "path dependency" that brought these regimes down. Each had its own unique features and imploded through a different combination of variables. Consequently, each has experienced varied experiences on the transitional path from communism to democracy,[12] while some communist parties have regenerated themselves into other forms of authoritarian regimes.[13]

Although communist party-states do not follow identical paths through their lifetimes or into extinction, implicit in this study is the belief that China's political evolution is best viewed through the comparative lens of Leninist systems. Many of the characteristics of and challenges to these regimes are generic and comparable in nature. Much about China and the Chinese Communist Party can be illuminated when viewed through this comparative lens. Recognizing this, I agree with Andrew Walder that in some ways China has outgrown the communist model and that one must also look to other nations' experiences and literatures as guides to forecasting China's future. As I note in chapter 1 and argue in chapters 5 and 7, it is particularly pertinent to draw on the lessons of other newly industrialized countries, because many challenges that China will face bear strong resemblance to the challenges of political aggregation and "public goods" experienced in Latin America and East Asia. So Walder is correct that the comparative communist paradigm has its limitations in explaining China today and into the future; yet I disagree that it has lost *all* explanatory relevance— because the Chinese Communist regime continues to wrestle with problems that derive from its distinctive Leninist structural and functional character. Thus, we should not throw the baby out with the bathwater—but rather should supplement our understanding of China's Leninist system with the broader comparative perspectives of modernization, industrialization, and sociopolitical change. Let us therefore begin with a discussion of the evolution of communist party-states.

The Evolution of Communist Party-States

Scholars of communist systems have posited various "stage theories" about the phases through which communist party-states all seem to pass. Many of these theories resemble each other in describing the stages' characteristics and substance, although the terminology used is often different. Most theorists of comparative communism agree that ruling communist parties pass from an initial stage that emphasizes ideology and social transformation (often employing classic "totalitarian" methods of terror and propaganda) to a second stage of guided economic development that emphasizes technical rationality and efficiency (which applies "softer" "authoritarian" methods that utilize bureaucratic management).

The German political scientist Richard Lowenthal identified this transition as that from "utopia to development."[14] Lowenthal also described it simply as the "post-totalitarian" transition in which the Communist Party "matures" by responding to pressures from "below" instead of imposing change from "above."[15] Chalmers Johnson observed that the shift from the first to second stage represented a movement from a "mobilization" to a "post-mobilization" regime.[16] Lowenthal, Johnson, and many other scholars recognized that the initial phase of communist rule was, in many ways, a continuation of the revolutionary struggle for power—whereby the new ruling regime sought to transform state and society alike using ideological inspiration and classic Leninist means. However, these regimes soon discovered that these mobilizational tactics were inappropriate for either nation building or enforcing social control. As a result, many regimes entered a new "totalitarian" phase characterized by terror and intimidation, bureaucratic retrenchment, and a command economy. During this second phase, the communist party-state morphed into enormous totalitarian bureaucracies that sought to extend their institutional writ to every corner of society. As the historian and Soviet specialist Robert Tucker aptly noted in 1965, "Totalitarianism carries the process of bureaucratization to its farthest extreme in modern society."[17]

Samuel Huntington and Zbigniew Brzezinski used different terminology to describe essentially the same phenomena, and each posited more lengthy spectrums of systemic change that took account of the increasing diversity and demands that develop in society as a result of the economic growth generated by the previous stage. Huntington identified a three-stage model of "transformation" (of the political system), "consolidation" (of regime control), and "adaptation" (of the ruling party to pressures generated by society).[18] Brzezinski, writing with great prescience in 1989, posited a four-stage model of evolution from "communist totalitarianism" to "communist authoritarianism" to "post-communist authoritarianism" to "post-communist pluralism."[19]

Thus Huntington and Brzezinski—writing later than Lowenthal, Johnson, and others—noticed that communist party-states evolved beyond the totalitarian bureaucratic phase described by scholars in the 1950s and early 1960s. They noted, in effect, that bureaucratism continued, but it became decoupled from classic totalitarian methods of political control as communist party-states began to loosen their grips somewhat in the post-Stalin period. Politically, this shift signaled the move from totalitarian to authoritarian regimes. Brzezinski noted that this second phase still initially included a strong ideological (Marxist-Leninist) flavor, but that this eventually gave way to nonideological authoritarianism (the third phase) as the classic canons lost their convincing appeal to cadres and masses alike. Rule became rule for rule's sake. The governing rationale was stripped bare to its core: maintaining power. Brzezinski recognized the hollowness and bankruptcy of such regimes, and he correctly identified this "post-communist authoritarian" phase as moribund and the precursor to the eventual implosion and collapse of communist party-states and their replacement with an entirely new phase, which he identified as "post-communist pluralism."[20] In fact, in his analysis, degeneration and collapse had long been a distinct possibility for the Soviet bloc, as it figured in his writings dating to the late 1960s. His analysis of this possibility was not based on some kind of naive Cold War optimism that capitalism would have to prevail over communism, but rather came from his own in-depth analyses of the maladies afflicting the Soviet and East European party-states.[21]

Although only Brzezinski predicted the collapse of communist party-states before the fact, there was no shortage of "Monday morning quarterbacking" among specialists in communist affairs in the wake of the 1989 uprisings in Eastern Europe (and China), and the collapse of the Soviet state in 1991. This is to be expected. Not only as scholars and analysts were they concerned with understanding the empirical reasons for these monumental political changes, but they were equally pressed to explain why none of them had predicted these globe-shaking changes. In the next section, we examine some of this introspection and the assessments of the reasons and factors that precipitated the collapse of these party-states.

The Causes of Implosion

Given the number of communist party-states that imploded over a two-year span (eight states in Eastern Europe, plus the Soviet Union split into fifteen states),[22] their divergent national conditions, and the number of scholars and analysts who attempted postmortems, there is little surprise that a wide variety of causes and theories were identified. Many such studies tended to emphasize four categories of factors:[23]

- the existence of an economic crisis,
- the loss of political legitimacy,
- Mikhail Gorbachev's policies, and
- the emergence of civil society.

Though these categories do capture several of the key variables, they do not capture the totality of factors. Table 2.1 identifies more than sixty such factors and causes that emerge from this literature. To be sure, not all factors were present in all cases, but this table does suggest the complexities at work in various societies and systems. They suggest several overarching commonalities that produced stresses in the systems and eventually led to their demise.[24] I would identify and cluster these factors as follows:

1. Economic variables:
   - problems of command economies,
   - distortion of the economy in favor of the military,
   - consequences of reform, and
   - international factors.
2. Political variables:
   - reforms from above,
   - reforms from below,
   - the erosion of party control over time (cognitive sphere, security sphere, party organizations, state sector).
3. Social variables:
   - the rise of civil society,
   - the decline of organized dependence, and
   - the social effects of economic change.
4. Cultural factors:
   - alienation from socialism,
   - the globalization of information, and
   - changing identities.
5. Coercive variables:
   - the decline of totalitarian controls, and
   - the rise of professional militaries.
6. International variables:
   - the impact of Gorbachev,
   - increasingly autonomous Eastern Europe, and
   - greater awareness of foreign political systems.

This categorization reduces the complex laundry list of relevant factors to a more manageable clustering of key variables. Even still, not all factors were present or precipitant causes of regime implosion in every East European nation, the USSR, or Mongolia. The distortion of economies in favor of the military-industrial complex was certainly a more significant factor in the former Soviet Union than in the East European satellites. All suffered the problems and inefficiencies of command economies, to a greater or lesser extent, and some encountered new problems owing to the economic reforms that had been undertaken. All had stagnant economies with low levels of wealth accumulation and consumer satisfaction. All were cut off from the Western and global financial and trading systems, and they were therefore unable to benefit from foreign direct investment and other sources of assistance from intergovernmental organizations such as the General Agreement on Tariffs and Trade, World Bank, and International Monetary Fund.

For those states that did embark on modest market reforms, this frequently produced a form of "rent seeking," whereby local governments became involved, usually in a predatory fashion, with the local private economy. Often it stimulated the asset stripping of state-owned enterprises by party-state elites. Sometimes, as in China, it produced mutual synergies between local governments and local economies. This became a means for local governments to channel investment into favored projects—but, more often than not, it exacerbated corruption and rent seeking. These phenomena *did* produce new revenue streams for the party-state, particularly at the local level, and the local state did supply new capital to the private sector, but they had the net effect of eroding the previous networks of organized dependence and party-state control over the populace.

Politically, in retrospect, it is clear that party organs in all countries had atrophied badly and far beyond what was recognized either at home or abroad. Party control had also badly deteriorated in people's minds (the cognitive sphere) and in the state sector of the economy. Ideologically, the party no longer inspired. Marxist-Leninist doctrine had become dogmatic, shallow, contradictory, and out of date in a modern world. Moreover, in many of these states, the party's ability to monitor citizens and enforce internal discipline and obedience had also atrophied, and concomitantly the compliance of the citizenry had diminished.[25] When compliance and discipline break down, an authoritarian state is endangered. Whether accomplished through intimidation or reward, a communist party-state must be able to count on the full compliance of its citizenry and discipline of its members.[26]

Table 2.1. Western Assessments of Factors and Causes in the Collapse of Communist Power

Economic Factors	Political Factors	Social Factors	Cultural Factors	Coercive Factors	International Factors
Economic stagnation	Gorbachev as an individual leader	Rise of semiautonomous or autonomous civic organizations (civil society)	Moral vacuum and public cynicism toward regime and its ideology	Decline of the "party-army"—rise of professional militaries	"Imperial overstretch" (USSR)
Consumer deprivation	Glasnost in the Soviet Union	Alienation from the workplace and the state	Alienation from socialist culture and rewritten history—search for the past	Uncertain loyalty of paramilitary and security services to ruling party	Collapse of the "Brezhnev Doctrine" (under Gorbachev)
Overspending on the military and resulting distortion of central government expenditures	Formation of autonomous trade unions (Poland)	Rising corruption	Increasingly noncompliant media	Corruption in coercive apparatus	*Ostpolitik* between East and West Germany
"Second economy" and black markets	Linkages between reformists elites and civil society	Increased labor mobility and alternative employment opportunities	Effects of globalization on popular culture	Decline in use of mass terror and intimidation tactics	Increasingly independent (from Moscow) foreign policies of East European states.
Nonintegration into international trade and financial systems	Delegitimization of Marxist-Leninist ideology	Decline in peer monitoring and surveillance	Declining appeal of moral incentives	Increased sensitivity to human rights concerns (post–Helsinki Accords)	Imposed party-states from without (by USSR)
Little inbound foreign direct investment (or foreign direct investment as an agent of change)	Official corruption and party privileges	(Frustrated) desires for foreign travel—but once exposure to the outside world occurs, comparisons are made	Ethnic tensions and seeking ethnically autonomous regions/states		Globalization
Inflation in some countries	Declining ability of party to enforce discipline within its ranks	Decoupling of political loyalty and tangible rewards in the enterprise (declining neotraditional dependency structures)	Increasing nationalist identity (as distinct from socialist identity)		
Nonconvertible currencies	New political elites emerge at the local level outside of party structure and cadres (at all levels) gain a vested interest in the "new economy"	Increasingly tense labor-management relations	Increasing appeal of religion and the role of the Catholic Church		

Insolvent banking sector and debt overhang ("triangular debt")	Bureaucratic unresponsiveness and inefficiency	Sporadic social protests, strikes, and slowdowns
Laggard agriculture and rise of smaller-unit or individual production	Decreased writ of the *nomenklatura*	Extrajudicial "taxes," levies, and fees
Inefficiencies of central planning	Despite transition to "technocracy," increasing incompetence and inability of cadres and bureaucrats to perform meritocratically in new economic climate	Pressures build to establish legitimate channels of interest articulation
Party intervention in planning process	Corrosion and disappearance of local party cells in work units	
Undeveloped and retarded market mechanisms	Disobedience of central party and government directives and/or feigned compliance	
Price distortions	Declining state capacity in provision of publics goods	
Subsidies and "soft budget constraints"		
Erosion of state monopoly on property rights—after economic reform was initiated individuals exercised de facto property rights over land and enterprises		
Little revenue sharing by central governments with localities, but reduced local government dependence on higher-level allocations due to extrabudgetary revenue		
Increasing government budget deficits		
Perestroika in the Soviet Union and market reforms in Hungary and Yugoslavia		
No going back once economic reforms had been begun, due to new vested interests of local cadres and empowered citizens (new form of "path dependence")		
New sources of revenue available to local party and state organs (and the military), and the resulting rise of govermental rent seeking		

Even in states like the former German Democratic Republic (GDR, East Germany), where totalitarian controls were strong (e.g., the Stasi),[27] the years before 1989 witnessed the development of numerous groups in the semi-public sphere: peace activists, Greens, human rights advocates, critical playwrights and artists, and the Protestant Church.[28] Once Gorbachev failed to back the GDR leadership in suppressing these nascent groups, they felt emboldened. As Corey Ross describes it: "The 'collapse from without' [Gorbachev] was the crucial precondition; the 'revolt from below' was the motor for change."[29] To be sure, other factors also contributed to the downfall of the GDR, including a split in the leadership and the ruling Socialist Unity Party, the flawed economic system, and the cumulative effects of *Ostpolitik.*[30]

Inner-party corruption was also a significant problem in these states, and the ruling party had become the ruling class. When limited political reform began (e.g., glasnost) in some countries, it exposed the inefficiencies in the system and raised expectations that could not be fulfilled. The competence of cadres and bureaucrats also had declined to a minimal level and, along with it, the party's governance and the ability to provide public goods.

Socially, the formation of semiautonomous civic organizations or in some cases, such as Solidarity in Poland, fully nonstate unions proved fertile ground for organized opposition against the party-state. In some East European states (Hungary, Czechoslovakia, and Poland), reformist politicians were able to work closely with such civic actors to push their mutual reformist agendas.[31] So, clearly, the rise of civil society was a key factor. So too was the decline of "organized dependence" on work units to allocate key goods and services to their members.[32] Previously, the party-states of the communist world maintained their power and privilege by allocating scarce and prized resources (salaries, bonuses, housing, transportation, consumer durables, food rations, etc.) to both party members and citizens. This "organized dependence" was a key component that held communist systems together. For those countries that did embark on economic reforms, this dependency eroded more quickly—as the goods and services formally allocated became available in the marketplace (or at least on the black market).

Culturally, there was the issue of ethnicity—particularly in the Soviet Union, but also in Yugoslavia, Czechoslovakia, and the Baltic states. As the eminent scholar and observer of socialist systems Seymour Martin Lipset pithily put it, "The Achilles' Heel of Communism has turned out to be nationalism."[33] The Soviet Union was an unnatural empire where proud ethnic and national identities were not assimilated or homogenized, but were suppressed.

Culturally, popular cynicism and alienation toward the party-states was also a critical factor in their delegitimization. This, too, was progressive and took place over time. Part of the alienation was due to the declining appeal of official ideology, part was due to rising corruption, part was the product of the declining provision of social and public goods, and part was related to skeptical political cultures (i.e., Europeans and Russians are more innately skeptical of government than, for example, Asians). As one observer noted, "If anything is clear about the sudden swoon of the hollow East European regimes in November and December 1989 is that those collapses were the result of moral rot at least as much as of economic and political failure."[34] Clearly, access to increased media and information about the West also played a role in popular perceptions of ruling regimes. In the German case, *Ostpolitik* and direct contact between East and West further raised comparisons and popular expectations.

Coercively, the communist party-states' internal and external security capacities remained strong, but they were increasingly challenged by domestic political dissent and ethnic discontent. Though they maintained a monopoly on the military and security services, and continued to intimidate their citizenry in very real ways on a daily basis, nonetheless the coercive features of the former totalitarian regimes had declined significantly. This was partly due to the transition from the early phase of such regimes, when terror was widespread, to the aforementioned second phase of development of communist party-states, when routinization of bureaucracy became more prevalent. After whole sectors of "enemies of the state" had been eliminated and society generally began to live with the new realities of suppression, both potential social targets declined and the instruments of proletarian dictatorship softened. This is not to argue that secret police or security services ceased to operate or intimidate—quite to the contrary—but the coercive atmosphere that characterized the early stages of communist party-states declined over time. Also, many communist militaries became more "professional" and less political tools of the party-state.[35] This process of professionalization of the armed forces made them less willing to rescue crumbling party rule by killing domestic demonstrators. Of course, some elements of the East German and Romanian militaries and paramilitaries did use lethal force, but other units balked at doing so and—in any event—such brutality was short-lived as the regimes quickly collapsed.

A final set of factors has to do with international circumstances and, in particular, the overextension of the Soviet imperial state. In much of the literature on communist implosions and transitions, the international factors are undervalued relative to domestic catalysts—but, as Juan Linz and Alfred Stepan argue, they should be viewed as much more central variables.[36]

The Soviet Union simply was not economically prepared to be a world power. Even the sphere of influence it controlled most closely, Eastern Europe, was an imposed type of occupation and form of neocolonialism. It was an artificial solidarity from the outset. This was apparent in the abilities of Yugoslavia and Romania to distance themselves from Moscow in the early 1950s, the Hungarian and Polish uprisings of 1956, the Prague Spring of 1968, the process of *Ostpolitk* between the two Germanys in the 1970s, and Gorbachev's abandonment of the Brezhnev Doctrine of intervention as the dénouement. Once the Soviet Union seriously began to spread its international tentacles into Asia, Africa, the Middle East, and Latin America during the 1980s, imperial overstretch began to exacerbate existing domestic economic strains—which, in turn, exacerbated sociopolitical tensions. At exactly the same time, the accelerated arms race with the United States compounded these strains. Then Moscow invaded and occupied Afghanistan, further aggravating stretched capabilities and strained resources.

Taken together, these and other factors collectively brought down the former Soviet Union and other communist party-states. Once the cracks in the monolith appeared, internal and external factors collectively reinforced each other and an inexorable dynamic gained momentum.

To be sure, it was the *confluence* of factors that produced the collapse of communist power in the former Soviet Union and Eastern Europe. For example, in separate studies, Ivan Szelenyi and Balazs Szelenyi, Andrew Janos, Leslie Holmes, Kenneth Jowitt, Daniel Chirot, Minxin Pei, Steven Saxonberg, and Jack Gladstone all put forward different comprehensive and sophisticated theories of disintegration and implosion—but all argue that a unique confluence of indigenous and exogenous factors interacted to create the particular dynamics that produced the collapse of the regimes.[37]

3

The Western Discourse on the
Chinese Communist Party-State

What about China's political system? Where does China fit on the continua of communist party-state evolution? How many of the Soviet/East European factors noted in chapter 2 are present in China today? And what do China watchers think is the current state of and future for the Chinese Communist Party (CCP) and the political system of the People's Republic of China (PRC)?

Surprisingly few China specialists have attempted to systematically apply comparative perspectives and address themselves to macro-level political change in the PRC.[1] Most studies of Chinese politics today focus on increasingly smaller units of analysis and fail to generate broader views or predictions about China's or the CCP's future. The China field in the United States seems to know more and more about less and less.[2] However, some China specialists have attempted to place China and the CCP in a comparative perspective.

In the aftermath of the collapse of the Soviet and East European communist party-states, some prominent China specialists publicly argued that it was only a matter of time before China went the same way as those regimes.[3] The Chinese communist regime was brittle, embattled, and on the verge of collapse, they argued.

But when the Chinese Communist party-state failed to collapse as the next domino after the East European, Soviet, and Mongolian regimes, and appeared to be strengthening its grip on power after 1991, such prognoses by China specialists tapered off. It was not really until the late 1990s that such speculation started afresh. Some journalists prognosticated and some popular books were published about the future of the Chinese political system, but it was mainly the scholarly community of China specialists that began to probe into the strengths and weaknesses of the Chinese Communist party-state. Chapter 8 considers those scholars who speculated about the future of the Chinese political system, whereas this chapter focuses on the (post-1989) past and present.

Not surprisingly, China watchers are not in agreement about what they see in China or the implications of their analyses. Two cleavages are apparent. The first is the division between those analysts who have focused on China's external posture—its economic power, growing military prowess, and increasingly influential foreign policy—and those who have studied the internal scene.[4] A major disjuncture became evident between the two groups of analysts beginning in the late 1990s. The former group saw a coherent and increasingly strong China that was making its influence and strength felt on the world stage. There was little, if any, questioning among such analysts that the internal Chinese political system might be weak and vulnerable (the only exception to this rule was Susan Shirk, who argued in her book *China: Fragile Superpower* that China was increasingly strong externally but weak internally).[5] In fact, for most in this school, the well-entrenched Chinese Communist state was one of the key components of the "rise of China" or the "China threat." By the mid-1990s, this "strong China paradigm," in the words of David M. Lampton, had replaced the "weak China paradigm" (which he defines as "China as a weak, developing, politically fragile, and transitional economy) that had been popular in the aftermath of 1989.[6]

The second cleavage became apparent among those who concentrated on China's domestic politics and internal scene. But it is interesting and important to note that the cleavage grew out of a more significant *agreement* among this community of analysts. That is, virtually *all* such analysts agreed that the Chinese party-state suffered from multiple problems and vulnerabilities. In fact, this group of scholars was virtually unanimous in agreeing on the problems (discussed further below): declining party legitimacy, eroding party organizations, increasing noncompliance with party directives, a hollow party ideology and moral vacuum in society, rampant corruption, parasitic officials who engaged in rent seeking and other predatory practices, and so on.

On these basics, there was widespread agreement that the CCP was in a state of atrophy. However, there was significant disagreement over the pervasiveness and *degree* of party atrophy, and even sharper disagreement among these analysts over what the party was doing to address these problems and how successful these reform attempts were in relegitimizing and shoring up the CCP's rule. One group, whom I call the "pessimists," identify these problems as extremely severe and the party's efforts to deal with them as wholly insufficient. The other group, whom I label the "optimists," identify the panoply of problems confronting the CCP as essentially manageable, and they further view the regime's initiatives and efforts to cope with them as (1) appropriate to the problems concerned and (2) successful in the short to medium terms (five to fifteen years). Thus, though the majority of foreign analysts of the CCP were in essential agreement over the atrophied condition of the party-state, they disagreed over the severity of the situation and the efficacy of the regime's responses.

The Pessimists

The pessimists see the Chinese political system as embattled and endangered. This perspective is shared by a number of leading scholars.

For example, Roderick MacFarquhar of Harvard University asserts starkly: "The political system is fragile."[7] Elsewhere he states, "In short, despite truly impressive progress in its economy, the PRC's polity is in systemic crisis. VIP visitors to Beijing are exposed to an impressive panoply of power, but this is a fragile regime."[8] Still elsewhere, in a well-publicized debate with Andrew Nathan at the Library of Congress, MacFarquhar starkly asserted: "The problems I shall analyze [in the debate] are likely to result in a breakdown in the communist regime in years rather than decades. . . . The CCP has acted as a competent fire brigade to date, imprisoning activists and appeasing their followers. By controlling the press, it normally manages to contain demonstrations locally. . . . At some point, in my view, one of these 'sparks' will ignite a national prairie fire. . . . All the elements for a really massive collapse are there. . . . The question is what will the trigger be?"[9] Later in this exchange with Nathan, MacFarquhar dismisses the CCP as a hollow institution: "What's the nature of the Party? It's a sort of Rotary Club of 70 million people who joined in because its good for their careers."[10]

Susan Shirk of the University of California, San Diego, has a similar view of China's political system and future. In her most recent book, she argues that "China may be an emerging superpower, but it is a fragile one. And it is China's internal fragility, not its economic or military strength, that presents the greatest danger . . . Chinese leaders are haunted by fears that their days are numbered."[11]

Richard Baum of the University of California, Los Angeles, also a noted expert on Chinese politics, similarly argues that that the CCP may be an emperor with no clothes: "There is a growing disconnect between a vibrant, dynamic economy and society, on the one hand, and a rigid, anachronistic system of governance and political control, on the other. . . . The regime's Marxist-Leninist philosophical underpinnings have been diluted virtually beyond recognition by 25 years of market reform and rationalization; and the Party is no longer able to offer an inspiring vision of China's future. Increasingly, the Party is seen by many groups and individuals in society as largely irrelevant in their daily lives—an annoyance to be avoided where possible and endured when necessary."[12]

Thus, these three leading specialists on Chinese politics think that the CCP regime's days are numbered. These views are also shared by a large number of Chinese émigré scholars (as noted below), who also perceive an increasingly incapacitated party-state. Among them, Minxin Pei has marshaled the most damning critique of CCP rule. Yet even Pei comes up short of predicting regime collapse—envisioning instead protracted stagnation. Only Gordon Chang and Bruce Gilley predict collapse and democratic breakthrough (respectively).

Chang's sensationally titled study *The Coming Collapse of China* posited cataclysmic change, standing in stark contradiction to a parallel wave of publications at the time on the "rise of China" or the "China threat."[13] Whereas these other studies focused on China's potential for external expansion and possible aggression, Chang looked inward at its potential for implosion. He argued that the signs of the CCP's "disintegration" were everywhere and that it was just a matter of time before the party was overthrown (he seemed to envision a revolutionary-type overthrow of the regime rather than a gradual demise). He summarized his prognosis as follows:

The Communist Party has struggled to keep up with change over the last two decades, but now it is beginning to fail as it often cannot provide the basic needs of its people. Corruption and malfeasance erode the party's support from small hamlet to great city. Central government leaders do not know what to do as the institutions built over five decades become feeble. Social order in their nation is dissolving. The Chinese are making a break for the future, and the disaffected are beginning to find their voice. The cadres still suppress, but that won't work in the long run. The people are in motion now, and it is just a matter of time before they get what they want.[14]

Chang's prediction was ridiculed by many scholars and China specialists. In 2006, five years after the publication of his book, he sought to defend his earlier prediction of Communist Party collapse by the end of the decade. He appears to begin his midterm assessment in the *Far Eastern Economic Review* somewhat chastened:

> *The Coming Collapse of China,* my book, predicts the fall of the Chinese Communist Party by the end of this decade. We are now at the halfway point. . . . So is China's leading political organization on schedule for a fall? It certainly does not look like it is. On the contrary, China's mighty one-party state is a wonder to behold. . . . By ascending the ranks of nations at an accelerated pace, China is altering our notions of political governance.[15]

After this deflection, Chang proceeded to defend his original analysis and prediction by ticking off a laundry list of domestic problems afflicting the CCP and government—notably rising social inequities and increasing incidents of unrest (both of which have become more pronounced since the publication of his book). Curiously, he says nothing about China's economy—which was the centerpiece of his earlier critique—and instead shifts his appraisal the political realm and the CCP in particular. He offers a dire assessment of party rule:

> The Communist Party has become incapable of reinvigorating itself. Once young and vital, it has been eroded by widespread disenchantment, occasional crises, and the enervating effect of the passage of time. The Party may be big, but it is also corrupt, reviled, and often ineffective. It is barely functioning in some areas, having been replaced by clans or gangs.[16]

Chang concluded his midterm assessment with the argument that socioeconomic change is outpacing the party-state's capacity to manage it: "No one should think that the Chinese people will let the cadres control the pace of transformation. At one time Beijing's officials were leading the change, but now they are struggling to keep up. . . . The combination of growing alienation and declining government strength should make the last years of this decade a time of even greater instability. . . . In sum, too much is happening too fast for any government—no matter how institutionalized—to hold on."[17]

Chang is not alone, however, in predicting the demise of the CCP—and the ultimate democratization of China. This includes a number of leading historians of China. Arthur Waldron has long been making such predictions on the lecture circuit and in the op-ed pages of U.S. newspapers.[18] Jeffrey Wasserstrom has looked for telltale signs of the CCP's "legitimacy crisis" and the erosion of state authority similar to declining imperial dynasties or the Nationalist Kuomintang regime.[19] Merle Goldman has spent a career tracking the seeds of political liberalism in China and has long advocated the democratization of China. In 2006, she argued that nascent signs of bottom-up democratization were increasingly evident.[20]

Bruce Gilley wrote a whole book about how the "democratic breakthrough" will occur in China, and how 2005 was actually the year that the beginning of the endgame for the CCP began.[21] He envisions a revolution from above as one group of fractured elites opts for the democratic option, following social "breakdown and mobilization."

In a thought-provoking book, the British journalist and author Will Hutton also sees China's political system, which he aptly describes as "Leninist corporatism," as structurally unstable and unsustainable.[22] He says: "It [China] has only a very limited ability to abandon the party-state and Leninist corporatism so as to become a successful bureaucratic party accepting constitutional constraints—but that is what must happen. How it is achieved is the story of the decades ahead."[23] Later, he argues that "the Party needs some justification for its control, whether of village elections or the media. All that stands between it and its own demise is its capacity to deliver economic growth and its control of the army and police. These are thin reeds on which to build long-term hegemony, especially as the economy is beset by the same weaknesses of the halfway house as the polity."[24]

A Chinese émigré scholar currently on the faculty of Nottingham University, Zheng Yongnian, agrees that regime change is both necessary and inevitable: "Today, more and more authoritarian regimes have democratized in other parts of the world. Will China buck the trend and become an exception? To be sure, the forces for regime change are there. The confluence of all these forces is likely to result in some meaningful regime in China."[25] But Zheng differs from Gilley and others in how China's democratization may come about. Zheng posits a range of four conceivable pathways to regime change, of which one is deemed impossible, one unlikely, one possible, and one probable:

- by external forces (impossible),
- collapse from above (unlikely),
- revolution from below (possible), or
- gradual political liberalization (probable).

Zheng does not affix a time frame for the probable political liberalization, and he qualifies his prediction by noting a variety of unstable factors that may precipitate an earlier revolution from below. But he seems to believe that, over time, the twin forces of the market economy and globalization will necessitate regime change from within.[26]

Other analysts argue that while the CCP is not necessarily in danger of imminent collapse, it nevertheless does face a severe "governance crisis." The most authoritative advocate of this thesis is Minxin Pei.[27]

In a series of articles, Pei identified several phenomena and statistics that collectively added up, in his view, to "state incapacity." He argued that unless these phenomena were reversed in relatively short order, through serious political reform, China's impressive economic growth will stagnate and, along with it, the regime's capacity to rule. He grouped the principal problems confronting the CCP in three categories:

1. the shrinkage of the party's organizational penetration,
2. the erosion of its authority and appeal among the masses, and
3. the breakdown of its internal discipline.

Pei also identified corruption and the personal patronage systems as chronic and cancerous problems that beset the party. He starkly but perceptively warns that "in many crucial respects, China's hybrid neo-authoritarian order eerily exhibits the pathologies of both the political stagnation of Leonid Brezhnev's Soviet Union and the crony capitalism of Suharto's Indonesia." He argues that these pathologies—such as pervasive corruption, a collusive local officialdom, elite cynicism, and mass disenchantment—are the classic symptoms of degenerating governing capacity.[28]

In a 2002 lecture "The Party's Crisis" at the Carnegie Endowment for International Peace (where he works),[29] Pei also argued:

> The CCP's base of social support has substantially eroded, and is now an elite-based Party. The Party suffers from an acute identity crisis and has no values or ideology, causing widespread cynicism and disenchantment

among the masses towards the ruling elite. There is a breakdown of accountability, widespread corruption, with collusion of officials at the local level. The Party has political rot. The erosion of the Party's authority impacts the state's ability to govern and provide public goods. There is a paradox of a rising economy but declining government effectiveness. The inability to deliver public goods will just deepen the alienation. Moreover, there are no regularized or institutionalized mechanisms for society to voice and vet grievances. This is all a recipe for the breakdown of the Party system.[30]

In 2006, Pei built on these earlier themes at considerably greater length in his book *China's Trapped Transition: The Limits of Developmental Autocracy.*[31] In this sophisticated and detailed study, he offers a much more systematic and systemic critique of the maladies afflicting the CCP. The essence of the problem, he argues, lays in "decentralized state predation" and "state incapacitation"—which had produced a "trapped transition" in China's reforms. The "trap" is that political reform had not accompanied economic reform and was becoming, he claims, a drag on development. Moreover, he observes that the party-state had become "predatory"—preying on society rather than facilitating economic growth and social betterment. The lack of political reform was no accident, he correctly notes, as it came from conscious decisions by the CCP elite to maintain power at all costs. Yet, while real political reforms were resisted at the top after 1989, he makes a strong case that at the bottom and throughout the system the party-state had become riddled with various cancers. It was into this "vacuum" of political reform from above that "decentralized predation" or "predatory autocracy" emerged, in his view. Manifestations of this include:[32]

- erosion of the party's mobilizational capacity,
- decline of the party-state's organizational capacity and decay of its organizational apparatus,
- entrenchment of rent-seeking local officials,
- widespread corruption within the CCP,
- rising tensions between state and society and mass disenchantment with the CCP,
- rural decay and discontent and rising incidents of unrest,
- institutional breakdown and substantially eroded state capacity,
- ineffective internal monitoring and no external checks and balances on the party-state,

- political patronage and collusion among party and state elites,
- erosion of institutional norms,
- fragmentation of judicial authority, and
- dramatically declining state capacity to deliver public goods and provide good governance.

Pei paints a bleak picture. Though different from and not quite as cataclysmic as Chang's assessment, in that he does not envision imminent breakdown or upheaval, Pei nonetheless perceives a serious crisis in China that has the potential to be the party-state's undoing. In the end, he argues that the most likely scenario of the "trapped transition" in which China and the CCP find themselves is *prolonged stagnation.*[33] Though he allows that implosion and regime collapse are possibilities, he rejects the possibility of political reform from above but leaves open the potential for reform from below.[34] The one alternative that he refuses to entertain is that the party-state could successfully adapt and reinvent itself *without democratizing* or introducing politically liberal reforms. In the end, he predicts prolonged stagnation.

The essence of Pei's analysis—stagnation amid predation—is unique. Other analysts do not share it (see "The Optimists" below). Indeed, though most analysts recognize some of the predatory characteristics that Pei identifies, his emphasis on this factor seems overdrawn. It is also difficult to agree with his thesis about stagnation when the economy is growing as it is. Moreover, despite declining capacity to deliver public goods in several spheres, the Chinese state is far more functional than he gives it credit for—and is far more efficient in its delivery of public goods than a large variety of other states in Asia, the Middle East, Africa, Latin America, and even some developed countries.

Yet, it is interesting that Pei's analysis of state incapacity is largely shared by other former Chinese citizens now resident abroad, such as Shaoguang Wang, An Chen, and He Qinglian.[35] The veteran Hong Kong China-watcher Willy Wo-Lap Lam is also pessimistic about China's political future, and his analysis has many elements in common with Pei and other Chinese émigrés.[36] Perhaps their exile reflects their disaffection with the Chinese Communist regime, but it is notable that these émigrés are pessimistic about China's political condition and future. Each of these analysts identify further factors—such as growing social stratification and the declining fiscal basis of the state—but all seem to agree that the CCP is currently facing significant and severe problems that are tantamount to a cumulative crisis for the party-state. Nor do they see the political reforms of Jiang Zemin or Hu Jintao, which are aimed at reversing the atrophy and strengthening the party-state's governing capacity, as having any positive effect.

The Optimists

Another set of Chinese émigrés, however, all of whom hold academic appointments in U.S. universities, are more upbeat about China's political-economic-social future and capacity to adapt to new challenges. For example, Dali Yang of the University of Chicago has written an excellent and detailed study of how various economic reforms have spurred various governance reforms that have strengthened the party-state,[37] and Cheng Li of the Brookings Institution has written a number of articles concerning the positive effects of generational change, leadership turnover, and the progressive social policies (which he labels the "New Deal") of the Hu-Wen government.[38]

Other analysts of the China scene are also circumspect about the evidence of the erosion of regime control, the potential for its collapse, and systemic political change in China. In a collaborative study that I edited in 2001 titled *Is China Unstable?* the contributing authors concluded that while there are signs of unprecedented social instability and political problems in China, the regime is not necessarily in danger of collapse.[39] The contributors to this study concluded at the time that China was in a state of "stable unrest" that could continue indefinitely. Much of the unrest and discontent in society were oriented against specific grievances in specific locales at specific points in time and were not more broadly aimed at the central party-state itself. Moreover, such outbreaks of social unrest that have appeared across China are disconnected from each other; that is, there is little "connecting tissue" between these "nodes" or pockets of unrest. Though the contributors to this study did agree that the party-state was being challenged on many fronts in unprecedented ways, and that many of the factors that had been present in the former Soviet Union and Eastern Europe *are* present in China today, it was equally noted that a number of important factors exist in China that were absent in these other former communist states, which have served, and can continue to serve, to buffer the CCP: a growing economy and increasing levels of wealth, extensive trade and investment ties to the outside world, a generally cohesive multiethnic society, a stable political leadership that has coped well with succession issues, and strong regime control over the military and internal security services.

Many observers emphasize the economic differences between China and the former communist states and argue that China is more likely to continue down the path of East Asian developing states—both economically and politically—than to follow the Soviet/East European model.[40] Yun-han Chu, a leading scholar of Taiwan's democratization, sees considerable political convergences between the present-day CCP under Hu Jintao and the Kuomintang under Chiang Ching-kuo during the late 1970s and early 1980s.[41] A comprehensive "balance sheet" assessment of China's strengths and weaknesses, collaboratively undertaken by China specialists at the Center for Strategic and International Studies and the Peterson Institute for International Economics in Washington, concluded that the regime's strengths far outweigh its weaknesses.[42]

Many others argue that the Leninist institutions in China remain strong and are undergoing a "reinstitutionalization." Andrew Nathan subscribes to this argument,[43] as do Alice Miller and Jing Huang.[44] I do as well (see chapters 6 and 7). A primary proponent of this view, however, has been the Boston University political scientist Joseph Fewsmith, who has spent years tracking the CCP and intraparty debates. Writing in early 2003, Fewsmith notes that, at the Sixteenth Party Congress in 2002, the CCP took a variety of political initiatives aimed at establishing a "more institutionalized, more formalized, and more procedure-based system."[45] These are all characteristics, he notes, of a "revolutionary party" (*gemingdang*) evolving into a "ruling party" (*zhizhengdang*). Though such political institutionalization took place under Deng Xiaoping's aegis in the 1980s, there have been *new* attempts to *re*institutionalize party rule under Jiang and Hu since the mid-1990s. Fewsmith continued to track these changes and, more than four years after his initial observation, he noted that these reforms had also been intended to "develop mechanisms to make government more responsive to demands of local society, but not to threaten the ruling status of the Party."[46] Though he allows that these political reforms are well intended, he is more guarded about their long-term prospects, observing that this dualism "may not be sustainable. The legitimacy issues the Party faces at various levels are real and long term."[47] Yet, at bottom, he concludes, "For better or for worse, this combination seems viable for the medium term."[48]

Richard Baum, a noted authority on Chinese politics at the University of California, Los Angeles, is more guarded in his assessment about the CCP's reinstitutionalization. "In the short term," Baum argues, "consultative

Leninism—bolstered by robust economic growth—has arguably extended the lifespan of China's authoritarian regime." But over the longer term, he concludes that "China's unreconstructed Leninists may already be living on borrowed time."[49] His "pessimistic impulse" grows out of his belief that the consultative mechanisms introduced by Hu into the party and in the party's dealings with society are insufficient to the need—and he deems them to be insufficient precisely because they are Leninist, united front tactics rather than genuine attempts to establish mechanisms to accommodate popular demands.

Bruce Dickson of George Washington University has also contributed a number of careful and detailed studies of the CCP. His first book, *Democratization in China and Taiwan: The Adaptability of Leninist Parties,* placed the CCP (and Taiwan's Kuomintang) in an explicitly comparative context.[50] This insightful study synthesized much of the previous literature on authoritarian and communist party-states up to that point (1997), but particularly applied Samuel Huntington's three-stage typology of the evolution of one-party systems—transformation, consolidation, adaptation—to the evolution of the CCP (and the Kuomintang on Taiwan). Dickson found that the CCP fits very well into Huntington's "adaptation" phase. But he concluded that a number of differences distinguish the CCP from the Kuomintang, and he argues that the former will not follow the latter down the path to democratization.

In a more recent book, Dickson carried his 1997 study further by examining the CCP's effort to recruit private-sector entrepreneurs (capitalists) as members.[51] This attempt and a new policy of actively recruiting such individuals into the CCP gained worldwide attention following the former party leader Jiang Zemin's July 1, 2001, speech announcing the initiative. This new policy, dubbed the "Three Represents" (Sange Daibiao) by Jiang and party propagandists, is an attempt to transform party membership—and hence the party itself—from a typically proletarian worker-peasant basis to a more inclusive one that represents "advanced" sectors of society and the economy. This initiative is consistent with the evolution of other East Asian ruling parties.[52] Dickson's analysis shows, however, that the recruitment of the entrepreneurial class into the party considerably predated Jiang's 2001 high-profile speech. Like so many other policy initiatives in China, the leadership had experimented with it at a subnational level for some time, before adopting it as national policy. In fact, this policy had apparently existed in the late 1980s but was suspended in August 1989.

This recruitment initiative is clearly an effort by the CCP to "adapt" it-self in order to save itself. In Dickson's earlier study, he was quite pes-simistic that the party was capable of such adaptation. In this study, though not going so far as to predict that it will enable the party to survive, he seems to believe that it is a pragmatic, adaptive measure. To be sure, there are far more variables than party membership that will ultimately determine the party's survivability, but he finds this initiative to be important. He further argues that entrepreneurs will be willing to join and support the party be-cause of a political culture where they (and perhaps other classes, too) feel secure when "embedded" with the party-state rather than separate from it. In his forthcoming study, which updates the nationwide surveys of CCP efforts to recruit entrepreneurs as members, he finds empirical evidence of success in the strategy—in contrast to the initial hesitancy of many busi-nesspeople to join the party following Jiang's 2001 initiative.[53] Dickson finds evidence that the CCP's strategy of "co-optation" is working.

Although perhaps new to the CCP, this tactic is not new to other com-munist parties. Several East European parties—notably in Hungary and Ro-mania—adopted such a policy. Even Nikita Khrushchev spoke of making the Soviet Communist Party a "party of the whole people." Such an "in-clusionist" tactic, to use Kenneth Jowitt's terminology,[54] is politically as-tute because if such advanced and progressive classes are not included in the party-state, they are highly likely to form the basis of external opposi-tion to it. Thus, such a move by the CCP is to be interpreted as a *preemp-tive* tactic as much as it is an adaptive one.

In her book *Capitalism without Democracy,* Kellee Tsai of Johns Hop-kins University shares Dickson's conclusion that private entrepreneurs and the emergent middle class are not going to demand regime change. Her study explores a variety of "adaptive informal institutions" that have per-mitted the CCP to rebuild and sustain its rule.[55]

Another adaptive initiative undertaken by the CCP, and widely written about by foreign scholars, is the transformation of CCP elites and leader-ship.[56] The establishment of retirement norms in the 1980s, as described first by Melanie Manion,[57] reached their zenith at the Sixteenth Congress of the CCP in October 2002 (when there was a wholesale turnover of the party's Central Committee and top leadership). This was followed by the same process in the government at the National People's Congress of March 2003. Taken together, these twin meetings brought to power the so-called fourth generation of party leadership. Though still largely "technocrats" trained in the engineering sciences, those of other professional backgrounds were also promoted.[58] The circulation of elites undertaken since 2002–3 is unprecedented in communist party-states and political systems.[59] Never since the Bolshevik Revolution of 1917 has a communist party leadership experienced such wholesale elite turnover, absent a purge. More than half of the party's Central Committee, Politburo, and Standing Committee stood down from office. The turnover in the state and military leaderships were of a corresponding magnitude. The Seventeenth Party Congress in 2007 witnessed a similar turnover. As communist systems have proven notoriously incapable of managing such successions peacefully and systematically, the Chinese example is noteworthy.

Some observers, such as Alice Lyman Miller, point to this example as further evidence of the steady "institutionalization" of the norms and rules governing political life in post–Mao Zedong China.[60] In an article in a 2003 special issue of *The Journal of Democracy,* Andrew Nathan also observes that the People's Republic of China has experienced "institutionalization of orderly succession processes, meritocratic promotions, bureaucratic differentiation, and channels of mass participation and appeal"—although he quickly adds that "the regime still faces massive challenges to its survival."[61] He goes on to argue, "In contrast with the Soviet and East European ruling groups in the late 1980s and early 1990s, the new Chinese leaders do not feel that they are at the end of history."[62] His argument is that China has simply passed from the totalitarian to the authoritarian stage, where "development" has replaced "utopia" (he invokes Richard Lowenthal's 1970 theory noted in chapter 2), and he foresees that this stage can last indefinitely. Though he does not rule out an eventual "democratic breakthrough," he assesses that this authoritarian regime is "increasingly stable."[63] Nathan's argument in this article is an important departure from his past pessimistic and critical views of the CCP and Chinese political reforms. Here, he argues that the CCP is undertaking a variety of institutional reforms that collectively are stabilizing and strengthening the party-state—which he appropriately labels "*resilient authoritarianism.*" He categorizes these reforms in four clusters: succession processes, meritocratic promotions, bureaucratic differentiation, and (improved) channels of mass participation and appeal.

Dickson, in the same special issue of *The Journal of Democracy,* seems to share Nathan's sense that the CCP will "muddle through."[64] But Dickson still has doubts, as expressed in his earlier book (noted above),[65] that the CCP—indeed, any Leninist party—can accommodate genuine civil society (as distinct from co-opted and controlled social groups) and the organized aggregation of social interests. Dickson's instincts (indeed those of most scholars of Leninist parties) are that Leninist parties are by nature intolerant and incapable of ceding such power to autonomous social groups. But Dickson's net assessment is based on his belief that the CCP's twin strategies of "corporatism and cooptation"—which add up to a "strategy of limited adaptation"—are working (for now).[66] The CCP's strategy of survival, he argues, is "designed to embrace the economic realm, suppress the political realm, and prevent the defection of the economic and technical elites to the opposition."[67] Elsewhere, he writes:

> The CCP is pursuing a variety of political reforms that are intended to enhance the capacity of the state to govern effectively, if not democratically. It has used a mix of measures to shore up popular support, resolve local protests, and incorporate the beneficiaries of economic reform into the political system. In turn, it also forcefully represses efforts to challenge its authority and monopoly on political power and organization. As a result, public opinion is surprisingly complacent: while many are unhappy with their current situation, they remain optimistic about the future. This is not a recipe for imminent revolution. China's leaders face a series of serious problems, but they are more chronic than acute, and absent a sudden and unexpected flare-up do not pose an imminent threat to the incumbent regime.
>
> In contrast to common portrayals of acute strife between state and society, anecdotal reports and survey research show a surprising degree of popular support for the existing political system and reform agenda. . . . Similarly, there is a widespread belief that democracy is not appropriate for China, at least not at its current level of economic and cultural development. This is, of course, the CCP's contention, and it is not challenged by most Chinese. It is challenged by many intellectuals and dissidents, but their calls for quick and immediate democratization are not only opposed by the regime but also by most of society. . . . Under these conditions, the CCP does not face strong societal pressure for democratization. Lacking an alternative political system that is both preferable and viable, the status quo seems secure for the near future. . . . Calls for better governance are likely to resonate with the public more than calls for democratization.[68]

Thus, the "optimists," like Nathan and Dickson, see the CCP as coping with and adapting successfully to its various challenges. I share this viewpoint. A Danish expert on the CCP, Kjeld Erik Brødsgaard, also shares this view. He and Zheng Yongnian argued in 2006 that, "as a result of [the CCP's] renewal and revitalization process, the Party and its governing apparatus appear better qualified and more technically competent than at any other time in the post-Mao period. The lesson from the collapse of the Soviet Union seems to have been learned. The response of the CCP leaders has been to introduce incremental reform at the grass-roots level while strengthening the capacity of the Party and state institutions at higher levels. The result has been to create a power system characterized by "authoritarian resilience."[69] Brodsgaard further argues that the CCP is "a revitalized party that has been able to consolidate its grip on the Chinese system."[70]

These observers do not deny the various challenges and problems that confront the CCP and the Chinese government, but they see the system as holding together rather than collapsing, and the party-state as successfully adapting rather than failing to do so.

A Middle Ground?

Although the pessimists and optimists are largely in agreement that the CCP is a vulnerable institution and that political reforms are needed to reverse the atrophy and rebuild its legitimacy and power, they differ—often significantly—over the scope and intensity of problems afflicting the CCP and how successful the political reforms of recent years (and many of the pessimists would argue that there have been *no* political reforms per se) have been. One group of specialists sees the vulnerabilities as manageable, with the party-state continuing to reinvent itself and strengthen its rule. The other group sees the party-state as inexorably losing its control—unless, and perhaps despite, adaptive measures are undertaken to:

- improve public governance and be more responsive to societal demands,
- revitalize local-level party and state organs,
- make the government and party more transparent and law-bound,
- reduce corruption and dramatically improve the quality of cadres,
- establish a clear set of property rights, and
- find some kind of coherent and persuasive vision to replace its discredited official ideology.

Unless these and other measures are undertaken, the pessimists see the CCP as continuing its progressive state of decay and degeneration. Their writings portray a sense of immediacy to the sclerotic party-state. Though only Gordon Chang and Bruce Gilley have explicitly predicted the nearing demise of the Chinese Communist party-state, this is an implicit element in many of the pessimists' analyses. Even the democratic transition specialist Larry Diamond predicts that this will likely be the case in China: "In ten years, I think that China will still be an authoritarian regime, but one in a serious state of crisis if it doesn't begin to liberalize much more than it has. China cannot remain a completely closed political monopoly and remain stable. Something is going to have to give. It may not be in ten years, but I am pretty confident it is going to be within 25, maybe 10 to 15."[71]

I would, however, caution the pessimists that it is important to understand decay as a *progressive* condition, and one that can take a very long time to reach a critical state. The *pace* of deterioration is variable, as is the degree of chronic sclerosis. Like patients who have terminal diseases, they can respond to medication and prolong life for some time, and even occasionally go into remission. As with some cancers, patients can respond to treatment and recover from the disease.

It is instructive, therefore, to conceptualize the atrophy of party control in China as an incremental process, a gradual process of decay, rather than a zero-sum implosion of power as occurred in the former Soviet Union, Eastern Europe, and Mongolia. In retrospect, the terminal symptoms of those systems, what Gabriel Almond described as the "tectonics,"[72] were apparent to many foreign specialists. But, in Sinology as in scismology, the ability to predict exactly when and how the tectonic plates will shift in tandem in such a way as to produce an eruption and systemic change is impossible to forecast with any precision. When it comes to reforming the CCP, there is also no blueprint, road map, or previous example to guide the way. As Richard Baum aptly observed, "There is no previous example—and hence no secondary literature—on successful Leninist transitions. So China and the field of China political studies is into sui generis territory. Previous examples of authoritarian transition are not sufficient to explain or predict the evolution of the CCP."[73]

Thus, the CCP today has moved into terra incognita. This study argues that it is in a simultaneous state of *atrophy and adaptation*. The adaptation can stabilize, and even reverse, the process of atrophy. The CCP has been in progressive decline for many years, yet it has been adapting since 1978 (with the hiatus of 1989–92). During this time, it has adopted various preventive measures to stave off the inevitable—some suppression, some adaptation, some co-optation, some genuine permitting of pluralistic tendencies—but all have been *tactics* meant to cope with a chronic condition that is inherent and systemic in nature.

Not all systems experience eruptions or implosions. Rather, many simply continue to muddle through, while others (like China) attempt to proactively cope with challenges and change. Some engage in full systemic, adaptive reforms. As long as they keep control of all means of coercive power, such authoritarian regimes—no matter how despotic—can remain in power for an extended period. The world is full of examples of such regimes that never do experience a "democratic breakthrough" (unless the regime is forcibly deposed by foreign powers).

If this is how many observers outside China see the state of the CCP today, what about the CCP itself? Does it have such a dire assessment of its own condition? How serious does the party-state think are the challenges to its rule? What courses of correction and adaptation does it believe are needed? To what extent have the experiences of the former Soviet Union and its satellites been studied by the Chinese, and what lessons were drawn from this analysis? To what extent has the CCP studied, and learned from, other single-party hegemonic and authoritarian ruling party-states? We turn to these questions in the next two chapters.

4

The Chinese Discourse on Communist Party-States

Understanding the reforms that the Chinese Communist Party (CCP) has undertaken, both during and since the 1990s, in an attempt to "reinvent," rescue, and relegitimate itself, requires understanding how it has assessed four sets of events: (1) the events of the spring of 1989 in China; (2) the events of 1989–91 in Eastern Europe and the Soviet Union; (3) the "color revolutions" in former Soviet republics and Central Asia; and (4) the political systems of a variety of noncommunist states in Asia, the Middle East, Europe, and Latin America. This chapter deals with the first three sets of events, and the next chapter assesses the fourth set. It is my belief that the CCP's understanding of these events and assessments of these political systems is absolutely central to appreciating what reforms it has undertaken (and not undertaken) and why.[1]

Although it is intuitively logical to surmise that China's understanding of these other systems and events would offer important insights into the CCP's own reform policies, remarkably few scholars have focused on this dimension. Other than Gilbert Rozman's study of Chinese assessments of pre-Gorbachev Soviet socialism,[2] and Nina Halpern's article on Chinese learning from the early East European reforms,[3] only one other study (by Christopher Marsh) has attempted to systematically explore this internal discourse in China and the lessons learned from the Soviet implosion (even Marsh's study only devotes one chapter to this dimension).[4] Though some other assessments, such as those by Minxin Pei and Peter Nolan, comparatively examined the systemic causes of the failure of Soviet reforms and successes of Chinese reforms, neither paid much attention to the internal discourse in each country about the other.[5] Yet, these postmortem assessments are fundamental to understanding CCP reforms in recent years. The CCP has devoted extraordinary and extensive effort in this process. Dozens of books and hundreds of articles have been written on the subject. Even an eight-volume DVD set, titled "Consider Danger in Times of Peace: Historical Lessons from the Fall of the CPSU [Communist Party of the Soviet Union]," was produced in 2006 by the Institute of Marxism of the Chinese Academy of Social Sciences and the National Party Building Research Association; classified secret (*jimi*) and restricted to inner-party circulation (*dangnei cankao pian*); and made mandatory viewing for all central, provincial, and municipal party organs.[6] Thus, this chapter tries to advance the understanding of these linkages by thoroughly examining this post-1989 internal discourse in China.

After the Storm: The Chinese Communist Party in 1989

During April and June 1989, the CCP, and China itself, was shaken to its core by the unprecedented popular demonstrations across the country, the violent suppression of them in Beijing on June 3rd and 4th, and the subsequent six months of martial law in the capital. Not since the Cultural Revolution had the CCP come so close to collapse. The party leadership was paralyzed and split at the very top (resulting in the purge of the reformist CCP general secretary, Zhao Ziyang). The leaders felt embattled and believed that their rule, and the People's Republic itself, were at genuine risk of collapse. It was, as Deng Xiaoping defined it at the time, a matter of life or death, survival or extinction, for the CCP. Yet Deng also evinced the view that there was something inevitable about the frontal challenge to the party-state. In a speech to his officers in Beijing on June 9, 1989, he explained that

> this disturbance would eventually have come in any event. Dictated by both the international climate and the domestic climate in China, it was destined to come, and the outbreak of the disturbance was independent of man's will. It was just a question of it happening sooner or later, and how serious the aftermath would be. . . . They [the demonstrators] were attempting to subvert our state and overthrow the Communist Party, which is the essence of the issue. If we do not understand the fundamental problem, it means we are not clear about the nature of the is-

sue. . . . It all became clear once the incident broke out. They [the demonstrators] had two key goals: one was to overthrow the Communist Party, the other was to topple the socialist system. Their aim was to establish a bourgeois republic totally dependent on the West.[7]

Immediately following the suppression of the Beijing demonstrations on June 4, 1989, the CCP Politburo began the predictable process of trying to understand and explain the causes of the upheaval.[8] This process became inextricably intertwined with the justification for the suppression and the purge of General Secretary Zhao.[9] The "party line" that emerged therefore had an inherently revisionist hue. In the immediate aftermath of the suppression, Chinese leaders were quick to attribute the uprising to a number of internal and external factors. Some of the explanations they offered foreshadowed their explanations six months later as similar popular uprisings spread rapidly across Eastern Europe, toppling one communist party-state after another. An internal speech given by then–Politburo member Yao Yilin is very revealing of the linkage (in the leadership's mind) between the June 1989 suppression, the evolving situation in East Europe, and alleged American attempts to undermine CCP rule. In a speech at a CCP Central Committee conference, attended by "responsible comrades of various departments," on June 13, 1989, Yao stated:

If we had yielded, China would have taken the road that Poland did. Both the Polish and the Hungarians were forced to follow the course they did. What has happened in Poland and Hungary is the result of repeatedly making concessions. Therefore, whether our party and state would have changed color depended on whether we made the first concession. This was a key and decisive step. Of course, making the first concession would not have necessarily meant the immediate collapse of our state, but it would have meant that the situation would have begun moving toward a bourgeois republic. . . . We must on no account take the Polish road or the Hungarian road that American Dulles designed in the 1950s for the gradual transformation of communist countries. Over the past decades the imperialists have never changed their original design. They came to cooperate with us and express friendship not only for the purpose of making money, but also for the purpose of changing the nature of our country and remodeling our country to be a capitalist society. Influenced by Western bourgeois ideology, some of our students and intellectuals actually planned to establish a Westernized bourgeois republic. Some of our cadres even planned to do so. . . . The bourgeois republic they planned to establish would eventually become a vassal state attached to a certain imperialist or capitalist nation. Without the leadership of the Chinese Communist Party and socialist system, it is impossible for China to exist in the world as a genuine independent state![10]

Secret speeches by other leaders also emphasized the subversive intentions and impact of Western countries, particularly the United States. According to then–CCP Propaganda Department chief Wang Renzhi, "Some Western countries and the anticommunist and antisocialist political forces have long cherished the hope of destroying us. In an attempt to incorporate China into the international capitalist system and place China under their control, they have done their utmost to realize the peaceful evolution of China."[11] Newly appointed CCP general secretary Jiang Zemin (who was summoned to the position from Shanghai following the purge of Zhao) adopted a somewhat different interpretation, blaming the deviant thinking of young people in China on the failures of CCP ideology and propaganda work:

> The concepts of so-called democracy, freedom, and human rights spread by the Western bourgeoisie have aroused sympathy among some of the young intellectuals in our country. It can be counted as one of the ideological roots of the recent student unrest and turmoil. Many young students have some confused ideas in this respect. . . . To them, "freedom" means they can do whatever they want. "Freedom of the press" was interpreted as meaning that one can express whatever views one wishes. How can that be possible? There is no absolute democracy or absolute freedom in any country.[12]

Jiang went on to call for intensified ideological indoctrination and vigilance against "bourgeois liberalization." This emphasis is not surprising, given the venue of his address (a national meeting of CCP Propaganda Department cadres), yet it is also interesting that he did not praise the military suppression or rail against hostile foreign forces, as other leaders did at the time. Having been catapulted into the top CCP post, he was in a very sensitive position at the time; this speech can be interpreted as an effort to distance himself somewhat from the repressive events of June 4th while shifting the focus on to "thought work" (*sixiang gongzuo*).

In the weeks and months following June 4th, the principal challenge for the leadership and CCP was to move assertively to try and "put Tiananmen behind them" and exercise damage control internally and externally.[13] This was, however, not so simple—as external events intervened. Not only did China find itself the pariah of the international community and subject to sanctions by the Group of Seven nations, but then the unimaginable occurred: Communist regimes elsewhere fell like dominoes in rapid succession.

Interpreting the Collapse of Communist Party-States in Eastern Europe

Throughout the autumn of 1989, the CCP leadership watched in shock and trepidation as the communist party-states in Eastern Europe experienced popular uprisings and, one after another, fell from power. Ironically, the first communist regime to lose power did so on June 4th—the very day of the martial law crackdown in Beijing. As the Chinese military shot its way through the streets of Beijing, voters in Poland peacefully went to the polls and gave the ruling Communist Party a resounding and humiliating defeat in the National Assembly elections.[14] The subsequent dénouements of other ruling communist parties across Eastern Europe were not as peaceful or smooth as in Poland.

Officially, China's Foreign Ministry put on a brave face and offered to establish "friendly and cooperative relations" with the new Polish government.[15] But the CCP was alarmed about the precedent the Polish elections might set. In an effort to gauge the situation, the Chinese government invited delegations from Czechoslovakia and the German Democratic Republic (GDR, or East Germany) to visit Beijing during September. The East German delegation, led by ranking Politburo member Egon Krenz, stayed on through the celebration of the fortieth anniversary of the People's Republic of China on October 1st (Krenz was one of the few foreign dignitaries present for the event).

As events in Eastern Europe were unfolding, Deng Xiaoping offered his view of the situation and prescribed China's response. In a meeting on September 4th with Politburo members Jiang Zemin, Li Peng, Qiao Shi, Yao Yilin, Song Ping, Li Ruihuan, Yang Shangkun, and Wan Li, Deng observed:

I think the upheavals in Eastern Europe and the Soviet Union were inevitable. It is hard to predict how far they will go; we still have to observe developments calmly. . . . There is no doubt that the imperialists want socialist countries to change their nature. The problem now is not whether the banner of the Soviet Union will fall—there is bound to be unrest there—but whether the banner of China will fall. Therefore the most important thing is that there should be no unrest in China and that we should carry on genuine reform and to open wider to the outside. Without these policies, China would have no future. . . . In short, my views about the international situation can be summed up in three sentences. First, we should *observe the situation coolly.* Second, *we should hold our ground.* Third, *we should act calmly.* Don't be impatient; it is no good to be impatient. *We should be calm, calm, again calm,* and quietly immerse ourselves in practical work to accomplish something— something for China. (emphasis added)[16]

Deng's advice may have been to remain cool, but by the end of September, events were beginning to mushroom out of control in Eastern Europe. As they did, the Chinese government scrambled to follow the events and understand their implications.[17] The exodus of East German refugees into neighboring countries during September quickly built pressure on the GDR regime and the Berlin Wall itself. As demonstrations grew across East Germany, the aging and hard-line GDR leader, Erich Honecker, welcomed the Chinese Politburo member Yao Yilin to East Berlin. In their meetings, Honecker thanked Yao for his briefing on the situation in China, and he observed that there was a "fundamental lesson to be learned from the counterrevolutionary revolt in Beijing."[18] Yao no doubt urged Honecker to hang tough. As popular pressure continued to mount and the crowds continued to swell in late October, Honecker urged his Politburo comrades to adopt the "Chinese solution," that is, the use of force. Unable to forge such a consensus, the ailing autocrat was forced to step down. Honecker was replaced by none other than Krenz—freshly back from his meetings with China's leadership in Beijing. Soon thereafter, as East Germans breached the Wall and flooded across the border into West Berlin on November 9, the government collapsed and Krenz resigned.[19] He later served a brief prison sentence for his role during the dying days of the GDR regime.

Throughout it all, the Chinese domestic media was silent about the events sweeping East Germany. It was similarly silent about the Hungarian renunciation of communist rule on October 7th. Seeking a closer look and to urge the remaining communist governments in Eastern Europe to hold the line, China dispatched Qiao Shi, a Politburo Standing Committee member and the internal security/intelligence czar, to assess the situation in Romania, Bulgaria, and Czechoslovakia. Qiao never made it to Prague because, two days into his trip to Bulgaria, the Czech Parliament voted to end the Communist Party's guaranteed monopoly on power.[20] Thereafter, a prolonged period of significant strain emerged in relations between Prague and Beijing as the new Czech government under dissident-turned-president Václav Havel embraced the causes of Tibetan and Taiwanese independence and became an ardent critic of the CCP.[21] For their part, the reform-minded Bulgarians sought to distance themselves from Qiao, who nonetheless warned his hosts that "maintaining socialism under the leadership of the Communist Party is the only way for China to develop."[22] As Qiao toured Eastern Europe amid the rapidly deteriorating situation, Jiang gave an internal speech on November 28, urging the CCP to heed Deng's September advice about staying cool amid "the rapid upheavals (*jiju dongdang*) in several East European countries."[23]

Romania was, however, the centerpiece of Qiao's trip. There, he attended the Fourteenth Congress of the Romanian Communist Party and met with the Romanian leader Nicolai Ceaușescu—a longtime and stalwart supporter of the CCP. Ceaușescu reassured Qiao that sometimes "the party and government of a socialist country must take measures to suppress counterrevolutionary rebellion."[24] Within three weeks, Ceaușescu would try to heed his own advice, as demonstrators laid siege to the provincial city of Timișoara. But some of the Romanian security services balked, causing a rift in the ranks and armed combat in the streets between rebellious army troops and Ceaușescu's Securitate internal security forces. On Christmas evening, Romanian (and international) television showed the bloody bodies of Ceaușescu and his wife Elena lying in the white snow, having been executed by military forces following a coup d'état.

This image, broadcast around the world on CNN, must have shaken the Chinese leaders to their core. On the surface, they tried to roll with the punch and adapt to the new circumstances. A Foreign Ministry spokesman declared it an "internal matter" for Romania and that "[China] respects the Romanian people's choice," while President Yang Shangkun and Premier Li Peng of China sent a telegram of congratulations to their new counterparts.[25] Such outward protestations belied, however, the internal alarm felt inside the Zhongnanhai (China's leadership compound) and outside in Beijing. Chinese leaders responded by tightening security around the capital, setting up roadblocks and checkpoints on all the approaches leading into the center of the city. The tension in Beijing was palpable.[26]

Following the rapid collapse of the East European communist regimes, there was a hiatus in internal interpretations, until the "line" was set by party authorities. The principal academic journal in the country, *Sulian yu Dong-Ou Wenti* (Soviet and East European Studies),[27] waited a full year before publishing articles interpreting the events in Eastern Europe. Within high party circles, however, the "blame game" began immediately. Though, over time, Chinese analysts produced a variegated picture of the multiple reasons for collapse of these regimes, the immediate assessment pinned the blame on a single factor: Soviet leader Mikhail Gorbachev. A series of Politburo meetings held shortly after the Romanian uprising apparently castigated Gorbachev.[28] Deng Xiaoping, Chen Yun, Jiang Zemin, Wang Zhen, and others all argued that Gorbachev had *intentionally* undermined the East European communist party-states, seeking just such a collapse. Jiang labeled Gorbachev a "traitor like Trotsky."[29]

Although the high-level intraparty debate must have been fierce, it is odd that no special guidance documents dictating the "party line" for interpreting the events in Eastern Europe appear to have been issued in the year following the uprisings. If such documents had been issued, they undoubtedly would have appeared in the CCP Central Propaganda Department's internal (*neibu*) compendiums of directives.[30] Instead, one finds only occasional mention of the East European situation in several documents during this year. One such document, Central Directive No. 21 of 1990 on improving external propaganda work, is illustrative of some of these themes.[31] Not surprisingly, it notes that the CCP's foreign propaganda work since China's "June 4 turmoil" and the East European "changes" (*dongbian*) has encountered "great difficulties" (*hen da de kunnan*). The document notes the potential dangers of reporting too fully inside China on the changes in Eastern Europe, lest "wrongful ideologies have a negative impact," thus suggesting that such coverage should adhere to the "principle of cautious and low-key news reporting." It goes on to assert that each East European collapse had its own causes, although the West's (read: the United States') "peaceful evolution" (*heping yanbian*) efforts were common to each—and thus China should be particularly on guard against similar subversion. Another inner-party document noted that foreign journalists based in China were deemed to be particularly pernicious threats to spread news about the events occurring in Eastern Europe, and they were to be subjected to extra monitoring by the Ministry of State Security (responsible for counterintelligence).[32]

Another document ruefully noted that, as a result of the events in Eastern Europe, "the international communist movement had encountered great hardships."[33] Yet another candidly admitted:

> The changes in Eastern Europe have had no small effect on us. The majority of people are asking: These countries have all changed, can China survive? Will China change, too? Is China able to resist [such] change? Ideologically, there are those that hope we go the way of Eastern Europe. Internally, we must resolutely resist this! During this stage, with external pressures and internal economic difficulties, including the suppressed turmoil and the aftereffects of the turmoil, it is possible to say that it is equally grim [*yanjun*].[34]

Following these candid admissions, the document then goes on to provide a rousing defense of how the CCP and the Chinese people can overcome all such difficulties by following their own road of "socialism with Chinese characteristics."

By mid-1990, Chinese analysts began to publish different interpretations of the causes. Not surprisingly, these began to appear in the pages of the journal of the Institute of Soviet and East European Studies of the Chinese Academy of Social Sciences (CASS). As we will see, this institute came to play a central role in assessing and determining the causes of the USSR's collapse. The institute has had a long and important history in Sino-Soviet relations, Sino-Soviet polemics, and subsequent assessments of the Soviet Union.[35] As such, the institute has been far more than an academic organization, performing an important intelligence function for the CCP and Chinese government. This function is exemplified by the fact that the institute has off and on, over the years, been under the "jurisdiction of the International Liaison Department of the Central Committee of the CCP."[36] After the dissolution of the Soviet Union in 1991, the institute changed its name to the Institute of East European and Central Asian Studies (winning a fierce turf battle with the Institute of European Studies within CASS for the continued coverage of East and Central European states[37]). By 2004, the institute's staff had grown to 106, including 85 full-time researchers.

Beginning in mid-1990, the institute's journal began to carry a variety of articles on the causes of the "drastic changes" (*jubian*) in Eastern Europe.

One of the first articles stressed four themes that would be repeated in many subsequent analyses:[38]

1. the deterioration of the economy, high levels of debt, and a poor standard of living;
2. "dictatorships" (*zhuanzheng*), ruling parties divorced from the populace, and a lack of local-level party building (*jiceng dangjian*);
3. unions that were not a "bridge" (*qiao*) between the party and the working class; and
4. "peaceful evolution" efforts by Western countries.

Subsequent analyses built on these initial themes. One criticized the East European communist parties for being too factionalized in their leaderships and too lax in their memberships (suggesting the need to tighten membership criteria, having trial periods for membership, and weeding out corrupt cadres).[39] This article also criticized the overcentralization of the party structure and the failure to institute "democracy" in local party branches. Many other articles took aim at the Solidarity independent trade union movement in Poland, arguing that it had abandoned the "real working class" and become a tool in the hands of Western powers intent on destabilizing the country.[40] Another article concurred that the unions were the principal target and agent of Western "peaceful evolutionists." The governments of the United Kingdom and Sweden, as well as the U.S. National Democratic Institute (NDI), the National Endowment for Democracy (NED), and the George Soros Foundation, were all accused of funneling monies, and offering training, to unions in Poland, Bulgaria, Czechoslovakia, Hungary, and Romania.[41] One classified (secret) inner-party document, "The Reasons for the Changes in Eastern Europe and Their Lessons," which was circulated in the summer of 1991 and cited by the BBC journalist James Miles (who claims to have been shown it), bemoaned the arrests, interrogations, and imprisonments of former East European communist officials.[42]

Curiously, the Chinese postmortems on Eastern Europe tended not to consider a variety of processes, forces, and causes of collapse emphasized by Western scholars (considered in chapter 2).[43] There is no (public and published) evidence that civil society, the Velvet Revolution, and the role of intellectuals were considered—nor the impact of economic reform in countries like Hungary, pressures to enfranchise opposition parties, the nature of civil-military relations and control of the security services, the Helsinki Process, Willy Brandt's *Ostpolitik* strategy, or for that matter the green light Gorbachev gave to demonstrators that the Soviet Union would not intervene against the East European demonstrations. Nor was there any real disaggregation of the nature and composition of the East European regimes, their historical circumstances, and variance in the paths to power of the opposition; Chinese analysts tended to treat them generically and as a group, and their analyses were thus oversimplified. This may reflect that, in fact, Chinese intelligence collection and understanding of the conditions in Eastern Europe was really rather poor at the time. An alternative explanation would be that Chinese analysts were very aware of these conditions but discouraged such discussion so as not to give the public in China any subversive ideas.

As time passed, however, the postmortems became more variegated and sophisticated. Perhaps this was the result of greater exposure to these countries after 1989. Also, the domestic political conditions inside China improved. In the wake of China's own June 4th incident, the intellectual and political climate was hardly conducive to analyses that discussed the various reasons for, and means of, the East European uprisings. One such comprehensive study compiled by a team of CASS researchers, undertaken a decade later in 1999, did a country-by-country assessment of the causes of the collapse of communist party-states.[44]

According to this study, the principal causes in Poland were said to be primarily economic—high foreign debt, rising inflation, imbalances in industrial development, a price structure that did not respond to supply and demand, and a low standard of living. All these economic conditions, plus the Helsinki pressures on human rights, were said to have stimulated demands for independent trade unions and the founding of Solidarity in Gdansk.

The sources of change in Hungary, however, were seen as political in nature. The Hungarian Socialist Workers Party had become factionalized in its leadership, but it had also decided to admit the entrepreneurial class (which had emerged as a result of economic reforms) as members of the party. Gorbachev's "New Thinking" (glasnost) of "humanism and democratic socialism" are said to also have had a substantial impact on Hungarian party elites. All these processes diluted and ultimately split the party, according to the CASS analysts. Support for the ruling party continually declined, reaching a level of only 36.6 percent in July 1989. Finally, the Hungarian Parliament passed a constitutional amendment on October 18, 1989, to establish a parliamentary democracy and separation of powers, create a real republic, and privatize state-owned enterprises.

East Germany's failures were deemed to have been a combination of economic (too wed to a planned economy) and political (ossified leadership and party organization). Czechoslovakia was said to have experienced "reform from below," stimulated by intellectuals. In Romania, the party leadership (Ceauşescu) lost control of the military and security services. Bulgaria, according to the CASS analysts, simply experienced a "domino effect."

In sum, these CASS analysts thought they saw a repetitive pattern across these different cases that included three common elements: (1) splits within, and the democratization of, the ruling party; (2) ordinary people's discontent, which was taken advantage of by opposition forces; and (3) the Western campaign of "peaceful evolution."[45] In brief, the CASS analysts succinctly summarized, the collapse of the East European regimes was due to "the combination of three forces, namely, political discontent, the West, and revisionism within the ruling Communist Party."[46]

Other analysts at other institutes emphasized other features. For example, some in the International Communist Movement Research Institute of the Central Editing and Translation Bureau of the CCP Central Committee blamed the collapse on the failure of East European regimes to adopt elements of West European social democracy.[47] These regimes were, it was argued, clones of the totalitarian (*jiquanzhuyi*) Stalinist model—what one author termed "Communist Fascism."[48] It is indeed interesting that such an institution—an organ of the Central Committee ostensibly devoted to researching classical communist theory and the history of the global communist movement—would become an ostensible advocate of the democratic socialist model. Yet, perhaps, simply because it had the authority to research all sorts of communist, socialist, and semisocialist systems worldwide, the institute's researchers may have enjoyed the latitude to advocate policies and models that were verboten in other party organs.

A 2004 visit by the author to a closely related institute, the Institute of World Socialism, also under the Central Editing and Translation Bureau (Zhongyang Bianyi Ju) reaffirmed this impression.[49] The director, Wang Xuedong, admitted that "in recent years the institute has concentrated on researching West European social democratic parties and systems—even though they are often critical of us [the CCP]. These parties have much to offer us by example. They recognize the importance of the market economy, their social welfare systems are particularly worthy of study, the way they deal with trade unions merits our attention, and even their system of checks and balances (*quanli zhiheng*) may be useful for us."[50]

Thus, as time went by, a more variegated set of analyses emerged from CCP researchers concerning the causes for the demise of East European communist party-states. Also, it is probably no accident that these more diversified and daring analyses began to emerge after Deng's 1992 fabled "Southern Tour" (Nan Xun) and his pointed criticisms of "leftist thinking."[51] As we will see below, the analyses of the causes of the Soviet Union's collapse reflected a similar diversification after Deng's 1992 tour and the Fourteenth Party Congress.

The Birthplace of Bolshevism Collapses

Then, two years after the East European communist regimes fell like dominoes, the "Mother" of all Bolshevik parties, the Communist Party of the Soviet Union (and the Soviet Union itself) came crashing down. These events, on top of the crisis of 1989 in China, left the Chinese leadership and the CCP profoundly shaken and worried about their own futures. Coming to grips with the collapse of other communist parties, particularly in the Bolshevik heartland of the Soviet Union, came as a profound and deeply disturbing shock to the CCP leadership and provided cause for considerable introspection among its rank and file. Indeed, the intra-CCP analysis of the causes of the Soviet collapse began well before the final implosion, insofar as Chinese analysts were carefully monitoring and critiquing the Brezhnev-Andropov-Chernenko transitional period, and then the reforms unleashed by Mikhail Gorbachev.[52]

The process of understanding the reasons and precipitating causes for the collapse of these other party-states was protracted (resulting in more than a decade of internal introspection and debate), but it was also infused with a sense of immediacy and urgency: What lessons should the CCP learn from the implosion and demise of these other regimes that might help it avoid a similar fate? Thus, the internal assessment was not an idle exercise in academic research among some theoreticians in the Central Party School—the research spanned a number of institutions and had very practical implications for the CCP's "general line" (*Zhongyang luxian*) and its longevity.

The internal Chinese analyses of the causes of collapse of the USSR produced debates and differing emphases over time. These analyses were undertaken in a wide range of institutions—including the Central Party School and party school system, the International Department of the CCP, the Organization Department of the CCP, the Institute of World Socialism, the Institute of the History of the International Communist Movement, the Institute of Russian and Central Asian Studies of CASS, the People's Liberation Army, and a number of universities.

In contrast to the immediate analyses of the East European collapses, there was broad agreement among Chinese analysts that a range of factors contributed to the overthrow of Gorbachev, CPSU rule, and the Soviet Union itself. Also in contrast to many Western analyses—which tended toward a singular emphasis on Gorbachev's individual actions and failings—Chinese analysts took a much broader view and offered a more systemic analysis of the multiple reasons for the collapse. In this regard, Christopher Marsh is only partially correct in his conclusion that "the themes that resonate throughout the Chinese literature on the collapse of the USSR focus on the role of the party and popular support."[53] Marsh is correct that Chinese assessments emphasize weaknesses in the Soviet party apparat and that Soviet policies progressively alienated the populace, but the Chinese discourse also points to many other precipitating causes.

Understanding China's analysis of the reasons that the Soviet and East European party-states collapsed also offers important insights into the ongoing debates and options considered inside the Chinese Communist Party. These "lessons" are of both a "positive" and "negative" nature for the CCP; that is, "If we carry out X reform we will be able to survive, but if we do Y it could lead to a similar collapse." Or: "Gorbachev did A and look what happened; we must not make the same mistake and should thus do B." Sometimes, as is elucidated below, these derivative "lessons" are explicitly stated and thus do not require deciphering; other times, they are implicit and require "decoding." In either case, these are issues and debates that go to the very core of CCP regime survival.

Unlike many of the debates over foreign policy "tendencies" in the Soviet Union twenty years ago,[54] when American analysts tried to establish nuanced differences between factions, institutes, and ministries, or among officials, the Chinese analysis of the causes and reasons for collapse of other socialist states really deal with core (political) life-and-death issues for their own system. The differences of analysis and opinion reflect institutional and factional differences within the Chinese system, which were very likely linked to higher-level discussions and positions among CCP officials. Yet, readers should be aware that many of the Chinese analyses and texts analyzed in this chapter were *not* intended for foreign consumption and were not "sugarcoated" for foreign readers. They were written for internal Chinese and inner-party (CCP) consumption, and some of them were published for restricted circulation (*neibu*), whereas others were intended for more general distribution inside China—but, in all cases, these materials were part of an internal and closed discourse.

Skepticism → Support → Suspicion → Shock → Systemic study → Conclusion

(1986–87)   (1987–89)   (1989–91)   (1991–92)   (1993–2004)   (2004–5)

Figure 4.1. Chinese Analysis of Soviet Reforms and Collapse

The Chinese discourse on the Soviet collapse passed through several distinct phases and, in each, different schools of thought are evident. As figure 4.1 illustrates, five distinct stages can be discerned. To be sure, the analysis and discourse continued long after the collapse of the Soviet Union.

A slightly different periodization was given by the leading Chinese Sovietolgist Lu Nanquan of CASS (himself a leading contributor to these analyses). Lu argued that the postcollapse analysis passed through three phases:

1. The first phase was 1991, when scholars first argued that the principal cause of collapse was the West's "peaceful evolution" tactics—but this only lasted a "short time," as it quickly became evident that there were multiple internal causes.
2. The second phase was 1992–96, when analysts focused on the various causes, both internal and external.
3. The third phase is 1996–the present, when questions were raised by Chinese leaders as to what the lessons for China were. "We are still in this phase," Lu reflected in 2004.[55]

Yet other observers detected other patterns. Zhang Jialin agrees with Lu that the prevailing immediate postcollapse view stressed "peaceful evolution," but he argues that by 1992 this had given way to those who maintained a "political determinism thesis" that Gorbachev's reforms were the principal cause, which in 1993 led to an "economic determinism thesis," which finally in 1994 led to multicausal explanations.[56]

Chinese analyses of the Soviet Union, and of Gorbachev in particular, also did not occur in the abstract. That is, they reflected the political climate inside China at the time. For example, it is evident that during the period 1986–87, when there was a cool political climate and campaign against "bourgeois liberalization" in the wake of prodemocracy demonstrations and the downfall of the CCP leader Hu Yaobang, Chinese analyses of Gorbachev's reforms were distinctly skeptical.[57] However, from 1987 to 1989, as Zhao Ziyang succeeded Hu as the CCP general secretary and the domestic political climate in China became much more liberal again, so too did Chinese analyses of the USSR.

The Twenty-Seventh Congress of the CPSU in February and March 1986 marked a major turning point in Chinese commentary on Soviet reforms. Liu Keming, then the director of the CASS Institute of Soviet and East European Studies, published an analysis of the congress in which he praised it (and Gorbachev) for attacking the "stagnation and dogmatism" during the Leonid Brezhnev era.[58] Liu praised Gorbachev's reforms as appropriate, but he warned that their success or failure rested on whether they could overcome the "inertia, conservatism, and dogmatism among officials and cadres."[59] A symposium in the institute's journal to assess the implications of the congress concluded that its major breakthrough had been the recognition that market forces were needed to rectify the stagnation of the Soviet economy.[60] Another bold article in the same issue of *Sulian yu Dong-Ou Wenti* offered the truly radical suggestion that, in order to deal with "the bureaucracy and mass inertia, . . . to be the master of the state, people should have the right to elect and recall their leaders at all levels. To realize these rights, the local Soviets should be broadened, mass participation in decisionmaking should be increased, and the autonomy of labor collectives should be guaranteed. To get rid of the bureaucracy, it is necessary to get rid of the appointment system [*nomenklatura*] and lifelong career for top officials."[61] Another opined that "the past experience of the Soviet political system has been too much centralization of power, too little democracy, and the masses have not had the practical right for democratic administration."[62] One cannot help but wonder if such radical suggestions and observations were not implicitly aimed at the CCP itself.

Postcongress analyses during 1986 tended to stress the problems confronting economic reform in the Soviet Union.[63] However, the emphasis in Chinese analyses began to shift from economic to political in 1987, and lasted all the way through the first half of 1989, leading up to Gorbachev's state visit to China and the Sino-Soviet Summit to consummate the renormalization of relations. Again, this also likely reflects the fact that in China this was precisely the time that Zhao Ziyang and his advisers were pushing political reform—thus, to praise Gorbachev's glasnost was simultaneously to rationalize and support political reform in China. We now know that there was a fierce intraparty debate within the CCP, and considerable swelling opposition to Zhao and his reforms, during this period leading up to the prodemocracy demonstrations of April through June 1989. During this period, Chinese analyses of Gorbachev's reforms mirrored Zhao's own political reform initiatives: separating party and government,[64] showing the errors of "leftism,"[65] demonstrating the need to retire and replace old cadres (we now know that Zhao was locked in a fierce battle with the CCP's conservative Old Guard at the time),[66] improving the educational qualifications of cadres,[67] introducing local-level elections,[68] and introducing competition and material incentives throughout society.[69] In short, Zhao's political manifesto began to sound increasingly like Gorbachev's, and vice versa. The two men were able to meet and share their simpatico perspectives during Gorbachev's historic visit to Beijing in mid-May 1989 (in the midst of the Tiananmen Square demonstrations).

However, Zhao's overthrow in late May and the violent suppression of the demonstrations on June 4th not only changed things in China—it also changed Chinese assessments of Gorbachev and the Soviet Union. A two-year period of suspicion and internal criticism ensued. On the surface, during this time, China and the Soviet Union attempted to maintain the semblance of normal state-to-state and party-to-party relations—what John Garver has described as "delegation diplomacy."[70] But underneath this facade of normalcy, the CCP leaders were themselves highly insecure and were deeply disturbed by what they were witnessing in the Soviet Union and Eastern Europe.

The failed coup d'état of August 19, 1991, the subsequent overthrow of the CPSU, and the full collapse of the Soviet Union shook the CCP to its core. There is some evidence that the Chinese leadership was aware of the coup plotting, as relayed by Defense Minister Chi Haotian (who was visiting Moscow in the week leading up to the attempted coup).[71] At first, the Chinese leaders rejoiced at the news of Gorbachev's arrest, but when the conspirators failed and Boris Yeltsin led the countercoup and succeeded in seizing power, China's perspective turned dour. The only thing that could be worse than Gorbachev, from the CCP's perspective, was his overthrow by noncommunist elements (Yeltsin had withdrawn from the CPSU at its Twenty-Eighth Congress in July 1990). Perhaps reflecting the fact that the Chinese had been tipped off about the coup plans, the official Xinhua News Agency reported the state of emergency within minutes of its declaration,[72] and the evening news on China Central Television, CCTV, was interrupted to report on the coup and the declaration.[73] That evening, an emergency Politburo meeting was convened at which General Secretary Jiang Zemin of the CCP is said to have hailed Gorbachev's overthrow,[74] although Deng Xiaoping is also reported to have warned Jiang at a Politburo meeting on August 20th that the coup might fail and thus to be prudent and take a more cautious, wait-and-see approach.[75] Deng's view seems to have initially prevailed (not surprisingly), as the CCP leaked inner-party directives urging caution and forbidding party members from publicly airing opinions on the situation in the Soviet Union.[76]

When the coup collapsed, the Chinese media initially went silent. Only the *People's Daily* reported Gorbachev's return to power, the CCP sent no official message of congratulations to him on his restoration of power. On August 23rd, the Soviet ambassador to China, N. N. Solovyev, paid a visit to Foreign Minister Qian Qichen of China and conveyed a three-point official message: (1) Gorbachev was in good health; (2) the Soviet Union would restore constitutional rule; and (3) the Soviet Union would soon restore political, economic, and social stability.[77] On the surface, the Chinese government continued to maintain its cool—but underneath, it was deeply concerned by the chain of events. Though the prospect of the overthrow of Gorbachev may have brought hope within the CCP leadership, the coup's failure and his restoration to power only deepened concern.

This was evident in an internal speech given by the *People's Daily* editor, Gao Di, on August 30th. In his speech to party editors and cadres, Gao, a noted ideologue himself, was surely relaying the spirit and decisions of high-level inner-party discussions.[78] In it, Gao began by telling his audience that he was conveying "the intent of the Central Committee," thus conveying the authoritative nature of how the CCP sought to have the events in the Soviet Union interpreted. It is an extraordinary speech, both with respect to the official interpretation of the coup and its failure and also because it signaled the main outlines of the CCP's postmortem interpretation of the reasons for the erosion and collapse of the Soviet Union itself.

Essentially, Gao gave two main reasons for the coup and its failure, and several broader reasons for the decline of the Soviet Union. Gao first blamed Gorbachev's erroneous policies of "New Thinking," which Gao claimed was political "liberalism" (*ziyouhua*). Gao alleged that liberalism had crept deeply into both the party and the military (particularly among young officers). Second, the coup plotters failed to preempt the countercoup elements. Gao claimed that they should have cut off Yeltsin's telephone, so he could not organize the resistance, and they "should simply have arrested Yeltsin and Gorbachev before they did anything else, just as we did the Gang of Four. . . . [The coup plotters] could never have achieved their ends by working within the framework of the Constitution. You do not ask a tiger politely for his skin—either you kill him or he will kill you! Revolution is merciless—if you do not overthrow him, he will overthrow you!"

More generically, Gao argued that the incident had been made possible by Gorbachev's "New Thinking" (glasnost), which had sown ideological confusion among the people. He also blamed the incident on the West's "smokeless warfare" campaign of "peaceful evolution." Gao claimed that "Gorbachev and Yeltsin are not true Communist Party members at all, but are traitors [*pantu*] and agents of the West [*Xifang dailiren*]—they have acted entirely in accordance with Western institutions and in accordance with orders from America." Gao further argued that the standard of living in the Soviet Union had declined badly, as a result of government misman- agement, excessive defense spending, and placing political reform before economic reform. He also blamed Gorbachev for beginning to "privatize" the economy, and thus "moving down the road to capitalism."

So, what lessons did Gao draw from his analysis for China? First, he claimed that "the August 19th Incident in the Soviet Union was so much like our own June 4th, and yet the result was completely the opposite. This was because we resolutely suppressed it [*jianjue zhenya*] without the slight- est mercy [*hao wu liuqing*], whereas the Soviet Committee of Eight was un- able to implement the dictatorship of the proletariat." Had force been used, and Gorbachev and Yeltsin purged, Gao insinuated, the Soviet Union would still exist. Gao concluded his speech drawing six specific lessons, in addi- tion to reaffirming the "correctness" of using force on June 4th; "it is cor- rect to quell disturbances," he opined. He concluded by listing six lessons for the CCP:

- Resolutely maintain the leadership of the party, and not develop a mul- tiparty or parliamentary system.
- Resolutely maintain party control over the gun, and not allow the devel- opment of a "national army" (*jundui guojiahua*).
- Resolutely maintain the dictatorship of the proletariat and never develop bourgeois democratic freedoms.
- Resolutely maintain the system of public ownership and not develop pri- vatization.
- Resolutely uphold Marxism and not allow ideological pluralism.
- Concentrate our energies and work hard for further reform and opening up.

Gao's analysis of the failed coup d'état and dissolution of the Soviet Communist Party, as well as his prescriptions for the CCP, were harbingers of years of further analyses to be undertaken within the CCP. We will see below the various permutations of this analysis, but it is striking that many of the variants echo Gao's initial analysis (and no doubt also the analyses of those much higher in the party apparatus than Gao).

More Postmortems

The subsequent analyses in China extended over *thirteen years* until 2004, when the lessons drawn were set forth in the form of the *Decision of the CPC Central Committee on Enhancing the Party's Ruling Capacity,* adopted at the Fourth Plenary Session of the Sixteenth Congress of the CCP in September 2004. This important document is discussed at length in the next chapter, insofar as it draws together many of the lessons derived from the collapse of the East European and Soviet communist parties. Over the intervening thirteen years, however, a considerable number of analyses were undertaken. Broadly speaking, the factors identified as having led to the Soviet collapse fell into four categories: economic, political/coercive, social/cultural, and international. These are explicated below but are summarized in table 4.1.

It is most interesting that the Chinese critiques of the failure of the CPSU and collapse of the Soviet Union were *systemic* in nature. That is, after the initial assessments in the immediate aftermath of the August 1991 failed coup—which blamed Gorbachev and Yeltsin for causing the dénouement of the USSR—Chinese analysts began to probe the precipitating causes more deeply, looking for the systemic factors that gave rise to the collapse. They found that, instead of a "perfect storm" of events culminating together in August 1991, in fact the sources of Soviet collapse lay in long-term Soviet decline, mismanagement, wrong judgments and policy mistakes, systemic distortions, an inability to react to failures and innovate, excessive dogmatism, bureaucratic inefficiency, an inappropriate foreign policy, and a variety of other maladies.

In this regard, the Chinese emphasis on *systemic causes* contrasts sharply with the prevailing Western analyses (described in chapter 2), which tended to emphasize *immediate causes*—that is, the role of Gorbachev and the immediate precipitating events of 1990–91. This is a most interesting difference. Most postcollapse analyses published in China were also historically retrospective.[79] They provide a fascinating set of insights into the CCP's self-assessment of its own past policy mistakes as well as its future challenges.

For example, one critique that emerged concerned Nikita Khrushchev's attempted reforms in the middle to late 1950s. Khrushchev was proclaimed by some Chinese analysts to have been the Soviet Union's first great reformer, and had he not been overthrown and his policies undermined, the Soviet Union would not have sunk into the prolonged thirty-year stagnation of the Brezhnev-Chernenko eras. The views of Li Jingjie, director of the CASS Institute of Russia and East Europe (later Eastern Europe and Central Asia), are illustrative of this revisionist viewpoint:

> Most Chinese scholars today believe that Khrushchev was the first reformist in the Soviet Union. Gorbachev was Khrushchev's successor, and his reforms were a continuation of Khrushchev's. The [Chinese] criticisms of Khrushchev's reforms at the time were not correct. His concept of *quanmindang* (party of the whole people) was a theoretical innovation. Many of us believe that if Khrushchev's reforms had continued, the Soviet Union would have turned out very differently. However, there is still a minority of scholars who believe that Khrushchev's criticisms of Stalin were not correct—but the vast majority believes that his Twentieth Party Congress speech was correct.[80]

The irony of this assessment, of course, is that it was none other than Chairman Mao and the rest of the CCP leadership who criticized Khrushchev so severely after the "Secret Speech" of 1956, praised Joseph Stalin's legacy, vigorously opposed Khrushchev's foreign policies toward Eastern Europe and the United States, and used these critiques to launch the 1957 Anti-Rightist Campaign, 1958 commune movement, and the 1958–62 Great Leap Forward. It was this set of mistaken Chinese judgments about Khrushchev at the time that led directly to the Sino-Soviet schism and the series of disastrous Maoist policy decisions that culminated in the Cultural Revolution. Thus, the collapse of the Soviet Union afforded the opportunity for historiography in the 1990s to address policy errors made more than three decades previously. Still, however, the effects of Chinese analysts' own self-censorship is apparent. That is, while able to praise Khrushchev and his reforms, they remained incapable of explicitly blaming Mao and his lieutenants (including Deng Xiaoping) for the policy errors on the Chinese side.

As noted above, though systemic and comprehensive in their nature, the Chinese critiques of the Soviet collapse can be disaggregated into four categories: economic factors, political and coercive factors, social and cultural factors, and international factors. Let us examine each in turn.

Table 4.1. *Chinese Assessments of Factors Contributing to the Collapse of the Soviet Union*

Economic Factors	Political and Coercive Factors	Social and Cultural Factors	International Factors
Economic stagnation	All features of "totalitarianism" (*jiquanzhuyi*)	Intimidated population due to totalitarian terror	"Peaceful Evolution" campaign of the West
Overly centralized economy and retarded market mechanisms	Overconcentration of political power in top leader; personal dictatorship	Low standard of living	Economic stresses caused by Cold War containment policies
Collectivized and large-scale state agriculture	Failure to replace political leaders systematically	Society cut off from outside world in all respects	Military stresses caused by the Cold War
Nonintegration into international economic systems and international financial institutions	No inner-party democracy	Alienation from workplace and party-state	Expansionist and hegemonic policies, especially under Brezhnev
Party dominance of government economic apparatus	Ideological rigidity and distorted Marxism	Low levels of worker efficiency, poor incentives, shoddy production	Soviet chauvinism within international communist movement
Low tax base	Party dominance of the state	Production slowdown and workplace unrest	Domination of Eastern Europe and other client states (Cuba, Vietnam)
Severe price distortions, owing to heavy subsidies	Prolonged "leftist" tendencies from Stalin until Gorbachev ("rightist")	Pervasive alcoholism	
Overdevelopment of heavy industry to detriment of tertiary industries	Party enjoys special privileges and becomes "ruling class"	Repression of, and chauvinism toward, non-Russian ethnic groups—including ethnic cleansing, forced labor, and forced relocation of ethnic minorities	
Overemphasis on defense industries and military sector of economy	Bureaucratic inefficiency	Rising autonomous nationalist identities separate from USSR	

State monopoly of property rights	Overconcentration of power in *nomenklatura*; overly large bureaucracy	Moral vacuum, public cynicism, and public "crisis in faith" in the system
Little revenue sharing between center and localities	Poorly developed mechanisms to police party members for breach of discipline	Persecution of intellectuals
Inefficiencies of scale of production	"Crisis of trust" in party leaders → "crisis of faith" in socialist system	Dogmatism among intellectuals
Dogmatic ideological bias against capitalism	Began political reforms (glasnost) before economic foundation was ready	"Pluralization" of the media under Gorbachev
Perestroika too little, too late, and too fast	Emasculation in role of Supreme Soviet and local Soviets → checks and balances of state on party became meaningless.	Breakdown in the relations of Communist Party of the Soviet Union with various social sectors.
	Falsehood of federalism—dominance of other republics and communist parties	Disillusion of youth
	Success of Western "Peaceful Evolution" campaign to usurp Soviet power	
	Gorbachev tried to democratize Communist Party of the Soviet Union (too much, too late), and remake it as a social-democratic party	

Economic Factors

The Chinese analyses of Soviet economic failings were a comprehensive indictment of its command economy and ideological dogmatism. Some used basic Marxist reasoning to blame the collapse of the political super-structure of the party-state on the failure of the economic base. "The collapse of the Soviet Union demonstrated a political and social failure, but the root cause was its economic system," argued Xu Zhixin of the CASS Eastern Europe, Russia, and Central Asia Institute.[81] The principal failing of the planned economy, Xu argued, was social deprivation owing to a shortage of consumer commodities. As a result of commodity shortages, "society lost vigor in production and technical innovation."[82] Moreover, consumer deprivation was not an accidental consequence of the planned economy—to the contrary, he argued, it was a consciously planned feature of the system! He also blamed the nonintegration of the Soviet Union into the global economy as a contributing factor.

Virtually all assessments were in agreement that the totalism of the command economy and the absence of market mechanisms were fundamental failings of the Soviet economic system. They also agreed that this failure was the result of economic determinism and excessive ideological dogmatism that dismissed certain reforms as "capitalist" and thus inappropriate. Soviet economic planners lacked flexibility and innovation, and they were never able to disentangle the command economy from the socialist political system.[83]

Many studies blamed the overemphasis placed on heavy industry and the resulting neglect of light industry and agriculture. This disproportional development began to actually contract the economy beginning in the 1960s.[84] Agriculture itself had been neglected since the forced collectivization of the 1930s and suppression of the kulaks—which was seen as Stalin's mistaken assessment of peasants and farmers as members of the petite bourgeois class.[85] As one assessment pithily put it, "Stalin did not trust peasants."[86] Not only was the overemphasis on heavy industry seen as a weakness, but the priority placed on military industries was seen as a particular distortion by many Chinese analysts.[87] The militarization of the national economy severely distorted the economic structure and bankrupted the society, argued Lu Nanquan of CASS.[88] A 2002 forum of experts also noted the inefficiencies of economies of scale, the state monopoly of property rights, severe price distortions (owing to heavy subsidies), a low tax base and little revenue sharing between the central government and regional governments, and a poor statistical system.[89]

By the time Gorbachev introduced his economic reforms, Chinese analysts argued, it was too late. The distortions and backwardness of the Soviet economy were too severe. Moreover, Gorbachev made the fatal mistake of trying to do too much, too fast. Chinese analysts were critical of his attempts to "telescope" the reform process—bypassing incremental reform (as in China) in favor of trying to rectify all economic maladies simultaneously.[90]

Political and Coercive Factors

Although Soviet economic failings were considered to be fundamental reasons for the collapse of the system, by far the bulk of Chinese analyses of the Soviet dénouement concentrated on political factors. As table 4.1 indicates, these included a wide range of characteristics.

Interestingly, some of the sharpest critiques echoed the strident Cold War rhetoric in the United States during the 1950s—the critique of Soviet "totalitarianism" (*jiquanzhuyi*). It is quite unusual to find this term in Chinese political discourse, but it featured prominently in postmortems on the Soviet Union.

Though a few argued that the origins of totalitarianism lay in the traditional tsarist political culture,[91] the majority of analyses traced Soviet totalitarianism to Stalin. Whereas Lenin was criticized for "underestimating the durability and adaptability of capitalism and being overly optimistic about the potential for revolution in European societies,"[92] it was Stalin who introduced the various features of totalitarianism: mass terror and intimidation;[93] dictatorship and the overcentralization of power;[94] establishing a cult of personality (*geren chongbai*) and abandonment of collective party leadership;[95] concentrating all power in the party with no separation between party and state bureaucracies;[96] glorifying the Russian race, equating ethnic tensions with class struggle, and suppressing non-Russian minorities;[97] severely suppressing all dissent;[98] and distorting the economy in all sectors through forced collectivization and overcentralization.[99] All these, and other, problems were perceived to be the result of the excessive concentration of power in the party and "dictatorship of the supreme leader."[100]

The impact of Stalinist totalitarianism was profound, comprehensive, and enduring. According to the veteran Soviet specialist Xu Kui, Stalinist totalitarianism resulted in a traumatized and morbid society.[101] According to Xiao Guisen, Stalinist totalitarianism had several lasting effects: stunted economic growth, a weakened attraction of socialism to the public, tight surveillance of society, a lack of democracy in decisionmaking, an absence of the rule of law, the burden of bureaucracy, the CPSU's alienation from people's concerns, and an accumulation of ethnic tensions.[102]

Several researchers labeled Stalin's totalitarian policies as "leftist" and "dogmatic," which deviated from true Marxism-Leninism.[103] Stalin's two major mistakes, argued Gao Fang of People's University, were dogmatism and feudalism.[104] Stalin's ideology was a "bastardization of Leninism," according to Zheng Yifan of the Institute of World Socialism.[105] Such leftist dogmatism became a "lethal problem" for the CPSU, according to the Sovietologist Yu Sui. Yu even went so far as to claim that "the collapse of the Soviet Union and CPSU is a punishment for its past wrongs!"[106] Hong Zhaolong of Beijing University argued that Stalin's worst mistake was his distortion of Lenin's concept of "democratic centralism" to concentrate dictatorial power in his own hands and thereby render ineffective all kinds of inner-party supervision and consultative mechanisms.[107] Hong noted the irony of personal dictatorships contradicting the essence of the idea of a proletarian, mass-based party."[108] Even Stalin's foreign policy was attacked. He was blamed for misinterpreting a temporary economic cycle in the West as a reflection of the "crisis of capitalism," thus distorting Lenin's theory of imperialism, and for supporting foreign revolutionary movements only when they served Soviet interests.[109]

Lu Nanquan, a senior Sovietologist at CASS, pinned blame squarely on the impact of what he called the "Stalin-Soviet Socialist Model":

> In my opinion, the fundamental cause for the drastic changes in the Soviet Union and East European countries at the end of the 1980s and beginning of the 1990s was the loss of dynamism in the Stalin-Soviet Socialist Model. . . . The demerits of this model were institutional and fundamental—not a single reform after Stalin's death brought fundamental changes to the Stalin-Soviet Socialist Model. This model, with its problems and contradictions accumulating day by day, was finally in crisis, and the people of the Soviet Union and Eastern Europe lost their confidence in it. The [only] way out was to abandon the Stalin-Soviet Socialist Model and seek another road for social development.[110]

Thus, the critique of political aspects of the Soviet collapse opened a deluge of criticism of Stalinist totalitarianism. The twin ironies of this invective are, of course, (1) that it closely mirrored Khrushchev's own critique of Stalinism in the 1956—which the Chinese roundly denounced at the time but were not admitted in these post facto assessments—and (2) the fact that none of the critiques drew any explicit comparisons to China's own Maoist totalitarian period. Implicitly, of course, this can be read between the lines of the attacks on Stalinism, but it remains remarkable that four decades after the events and three since Mao's death, Chinese intellectuals still cannot explicitly criticize these mistakes of Mao.

Many Chinese analysts were critical of the CPSU's failures in "propaganda work." Hu Yanxin summarized these failings as principally five:

1. Propaganda was tedious in content, monotonous in form, and disconnected from reality.
2. The authorities concealed the truth by only reporting good news, which lost the people's trust.
3. The CPSU dealt with intellectual circles by administrative and repressive means.
4. Real information had to come from abroad, but this only made Russians further disbelieve their own media.
5. The CPSU failed to accurately analyze the new changes in the West objectively, thus losing the opportunity to develop in line with the new scientific and technological revolution.[111]

The issue of ideological dogmatism was also taken up by a number of scholars in critiquing the post-Stalin period.[112] Whereas Khrushchev was seen as reformist and ideologically flexible, and some viewed Yuri Andropov as potentially so, Brezhnev, Mikhail Suslov, Aleksey Kosygin, Konstantin Chernenko, and other Soviet leaders were all depicted as having dogmatic, ossified, inflexible, bureaucratic ideology and thinking.[113]

Gorbachev, of course, was not seen as ossified and dogmatic in his thinking. Quite to the contrary. Almost without exception, Chinese analysts labeled his policies of glasnost (new thinking) and perestroika (restructuring) as ideologically "rightist"—as distinguished from the totalitarian "leftist" policies of Stalin. Chinese critiques of Gorbachev's ideology were particularly critical of his advocacy of "humanistic and democratic socialism" (*rendao he minzhu de shehuizhuyi*) after a January 1987 CPSU Central Committee meeting and formal adoption of the concept at the Nineteenth Party Congress of June 1988.[114] In China at the time, the dissident intellectual Wang Ruoshui and others close to the reformist party leader Zhao Ziyang were simultaneously advocating "humanism" (*rendaozhuyi*).

Gorbachev's ideological deviation on this issue was seen to have been his core error, for it was rooted in two profound misjudgments. First, Chinese analysts argued, it was based on West European social democracy and a worship of the capitalist system. Second, it advocated pluralistic politics, which opened the door to his subsequent advocacy in February 1990 of amending the Soviet Constitution to allow for a multiparty and presidential-style system—thus directly undermining the political hegemony of the CPSU.[115] According to one analysis,[116] glasnost (which the Chinese translate as "opening" or *gongkaixing*) led to the "eight negations" (*ba ge fouding*) in the Soviet Union:

1. negating the leadership position of the Communist Party,
2. negating the socialist economic system as the dominant sector of the economy,
3. negating the public ownership system as the dominant ownership system in the economy,
4. negating the existence of classes and class struggle,
5. negating the ultimate socialist goal of realizing communism,
6. negating the leadership position of Marxism-Leninism as the guiding principles of socialism,
7. negating democratic centralism, and
8. negating the international appeal of socialist ideals.

After first advocating the concept of humanitarian and democratic socialism internally, in 1988 Gorbachev then applied it externally to relations with Eastern Europe. This "New Thinking Diplomacy" (*Xin Sikao Waijiao*) undermined these regimes by emboldening antiparty elements,[117] fractured the solidarity of the Warsaw Pact, gave scope for the West's "peaceful evolution" policies to make further inroads, and represented a complete capitulation to the West.[118] "Humanitarianism" was seen as a ruse for the total embrace of Western values,[119] because it played directly into the hands of the West's "peaceful evolution" strategy,[120] and it sought to copy West European social democracy.[121] Opening the door to "ideological pluralism" was just the prerequisite step to political pluralism.[122]

Having thus abandoned the CPSU's hegemony over ideology, the next logical step was to undermine the most fundamental of all Leninist principles—the party's absolute monopoly of political power. Gorbachev thus set out to actually dismantle the party apparatus (it was asserted). According to Wang Changjiang, a leading Central Party School researcher, Gorbachev's two fatal errors were to separate the party from the government and to introduce inner-party democracy without controlling it. "The two trends,"

Wang argued, "were lethal to the fall of the party. Unlimited democratization led to the emergence of multiple parties and political organizations and intraparty groups within the party, while the party lost control over the government."[123]

According to many Chinese analysts, party reform *was necessary,* because the CPSU had become "ossified" (*chuisixing*) and a "crisis of trust" in party leaders and a "crisis of faith" in the party's ideology had developed among its rank and file.[124] As one researcher at the People's Liberation Army's National Defense University ruefully reflected: "Gorbachev had no choice but to reform the party—the problem was how he did it. . . . While Gorbachev's reform policies did not intend to bring about the dissolution of the CPSU or Soviet Union, it nonetheless was an inevitable tragedy precipitated by his reforms."[125]

Another analyst in the CCP Organization Department agreed: "What Gorbachev in fact did was not to transform the CPSU by correct principles—indeed the Soviet Communist Party *needed transformation*—but instead he, step-by-step, and ultimately, eroded the ruling party's dominance in ideological, political, and organizational aspects."[126] This assessment identified four successive steps, undertaken by Gorbachev, which progressively usurped CPSU rule:

1. advocacy of pluralist ideology;
2. advocacy of political pluralism via constitutional amendment;
3. issuing new party guidelines (at the Twenty-Eighth Session of the Supreme Soviet) that changed the nature that allowed factions within the party and autonomy of local party organs, thereby transforming the CPSU into something like a parliamentary party under a Western-style multiparty system; and
4. dissolving the Central Committee, yet retaining supreme authority as CPSU secretary-general.[127]

The same annual assessment published eight years later accused Gorbachev of progressively usurping CPSU authority and control through five different steps:

1. reforming central organs in line with the principle of "separating party and state" (*dang-zheng fenkai*), which had the effect of transferring all authority and functions of the political regime from the CPSU to the Supreme Soviet, making it the core of the state apparatus. (Another study

agreed that the attempt to empower the Supreme Soviet was a step away from CPSU dominance, but it also argued that because the Supreme Soviet had been a weak "united front" body for so many years it was not ready to absorb the new powers granted to it, thus creating a power vacuum at the center which permitted the republics to push for their autonomy);[128]

2. reforming the party Politburo in order to mandate that leaders of the Communist Party in each republic automatically be granted Politburo status, thus removing the Soviet Confederation from decisionmaking;

3. amending the Constitution to permit a multiparty and presidential system;

4. dissolving the CPSU in 1991; and

5. forcing party elders into retirement and realigning the membership of the Politburo and Secretariat—such a large-scale replacement of party leaders contributed to instability among rank-and-file cadres and brought many "opportunists" into party leadership positions at all ranks.[129]

One particularly comprehensive analysis by a Central Party School researcher, Zhao Yao, argued that everything Gorbachev did was misguided.[130] He tried to telescope economic reforms. He blindly copied a Western political model of democratic socialism. He degraded the party, by allowing a privileged class to form within it. His reforms permitted party leaders to betray each other and not follow discipline. He lost belief in communism. He did not understand ethnic separatism. He did not foster the rule of law. He permitted subversion by domestic and foreign enemies. Zhao, like others, argues that by the time Gorbachev introduced these measures the system was already too distorted from the Stalin and Brezhnev eras, and the system could not absorb the totality and rapidity of these changes.

Interestingly, in May 2006 one Chinese journal carried an interview with Gorbachev, in which he is quoted as warning:

My advice to my Chinese friends is: Do not practice so-called "democratization" because it will not end well. Never allow the situation to become chaotic. Stability comes first. . . . On the collapse of the Communist Party of the Soviet Union, I now deeply realize that, during the period of *perestroika,* strengthening the party's leadership over the state and the process of reform is the core of all important issues. Here, I would like, with our painful errors, to remind my Chinese friends: If the party loses its control over society and reform, there will be chaos, and that is very dangerous. Before we were prepared, we allowed Soviet society to greatly liberalize.[131]

It is hard to know if this is an accurate quotation from Gorbachev. It certainly accords with the CCP's general line, but it does not coincide with other statements made by Gorbachev in the international media and his memoirs.

Although these assessments emphasized top-level changes initiated by Gorbachev, others stressed lower-level problems in the CPSU. For example, an "investigation team" (*kaochadui*) was dispatched by the CCP Organization Department to Russia and Cuba from September 22 to October 9, 2003, at the invitation of the Russian and Cuban communist parties, with the expressed purpose of discussing the reasons for the CPSU's demise and the Cuban Communist Party's longevity. Its report noted a number of contributing factors, some of which have been noted above (e.g., the dogmatization of Marxism and Gorbachev's "humane and democratic socialism"), but it also stressed failures in grassroots party building. It is not surprising that such an investigation group from the CCP Organization Department would focus on this factor, but in its post-trip report the group noted that party cell development inside the CPSU had been very weak and party members were of low quality. This, the report argued, was the case before Gorbachev's assumption of power, but he contributed to the trend by issuing inner-party regulations that banned the formation of party cells in enterprises, rural areas, schools, and universities—all of which caused the party to lose its "base" with the "people."[132] The report, like many others, also stressed that the CPSU had become too commandist and did not have any inner-party democracy (*dang nei minzhu*).[133]

Still other studies focused on the composition of the CPSU's membership. Some blamed the party for having become a "technocracy,"[134] while not recruiting (and ignoring the interests of) average laborers, farmers, and intellectuals.[135] Some were particularly critical of the Soviet *nomenklatura* personnel system, which overcentralized and perpetuated rule by a small, self-selected elite.[136] Others ridiculed the CPSU in a Milovan Djilas–like fashion,[137] for having created a "managerial class that pursues its own privileges and interests."[138] Huang Zongliang of Beijing University explicitly endorsed Djilas's analysis and argued that the creation of a "corrupt and privileged class" had structural roots in the *nomenklatura* system.[139] On this basis, Huang issued a warning for the CCP: "We can see clearly that the ruling group in the Soviet Union became a ruling class, a bureaucratic class. There is a consensus among Chinese scholars on this point. As we promote social and political reform in China, we need to be very aware of the dangers of a bureaucratic class arising here."[140]

Such accusations opened the way for a few critiques of corruption within the CPSU and personal perquisites enjoyed by its members.[141] Though not many analysts focused on the issue of corruption or party privileges (perhaps because it struck too close to home), one 2002 analysis was explicit:

> There were many causes of the collapse of the Soviet Union, but one that has been overlooked was corruption among the CPSU's leadership. We can thus conclude that the death of the CPSU was not caused by anticommunist forces, but rather by corrupted members within the Party. . . . To a certain extent, the Soviet disintegration was brought about by the "self-coup" of the privileged [party] class.[142]

Another analysis specified six different types of special personal perquisites that CPSU cadres enjoyed: special housing, special supplies, special education, special benefits for family members and relatives, special guards, and special expense accounts.[143] This assessment of corruption in the CPSU also argued that "money politics" had become rampant in the party, and that cronyism and nepotism were widespread among the leadership.

Another analysis pinned the blame for corruption on the progressive atrophy of the CPSU's vaunted *nomenklatura* personnel system—which was intended to constantly inject new blood into the party apparat. The author alleges that this core system of the CPSU underwent long-term atrophy from Stalin to Brezhnev, and he describes five attempts at "organizational surgery" (*zuzhi shoushu*) undertaken by the CPSU personnel organs under Gorbachev between 1985 and 1991. All the attempts proved unsuccessful, and they in fact exacerbated the already-atrophied system.[144]

Finally, one other political factor figured in Chinese postmortems: the role of the Soviet military and its relationship with the CPSU. While a number of analyses pointed to the negative effects on morale and discipline within the armed forces owing to the Soviet invasion of Afghanistan,[145] and others noted the excessive relative spending on the military-industrial complex, some focused on internal problems in the Soviet military. A large number of problems were noted: the unilateral downsizing of the military without appropriate preparations for absorbing demobilized soldiers back into society, pervasive alcoholism and laxity of discipline in the rank and file, wage arrears and truancy, ethnic tensions between Russians and non-

Russians; the rise of separatist insurgencies in the Caucasus, mass media exposure of military mismanagement, the decline of the political commissar system within the military, and the breakdown of party control over the military.[146]

All these, but particularly the last factor, were seen as contributing to the corrosion of the once-vaunted Soviet military. One assessment noted that the process of "nationalization" (*guojiahua*) and the depoliticization of the armed forces during the latter half of the 1980s under Gorbachev, and particularly the 1990 decision to shift control of the Soviet commissar system from the party to the state in 1990, were the death knell of the CPSU's "command of the gun."[147] These processes led directly, the critique argued, to the (failed) August 19th coup d'état attempt.[148]

Social and Cultural Factors

A number of assessments pointed to the Soviet leaders' and governments mishandling, and suppression, of non-Russian ethnic groups. Such suppression was said to have arisen out of Stalin's mistaken belief that ethnic tensions equated with class struggle, and thus should be handled coercively.[149] While criticizing the Soviet leadership for being *too harsh* on ethnic groups, other assessments criticized the very nature of the Soviet federalist state that granted limited autonomy to the republics as the problem. What was needed instead of federalism was a unitary state, they argued.[150] A basic mistake was made by Lenin, others claimed, who encouraged self-determination by ethnic groups—a decision that led to the federalist structure, which in turn gave rise to separatist movements and the ultimate disintegration of the union.[151] Others reinforced this notion, arguing that there had always been an inbuilt systemic tension between the central Soviet state and the republics, a tension that would not have existed if the USSR had been created as a unitary state from the beginning.[152] Others disputed this, arguing that the Soviet Union was "federal in form, but unitary in reality." Federalism, according to Zuo Fengrong, was a matter of formality that was never implemented—indeed, that was usurped by Stalin and successive Soviet leaders, despite the constitutional provision that all republics enjoyed full autonomy and the right to secede from the union if desired.[153]

A number of critiques pointed to the "crisis of faith" (*xinyang weiji*) that pervaded Soviet society. This social condition was said to have been the cumulative result of years of "leftist" and totalitarian policies,[154] an unappealing and overly dogmatic party ideology, the alienation from the party of the proletariat (its core constituency),[155] the low level and decline of living standards, a nonexistent incentive structure in the workplace, and the suppression of intellectuals.[156] All these conditions led to widespread social alienation against the Soviet state and party.

By the time Gorbachev attempted to rectify these maladies, it was deemed to be too late. In any event, his freeing of the media from party supervision was alleged to be a catastrophic mistake—both because it exposed the party's failings and because it opened venues for "antisocialist voices" to vent their frustrations and attack the party-state.[157] Moreover, once the media had been cut loose from party control, the way was opened for Western propaganda to "penetrate it and plant articles that sowed chaos."[158]

International Factors

The final category of factors that Chinese analysts allege contributed to the collapse of the Soviet Union lay in Soviet foreign policy and the international domain. Some analyses stressed factors intrinsic to Soviet foreign policy, while others emphasized the role of the United States.

With respect to Soviet foreign policy, the key critiques blamed a succession of Soviet leaderships with:

- external expansionism and aggression;
- pursuit of international hegemony;
- the export of revolution;
- the establishment of client states;
- interference in the internal affairs, and the occupation of, other states;
- a "militarized foreign policy" (*junshihua de waijiao*);
- great power chauvinism toward other fraternal socialist and communist parties; and
- Cold War competition with the United States.[159]

These critiques are widely shared by Chinese analysts. As the leading CCP theoretician and Politburo adviser Zheng Bijian put it in 2005: "The Soviet Union pursued a path of military hegemony under the banner of 'world revolution' that was a dead-end."[160]

Some assessments credited Gorbachev and his foreign minister, Eduard Shevardnadze, with recognizing the bankruptcy of these policies and embarking upon a serious policy of détente with the West. They also note that such a relaxation of the Soviet Union's external environment was necessary for Gorbachev to pursue his internal reforms.[161] But, these analyses point out, this relaxation of tensions played right into the "peaceful evolution" policies of the United States.[162]

Peaceful evolution plays a central role in many Chinese assessments of the causes of the collapse of the USSR and the East European communist regimes. Several detailed analyses of the alleged U.S. strategy to undermine and peacefully evolve these regimes were published.[163] Chinese analysts, and the CCP itself, have been obsessed with this subject and have alleged a U.S. strategy for years—dating back to John Foster Dulles's first use of the term in the 1950s. Peaceful evolution strategies are said to employ a variety of what today would be described as "soft power" tools: shortwave radio broadcasts, the promotion of human rights and democracy, economic aid, support for nongovernmental organizations and autonomous trade unions, spreading the ideology of capitalism and freedom, supporting underground activists, infiltrating Western media publications into closed countries, academic and cultural exchanges, and so on.[164] Peaceful evolution was said to be the "soft twin" of "hard containment."

Lessons Learned

So, what lessons have Chinese analysts and the CCP drawn from all these analyses of the collapse of the Soviet Union and the East European regimes? To some extent, the lessons are *implicit* in the foregoing analyses, that is, criticisms of what policies and practices Soviet and East European leaders and regimes adopted over time before their demise. But some analyses were *explicit* about the lessons to be drawn by China and the CCP. This section summarizes these explicit prescriptions. They fall into two general categories: (1) general and comprehensive prescriptions, and (2) prescriptions specific to the Communist Party as an institution.

General Lessons

The following sample from six scholars is illustrative of the broader published discourse in China. Though a substantial range of views existed on the causes of collapse of the CPSU and the USSR, there is considerable consensus among Chinese analysts about the general lessons to be learned by the CCP and China. Some of these are both obvious and seemingly trite, but nonetheless they reflect the inner-party discourse on the subject.

Li Jingjie, the director of the former Soviet-Eastern Europe Institute at CASS and one of China's most well-respected and astute analysts, offered eight lessons to be learned from the failure of the CPSU:

1. Concentrate on productivity growth.
2. Be ideologically flexible and progressive—there is no set model for a socialist society.
3. Learn from the advancements of capitalism, and particularly practice an "open door" policy.
4. Seek not only to strengthen the comprehensive power of the state but also, more important, the material living standards of the people.
5. Correctly implement democratic centralism, expand inner-party democracy, and carry out the struggle against corruption.
6. Treat intellectuals fairly.
7. Fully comprehend the complexity and fundamental causes of ethnic issues and tensions, ensure equality and the right of self-determination to all ethnic groups, and expedite economic growth as the fundamental way to solve ethnic tensions; but recognize the danger in implementing political pluralism in a multiethnic region.
8. Begin reforms in the economic realm but also carry them out in other fields—including the political realm.[165]

In an interview with the author in 2003, Li Jingjie elaborated on some of his earlier viewpoints and, in some cases, offered some new reflections and insights.[166] He began by recalling how the collapse of the Soviet Union and CPSU rule had gripped and haunted the Chinese leadership ever since:

> The collapse is the most important development that has affected the internal and external development of China. It shocked both our leaders and intellectuals. Even before the collapse, our leaders were worried about chaos in Russia. Our leaders are still, to this day, trying to understand the implications and lessons, so that they don't make the same mistakes as Gorbachev. . . . After the collapse Russia has been in a state of crisis—this has lessons for us. . . . Almost all Chinese intellectuals have concluded that democracy is a good thing, but it needs to be carried out according to a country's characteristics and to maintain social order. . . . The CPSU was a ruling party for seventy years, same for the KMT [Kuomintang, on Taiwan], and the PRI [Partido Revolucionario Institutional] in Mexico—we must study and understand all of these cases care-

fully. Generally speaking, Chinese intellectuals have three mirrors (*san jingzi*) to learn from: (1) the Soviet Union / Russia, where democratization preceded economic modernization—this cannot be accepted in China; (2) the powerful economies of Asia (e.g., Japan, South Korea, Taiwan, Singapore), where economic modernization was carried out before democratization—they were successful and we should learn from them; (3) India, which is similar to China in many ways, but not a good political example for us.[167]

Concerning the causes of collapse of the USSR, Li opined that, for most Chinese analysts, the *internal causes* of collapse were primary and more important than the external ones. Yet, he allowed that "the arms race put a large burden on the Soviet economy. Further, Soviet expansionism and hegemony toward other socialist and developing countries exacerbated these stresses. In addition, 'peaceful evolution' from the West was an important cause, particularly in Eastern Europe. Also, the former Soviet Union was cut off from the outside world—the Soviet people just took for granted that their system was the most advanced in the world, when in fact it was not."[168] In another setting, at a joint U.S.-China conference on the collapse of the USSR in 2004, Li further observed that "the collapse of the USSR was the inevitable collapse of the CPSU. It was the CPSU that collapsed first. CPSU leaders did not understand economics and they steadfastly avoided reform because they dogmatically believed in their model. The CPSU never renewed itself and did not adapt with the times. From the Stalin era on, the CPSU became too dogmatic. In seventy-plus years, there was no development of democratic politics. Once they began, under Gorbachev, they were too late and the reform strategy was erroneous—which was the direct precipitating cause of the collapse."[169]

Li Jingjie's colleagues at the Institute of East European, Russian, and Central Asia Studies, Ma Shufang and Li Jingyu, offered four general lessons to be learned:

1. Concentrate on economic development and continuously improve people's standard of living.
2. In undertaking political reform, honestly face up to and admit past mistakes; observe and manage all problems from a political (ruling) perspective; strengthen party leadership; and steadily push for democratic political reform.
3. Uphold Marxism as the guiding ideology, and strengthen propaganda work and thought education (*sixiang jiaoyu*).

4. Continuously strengthen efforts on party building—especially in the areas of ideology, image, organization, and democratic centralism—in order to safeguard the leadership power in the hands of loyal Marxists.[170]

A group of leading experts assembled from the Central Party School, CASS, the CCP International Department, the China Institute of International Studies, and Renmin (People's) University presented eight lessons:[171]

1. Do not be hasty in reform—concentrate on building the productive and capital base, in order to build the cultural and political superstructure.
2. Constantly reform and adapt with the times.
3. Borrow lessons from capitalism.
4. Socialism must be wealthy and democratic.
5. Enhance party building by developing ideology with a focus on science and technology, building democracy within the party, and combating corruption.
6. Manage relations with intellectuals well and value their function and role in society.
7. Manage ethnic issues well—economic development is the basic solution to ethnic tensions.
8. Develop a comprehensive and correct strategy of reform, be patient in the process, and allow for multiple views to be expressed and dissent within the party.

Li Zhengju of the Institute of World Socialism under the CCP Central Committee offered ten concise and insightful lessons that the CCP should learn from the Soviet collapse:[172]

1. In the area of leading ideology, constantly uphold but adapt Marxism-Leninism to developing conditions.
2. In the area of organization work and system construction, constantly adapt to changing conditions and requirements, and strengthen the inner-party supervision system and democracy.
3. In the area of work style, constantly uphold the principles of the party serving the public and the government serving the people, while combating the manifestations of corruption and special interest groups.
4. In the area of leadership, make the adaptation from a revolutionary party to a ruling party, and constantly adapt the leadership system and governing procedures.

5. In the area of production work style, constantly adapt the productive forces to laws and regulations, take economic construction as the central point, and ensure that a strong country serves the people's real interests.
6. Place priority on solving ethnic, religious, and other social problems.
7. Must control the military's leading power, and do not weaken the party's control over the military, the People's Armed Police, and other "power organs" (*qiangli bumen*).
8. Do not succumb to the Western countries' "peaceful evolution" strategy.
9. Accurately address the problems of peasants and intellectuals.
10. Carry out a foreign policy in accordance with the people's fundamental interests.

Finally, the International Department of the CCP came up with its own five lessons:[173]

1. Mistakes are inevitable in building socialism, but they should be admitted rather than ignored and negated.
2. Firmly adhere to the Communist Party leadership, but continuously seek to improve the party leadership's capabilities—through organizational party building, strengthening propaganda and thought work among cadres, implementing democratic centralism and a system of inner-party supervision, improving the quality of cadres, and the like.
3. Take economic development as the core, seek to improve productivity and the standard of living *before* embarking on political reform (this was Gorbachev's greatest mistake).
4. Emphasize the unity of different ethnic groups and fight separatism.
5. Beware of the West's "Westernization" and "division" strategies (*Xi-Hua, fen-Hua zhanlue*) and be highly alert to the West's "peaceful evolution" strategy.

Thus, those who offered a series of comprehensive lessons to be learned by the CCP from the collapse of the CPSU were in general agreement about the principal lessons to be drawn and adopted in China. As one source succinctly put it, "In short, the collapse of the Soviet Union was precipitated by political autocracy, economic dogmatism, ethnic chauvinism, and international hegemonism."[174] As we will see in subsequent chapters, and have seen in China itself over the past fifteen years, these lessons have all worked their way into actual policy initiatives undertaken by the CCP and government.

Lessons Specifically for the Development
of the Chinese Communist Party

Some more specific lessons for the development of the CCP were also elaborated by some analysts. Several themes were prominent.

The CCP theoretician Huang Weiding and others zeroed in on the problem of corruption.[175] Huang argued that corruption could spread like a cancer throughout the party and posed several dangers. It posed twin dangers to the party and state by weakening the party leadership and stimulating the formation of special interests within the party and state apparatus. Vis-à-vis society, corruption exacerbates inequality, thus stimulating rising crime rates and other social tensions—leading to instability and increasing the potential for separatism. Corruption, Huang argued, also leads to inefficiency within the bureaucracy and economic losses. Thus, for Huang, corruption inside the CCP was the No. 1 issue: "If corruption isn't effectively managed, the end of the party and state is likely. We must struggle to stop the history of the Soviet Union from reoccurring in China! No one but the CCP could defeat itself!"[176]

He Qiugang of the New China News Agency also emphasized the problem of corruption inside the party, arguing that regulations should be passed to make transparent the leadership's personal assets.[177] Bribery was rampant inside the party, he noted. He also astutely observed that corruption is not just a systemic problem but also a social problem in Chinese culture. That is, corruption is a function of the culture of *guanxi* (connections) in Chinese society, He argued. Within the party, this becomes manifest in the criteria for promotion—which, he asserted, is based more on *guanxi* than merit. Thus there was an urgent need, he argued, for the establishment of a "scientific," meritocratic cadre management system inside the party and state apparatus. The lack of such criteria, he further noted, had led to factionalism within the party, as well as "unscientific" leadership succession (a not-too-veiled criticism of the arbitrary methods by which senior Chinese leaders hand-picked their successors).

Some analysts from the CCP Organization Department, not surprisingly, picked up on this theme of improving the cadre management system, and they advocated the implementation of more merit-based and "scientific" promotion criteria in order to improve the party's "governing capacity" (*zhizheng nengli*)—a term that would become the CCP's theme in 2004. Similarly, many analyses noted the need to strengthen grassroots party cells and organizations—as this had been seen as a long-term weakness of the CPSU.[179] Other analysts pointed out the need to establish a collective party leadership and a consultative decisionmaking system, and not to allow power to be concentrated in the hands of the few.[180] Many others, such as Jiang Changbin of the Central Party School, reiterated the need for improved "inner-party democracy" (*dangnei minzhu*) and improving inner-party life (*dangnei shenghuo*)—which, in essence, means improving consultation at all levels of the party apparatus and rooting out remnants of dictatorial decisionmaking.[181]

Control of the media was another lesson learned. A study by the CCP International Department observed that the pre-Gorbachev control of the Soviet media was too tight, and thus (for China) "innovative means of propaganda that appropriately reflects relations between Marxism and the realities of society must be found."[182] Gorbachev's media reforms, conversely, went too far—making the party "deaf mute" to society's concerns, allowing attacks that undermined the authority of the government and the military, distorting reality, giving nonparty voices a mouthpiece, and providing direct opportunities for Western penetration of Soviet news agencies. Thus, the authors concluded, "The Party [CCP] must maintain tight control over the mass media in order to maintain the dominance of Marxism in the ideological arena, closely watch the impact of propaganda on national security, but grant the mass media and broader communication and inspection functions."[183]

A final theme was the conclusion that European-style social democracy should be avoided at all costs. As the former CCP Propaganda Department czar Wang Renzhi bluntly stated, "We have no alternative but to reform. One option is to reform following the democratic socialist and capitalist path—but that has proven disastrous!"[184] Wang, a noted hard-line and conservative ideologue, was not the only one to conclude that a move down the path of European democratic socialism was a firm step down the slippery slope to political extinction for the CCP. Gorbachev's embrace of "humanistic and democratic socialism" was unanimously viewed as the coup de grâce for the CPSU—because it represented a fundamental philosophical abandonment of Marxism-Leninism, "confused cadre's thinking," and opened to door for political pluralism and the multiparty system.[185]

The Survivors: North Korea, Vietnam, and Cuba

Although analyses of the East European and Soviet collapses have consumed the CCP's researchers, they have also paid attention, and have devoted analyses, to those few communist parties that have survived: North

Korea, Vietnam, and Cuba (Laos receives little attention in Chinese analyses). This section samples some of this analysis. Generally speaking, Chinese analyses of these three cases are descriptive but not judgmental. The Chinese are interested in the reasons why these regimes have survived, when so many others have not. Nor do they tend to be pessimistic about the chances for survival of these communist party-states. As one analysis described it, "Obviously, the drastic changes in Eastern Europe and the Soviet Union in the late 1980s and early 1990s have seriously hampered the international socialist movement. However, after several years, the 'period of shock' [*zhendang qi*] has passed and many signs of revival have emerged. The shocks that resulted from the collapse have already passed; we [the international socialist movement] have gone through a period of emergency and into a period of moving forward amid difficulties" (the article then describes reforms in Cuba, Laos, and Vietnam).[186]

North Korea

Although China's North Korea watchers no doubt know more about the Democratic People's Republic of Korea than any other country, they tend not to commit their views to print. A scouring of the literature reveals very little beyond superficial descriptions of North Korea and China–North Korea relations. Even studies by the CCP International Department, which has more extensive interactions with Pyongyang than any other organization in China, contain no analysis of North Korea, although they do contain an interesting description of party-to-party exchanges between the two sides over a half century.[187] North Korea is clearly a proscribed topic to write about, even in internal (*neibu*) publications. The only insights to be gleaned are a few analyses of North Korean economic reforms, which are said to have begun in 2001—with the establishment of some special economic zones and the acceptance of some foreign investment, the abolition of the ration system for certain controlled commodities, some price reform, and the permitting of some small-scale free markets. These developments are said to be in line with the government's decision to move from a planned to a collective and mixed economy.[188] These reform efforts are specifically credited to Kim Jong Il.[189]

Unlike in publications, Chinese analysts of North Korea are much more candid—and critical—in discussions. They often speak with disdain, despair, and frustration when discussing North Korea and China's relations with it. They often deplore the sycophantic cult of personality surrounding the Kim dynasty (they are also critical of the family political dynasty), the Stalinist security state, the command economy, the impoverishment of the population, the use of scarce resources for military purposes, the regime's mass mobilization techniques, its autarkic paranoia about the world beyond its borders, and so forth. Some of China's Korea watchers go so far as to draw explicit parallels to Maoist China (particularly during the Great Leap Forward and Cultural Revolution), and they argue that North Korea's only viable option to avoid national suicide is to emulate China's reformist example.[190]

To this end, the International Department of the CCP and other organs have brought a series of delegations of North Korean bureaucrats, managers, economists, and officials to China to receive briefings and view the economic reforms first hand. This kind of "economic reform diplomacy" has also involved North Korea's enigmatic and reclusive leader Kim Jong Il, who made four such visits to China between 2000 and 2006. Kim has been shown an array of sites aimed to impress him about the key components of China's economic reforms: China's "Silicon Valley" in Zhongguancun, Beijing agricultural research institutes, the Shanghai skyline, the Three Gorges Dam, the bustling seaport of Yantian in Guangdong Province, the five-star White Swan Hotel in Guangzhou, and the export-processing Zhuhai and Shenzhen Special Economic Zones.[191] Kim's January 2006 visit, which took him for the first time to the booming southern province of Guangdong, clearly had an impact on him. "The progress made in the southern part of China, which has undergone a rapid change, and the stirring reality of China deeply impressed us," he proclaimed in a banquet toast to Chinese president and CCP general secretary Hu Jintao, at the end of his visit.[192]

Clearly, it is China that is trying to impress North Korea with its "model," rather than vice versa. In this sense, North Korea is a largely negative example in China's evaluation of foreign communist party-states.

Vietnam

China is more interested in the Vietnamese Communist Party (VCP) and the situation in Vietnam. Chinese analysts credit Vietnam and the VCP with having weathered the storm of the Soviet collapse and having pushed forward on a reformist path. It is noted that the VCP formally adopted a policy of reform (*Doi Moi*) at the Sixth Congress of the VCP in December 1986. This policy decision placed an emphasis on economic development, trade liberalization, reforming the planned economy, and permitting a diversified economic structure.[193] Agricultural reform began in 1988 with the implementation of the Chinese-style "household responsibility system," and in 1989 the grain market was totally privatized, along with the acceptance of private ownership in farming, fishing, and forestry. As a result, grain production jumped, and Vietnam became the second-largest rice exporter after Thailand. Industrial reform followed. The Vietnamese government closed down a number of inefficient state-owned enterprises and abolished the monopoly that the enterprises had in the national economy. The ownership structure was then reformed, with an emphasis on "national capitalism," foreign investment, and export processing. All these policy reforms are discussed approvingly by Chinese analysts.

In terms of political development, the VCP is credited with having launched a series of party-building and rectification (*dangjian zhengfeng*) initiatives from 1999 to 2001, which rectified the "moral degeneration" and countered "peaceful evolution" inside the party.[194] The VCP's primary goals are said to have been to strengthen ideological education, improve the moral quality and lifestyle of party cadres, combat corruption and bureaucratism, promote self-criticism and democratic centralism within the party, and streamline and consolidate basic-level party organs.[195] Chinese analysts are quite generous in praise of Vietnam's economic reforms and party rectification and revitalization efforts.[196] They are also closely following the VCP's experiments with multicandidate elections to local party committees.

Cuba

The CCP and Chinese analysts have also shown a considerable degree of interest in the Cuban Communist Party and its policies. Entire books have been published on the successes of Cuban communism.[197] These offer comprehensive assessments of the Cuban system: health care, education, politics, military affairs, foreign relations, the economy, society, and culture. There seems to be a particular fascination in China with the "Cuban Way." Fidel Castro is admired for his tenacity and longevity, in the face of intense pressure from the United States and other obstacles.[198] Other articles detail Cuba's economic system and reforms, praising them for their distinctiveness.[199] To be sure, the admiration is not only one way, because Castro and the Cuban Communist Party have looked to China as a reformist example as well.[200]

The Cuban Communist Party's methods of rule and reasons for longevity have been analyzed particularly closely. One study by the CCP Organization Department attributes the Cuban Communist Party's longevity to three principal factors: fusing party building with anti-American nationalism, keeping close ties to the people, and promoting social equality.[201] Another study by an official in the CCP International Department credits a series of other factors: the promotion of younger officials and cadres; new party recruitment campaigns; the downsizing of government agencies to improve efficiency; frequent inspection trips by party leaders to the countryside; encouraging national discussion of policy alternatives prior to adoption; encouraging inner-party democracy; the strong monitoring of party members and enforcement of anticorruption measures; and the establishment of party branches in all schools.[202]

Another analysis, by China's leading "Cuba watcher," Mao Xianglin of CASS, agrees with many of these observations, but he stresses the priority placed on "inner-party democracy," party and government dialogue with different sectors of society, control over the military and security services, and strong nationalism.[203] Yet another assessment by the International Department of the CCP is effusive in its praise for the Cuban Communist Party's accomplishments, including combining indigenous ideology (Marti Thought) with Marxism-Leninism, refusing to adopt a Western multiparty system, rejecting the Soviet model as incompatible, stressing social stability above all, organizing special study sessions for party members, using the mass media to mobilize patriotism, creating party organizational linkages to urban neighborhoods and rural villages, establishing a system whereby party officials must meet with and "report back" (*hui bao*) to citizens and conduct opinion polls among the population, allowing two or more candidates to stand for local party elections, not permitting special privileges among officials and senior party members, maintaining a "zero tolerance" policy toward corrupt officials; promoting party members based on merit and careful vetting, and streamlining central and provincial-level governments to promote efficiency.[204]

Clearly, the "Cuban model" is of great interest to the CCP. Exchanges between the two sides have increased considerably since the early 1990s. Hardly a month passes without an official party or state visit in one direction or the other.[205] The CCP leader Hu Jintao is said to have heaped praise on the Cuban Communist Party at the Fourth Plenum of the Sixteenth Party Congress in 2004, which discussed the lessons of other ruling parties for the CCP.[206] When the Politburo member Wu Guanzheng visited Havana in April 2007, and met with Castro in his hospital room, Wu gave Castro a letter from Hu Jintao, which stated: "Facts have shown that China and Cuba are trustworthy good friends, good comrades, and good brothers that treat each other with sincerity. The two countries' friendship has withstood the test of a changeable international situation, and the friendship has been further strengthened and consolidated."[207]

Casting a Wider Net

Although the analysis of the collapse of the former communist party-states has attracted the greatest attention in China, with the analysis of the "survivors" attracting some, the CCP and Chinese analysts have also shown a growing interest in noncommunist and ex-communist political systems. We turn to these assessments in chapter 5.

5

The Chinese Discourse on
Noncommunist Party-States

The Chinese Communist Party (CCP) has not limited its survey of foreign party-states and political systems to former and existing communist systems. The CCP is relatively open-minded about studying and trying to learn lessons from various political systems. As the CCP leader Hu Jintao himself has said, "Fresh experiences during the Party building process should be carefully summarized, and helpful practices of foreign political parties should be studied and borrowed from to enrich and develop the CCP's governance theories."[1] Single-party systems (particularly those that have endured for some time) have, of course, been of greatest interest, but CCP analysts have not limited their study to authoritarian or single-party states; they have cast their net widely to study and absorb lessons from a wide variety of ex-communist systems, single-party authoritarian systems, multiparty authoritarian systems, and multiparty democratic systems. This chapter samples some of this discourse and analysis.[2]

The "Color Revolutions"

Although the CCP may have taken some solace from the fact that the Cuban, Vietnamese, and North Korean communist parties have endured, Chinese analysts and leaders were deeply alarmed by the so-called color revolutions that swept through the ex-communist, post-Soviet Central Asian republics in 2003–4, which were seen as having important implications for China's external security and internal political stability. The term "color revolution" originated with the "rose revolution" that overthrew President Eduard She-vardnadze in Georgia in 2003, followed by the "orange revolution" in Ukraine in 2004, and the "(yellow) tulip revolution" in Kyrgyzstan in 2005. Substantial analysis has been devoted to assessing the color revolutions and their implications, and these analyses make clear that a considerable amount of hand-wringing has taken place behind the scenes—the CCP is very worried about the causes and implications of the color revolutions for China and its own rule.

Six major lines of emphasis emerge from Chinese analyses of the color revolutions. The first concerns the nature of the "revolutions" themselves. The second concerns the role of the United States in fomenting them. The third involves the role played by nongovernmental organizations (NGOs). The fourth concerns the potential for more color revolutions in Central Asia. The fifth considers the revolutions' implications for Russia. The sixth considers their implications for China.

First, Chinese analysts are very skeptical that the regime changes in these countries truly constituted "revolutions." Rather, analysts at the China Institute of Contemporary International Relations (CICIR), which is affiliated with the Ministry of State Security, alternatively label them as "power struggles," "coup d'états," and "halfway revolutions."[3] As one put it, "The 'color revolutions' represent an effort to use the halo of 'revolution' to cover up illegal regime change."[4] Chinese analysts dismiss movement toward establishing democratic institutions in these countries as an artificial ruse for post-Soviet power struggles within these states, and for the strategic designs of the United States. They deny that any real systemic change has occurred. As Ding Xiaoxing of the CICIR observed, "Leaders of those [new] states have instituted autocracies behind a facade of democratization."[5]

By far, the most analysis and greatest degree of consensus among Chinese analysts concerns the motives and roles played by the United States. There is unanimous agreement among Chinese analysts that the color revolutions would never have occurred were it not for U.S. subversive efforts. The CCP has long argued that the United States has pursued a policy of "peaceful evolution" toward communist countries in general and China in particular.[6] In the case of Central Asia, there are three primary aspects of American subversion cited by Chinese analysts. Two concern U.S. strategic designs, while one concerns tactics.

The first aspect is said to be America's geopolitical interests in Central Asia, as part of its global strategy and pursuit of global hegemony. As

Chen Xiangyang of the CICIR views it, "By encouraging and supporting 'color revolutions,' the United States spares no effort to expand its influence in CIS [Commonwealth of Independent States] states, actively scramble for dominance and commanding point in the hub zone of the Eurasia continent . . . in order to expel Russia's traditional influence and safeguard and promote U.S. world hegemony."[7] Chen's CICIR colleague Jiang Li agrees that the U.S. and Russia are engaged in strategic competition in the region:

> The so-called "color revolutions" in the CIS states are actually a fierce competition between America and Russia since the end of the Cold War. It is also a means for the West to launch a deadly blow on Russia's strategic hinterland, revealing the posture that America is on the offensive while Russia is on the defensive. Currently, Russia is in an unfavorable position, whose sphere of influence has been nibbled away and whose strategic space has been incessantly squeezed by the United States. . . . Russia has been trapped into a ring of encirclement by NATO and the EU. Russia's security is facing a severe challenge. Meanwhile the United States will continue to promote the strategy of democratic transformation in the CIS, provoking the redline of Russia's security interests.[8]

Qi Zhi of the China Institute of International Strategic Studies, a think tank affiliated with the People's Liberation Army General Staff's Second Department (Intelligence), concurs with the strategic basis of U.S. involvement in the region: "The U.S. has cherished a very clear strategic intent, which is to put the heartland of Eurasia under its control by further squeezing Russia's strategic space so as to prevent it from staging a comeback. In short, the 'color revolutions' are of an inestimable significance to the U.S. in isolating and containing 'potential' adversaries, and to finally gain all-round control over Eurasia."[9]

Other analysts view the color revolutions and U.S strategic objectives in a more global context. As Liu Jianfei of the Institute of Strategic Studies of the Central Party School describes it, "Emphasizing 'promotion of democracy' is not just a tactical consideration, but it also has a strategic intention. . . . It organically combines 'promotion of democracy' with maintaining U.S hegemony. According to American logic, the United States is the most powerful democratic country, so it is naturally the leader of the 'democratic world'; if all countries in the world go democratic, they will all accept U.S. leadership. Thus, the U.S. hegemonic position will be still more consolidated."[10]

The second strategic objective of the United States in fomenting the color revolutions, according to Chinese analysts, is to export democracy all around the globe. Though Chinese analysts recognize that this has been a long-standing U.S. objective, they also note that the George W. Bush administration, during its second term, shifted its main foreign policy priority from counterterrorism to "promoting democracy." "This is the first time that a Republican administration has raised 'promotion of democracy' to such a height," noted Liu Jianfei of the Central Party School.[11]

Tactically, all Chinese analysts emphasize the role played by NGOs in fomenting the color revolutions in Central Asia. Much analysis has been devoted to this issue. Many writers note the activities and influence of the Soros Foundation, Eurasia Foundation, Ford Foundation, Carnegie Endowment for International Peace, Freedom House, National Democratic Institute, International Republican Institute, Carter Center, and other NGOs.[12] These organizations are said to "disseminate propaganda about democracy and freedom, so as to foster pro-Western political forces and train the backbones for anti-governmental activities," as well as to "take advantage of their experiences from subversive activities abroad to provide local anti-government forces with a package of political guidance from formulation of policies to schemes of specific action plans. . . . All that the NGOs have done have played a crucial role in both the start and final success of the 'Color Revolutions.' "[13]

According to Chinese analysts, these NGOs do not just act on their own but are closely linked to work being carried out by various U.S. government agencies, including, allegedly, U.S. intelligence agencies. "An important part of CIA espionage training is just how to make use of NGOs, and indeed some of them have served as the Trojan horses planted in other countries by the CIA," asserts Qi Zhi of the China Institute of International Strategic Studies.[14] The U.S. Departments of State, Defense, Agriculture, and Commerce are all alleged to have played roles in contributing to the color revolutions.[15] From supporting Radio Liberty and Radio Free Europe, to inviting an estimated 90,000 intellectuals and officials to the United States, to training CIS militaries, to granting aid, the U.S. government is said to have contributed directly to the color revolutions. In the words of one CICIR analyst, "America's financial assistance is the *direct cause* of the 'color revolutions' " (emphasis added).[16] Over ten years, the United States is said to have provided $21 billion in economic aid to CIS countries to "help those countries in their democratic reforms."[17]

What do Chinese analysts think is the potential for further such "color revolutions" in other Central Asian states? In the view of the CICIR analyst Feng Yujun, "The possibility of outbreak of 'color revolutions' in other CIS countries cannot be ruled out."[18] Feng thinks the chances are highest in Kazakhstan, where "the strength of opposition forces should not be underestimated." Belarus,[19] Armenia, and Tajikistan, he and others argue, are the next targets of the United States.

Finally, what have been the implications of the "color revolutions" for Russia and China? In addition to the detrimental strategic impact on Russia, noted above, Chinese analysts approvingly note that President Vladimir Putin and the Russian government have begun to examine the potentially disruptive roles played by NGOs in Russia—banning some, expelling others, bringing closer scrutiny by the Russian Federal Security Bureau, having the Duma pass new regulatory laws, causing all to reregister with the government.[20] (These efforts also attracted attention in the Western media,[21] and they have been criticized by the U.S government.[22])

As for China's reaction to the color revolutions, writings by and interviews with Chinese analysts evince a great deal of alarm, fear, even paranoia.[23] Simple reporting about the color revolutions in the Chinese media itself carried certain risks. As Shi Zhongyun, the head of the watchdog State Press and Publications Administration, stated candidly, "When I think of the 'color revolutions,' I feel afraid."[24] As a result, Beijing suspended plans to allow foreign newspapers to be printed in China.[25] The domestic Chinese media were also forbidden to report on a visit to China in October 2005 by George Soros, president of the Soros Foundation and Open Society Institute. Upon his arrival in Beijing, Soros found that his scheduled lectures and meetings had all been cancelled.[26] In the wake of the color revolutions, the Chinese government also began to scrutinize foreign NGOs operating in China—both as a result of their role played in the color revolutions in Central Asia and also apparently because President Putin warned President Hu Jintao of China at a 2005 Shanghai Cooperation Organization meeting about their subversive impact.[27] "If you don't get a grip on them [NGOs], you too will have a color revolution!" Putin is said to have warned Hu.[28]

Liu Jianfei of the Central Party School also notes several other concerns for China. Liu believes that the "Community of Democracies," made up of 124 countries, will gain an increasing voice in the United Nations, "and those countries who are not members will be in a clear minority and a weak position. If this goes on, China's role in the UN will be severely constrained," Liu argues.[29] He also thinks that elevating the promotion of democracy within U.S. foreign policy will "stimulate the anti-China tendencies of the American neocons [neoconservatives], . . . and the policy of 'ending tyranny' will cause some problems for Chinese diplomacy."[30] Finally, Liu writes that the Taiwan issue would become "more complicated" as the "tendency of the neocons and the military-industrial complex to support Taiwan independence will play a role of stimulating and encouraging pro-independence forces by urging them to play the 'democratic reunification card.' "[31]

All in all, the "color revolutions" in Central Asia during the period 2003–4 had an effect on the CCP similar to that of the revolutions of 1989 in Eastern Europe and the collapse of the Soviet Union in 1991. The events in Central Asia only seemed to renew earlier fears and to reinforce the CCP mindset that the U.S. strategy of "peaceful evolution" was alive and well.

Views of Noncommunist Party-States

A number of Asian political parties have been of great interest to the CCP, and every party has been examined in some depth.[32] This began with the pre–Tiananmen Square incident interest in "neoauthoritarianism" (*xin quanweizhuyi*) and the post-Tiananmen interest in "neoconservatism" (*xin baoshouzhuyi*).[33] Both schools of thought grew out of the Chinese study of (primarily) Asian political systems during the late 1980s and early 1990s, respectively. Though the former school embraced far greater pluralism than the latter one, *both* schools were interested in a single party state with the state guiding development in all facets: economic, political, intellectual, cultural, and so on. Laissez-faire liberalism was rejected by both, for both schools thinking resonated with the century-long Chinese belief that a strong Chinese state was crucial to attain wealth and power (*fu-qiang*) as well as social stability.[34] To be sure, there were many permutations of each school, and there were certainly other Chinese intellectuals who embraced a more liberal "Enlightenment tradition," as the Sinologist Joseph Fewsmith describes it,[35] but the mainstream all worshiped a strong state that could guide and facilitate the development of China into a major world power.

Singapore has always been of particularly keen interest to the CCP, which has been sending delegations to Singapore since the early 1980s to study every aspect of the People's Action Party's (PAP) methods of rule. Chinese observers of the PAP are particularly intrigued by the party's low-key presence, but total control.[36] "They are particularly intrigued by how it is that the PAP isn't seen, but is everywhere," observed Singapore's founding president and elder statesman, Lee Kuan Yew, in noting Chinese interest in the "Singaporean Model."[37] This is accomplished, the CCP International Department concludes, by the PAP's "well-developed social network, which controls constituencies effectively by extending its tentacles deeply into society through branches of government and party-controlled social groups."[38]

Chinese analyses of Singapore also evince admiration of Singapore's clean and efficient government, social order, rule of law, moral education, higher education, and high level of technological development.[39] Chinese analysts certainly understand that Singapore is a democracy, but they view it as "guided democracy,"[40] and they attribute the PAP's longevity of rule to (1) successful policies and (2) co-optation of the opposition.[41] Party recruitment and continuous midcareer training of officials is also noted to be a particular strength of the PAP system.[42] Another analysis by the Chinese Academy of Social Sciences scholar Li Wen attributes the PAP's success to the creation of the "administrative state," (*xingzheng guojia*), the merger of party and government (*dangzheng heyi*), and the tolerance of some Western culture as a "necessary evil" (*xinyao de è*) while not tolerating pornography, criticism of the government, defamation of leaders, or political subversion.[43]

In 2005, a very unusual article concerning the "Singaporean Model" was published by Cai Dingjian in *China Youth Daily,* following his four-month stint at the National University of Singapore's East Asian Institute.[44] His observations are unusual not because he noted all the elements of PAP rule identified by other Chinese observers (as described above), all of which he did, but because he dug more deeply into how the PAP operates and found that, among other things, democracy plays a role in Singapore—and should in China. His astute observations in this article about the PAP deserve quotation at length, and include the following:

> In my opinion, Singapore's success is not the result of its authoritarian system, but is the result of its abiding sense of crisis and its spirit of working hard to make the country strong. In particular, it is the result of the PAP serving the people wholeheartedly within the framework of the democratic system in order to win their support. . . . What sort of system

does Singapore really have? Is it a democratic system or an authoritarian system? It is a parliamentary democratic system that is thoroughly British in style. Yet it is also a Leninist political party.

Some of Cai's most interesting observations concern comparisons between the PAP and the CCP:

> The PAP is similar to the CCP in many ways. Like the CCP, its goal is to serve the people. It has a tightly knit organizational structure. It also boasts such peripheral organizations as the federation of trade unions, youth league, and women's federation. The party has branches at the grass roots. The PAP has a rigorous recruitment system similar to what the CCP had in the latter's early days. The PAP has a formidable organizational and mobilization capability. However, the PAP differs from the CCP fundamentally in that it is not a political party based on the working class—instead it is a political party of the elite. . . . It is also a political party of the parliamentary system, not a revolutionary party. It came to power through multi-party elections. Moreover, it will remain the ruling party only if it wins the parliamentary elections that take place every five years. . . . As the ruling party, the PAP uses the power of incumbency to write the rules of elections and exploit the financial and government resources at its disposal to manipulate the election process. It can shape public opinion by controlling the media and does not shrink from muzzling the opposition parties through the judicial process. . . . But the PAP cannot force people to give it their votes. The only way the PAP could become the ruling party is to woo the people and earn their trust. Herein lies the fundamental reason why the party has remained the ruling party for a long time and why its legitimacy has been recognized by the people and the international community. . . . Despite its Leninist party structure, the PAP has always maintained inner-party democracy and allowed open ideology and different viewpoints within the party. . . . In view of the foregoing, therefore, Singapore is basically a democratic system that practices authoritarian rule. In the final analysis, the PAP bases its rule on the support of the people, which is precisely what has given Singapore's authoritarian rule its legitimacy.

On the basis of his exposure to and analysis of Singapore, what does Cai think the lessons are for China and the CCP?

Singapore's success has more to do with truly serving the people than authoritarianism. If we emphasize only the authoritarian aspect of the PAP while ignoring its democratic foundation, if we emphasize only its strict laws while overlooking its corps of high-caliber civil servants and its high level of rule of law, we would be grossly misinterpreting the Singaporean experience. . . . Singapore has a democratic system but lacks full political freedom. While it strictly practices the rule of law, it does not fully safeguard modern human rights. It has a mature market economy, but government control is everywhere. What *can* China learn from Singapore? We will be grossly misreading the Singaporean experience and may end up going down the wrong path if we emulate just the latter [features] without studying how Singapore has built a basis of populism by building on a democratic system and working through the organs of state power.

Then Cai gets to his main conclusion:

What we must understand is that the PAP has established its modern authoritarian rule and put itself in an impregnable position only because it bases its rule on a democratic system and populism. General elections, which take place every five years, are the Damoclean Sword hanging over the party. The danger that it may lose state power has always filled the party with a sense of crisis, always reminding it not to forget the people. This awareness is the in-built force that drives the party to truly serve the people at all times.

I quote Cai's analysis and prescriptions at such length both because of the long-standing CCP interest in the "Singaporean Model" but more so because of his conclusions about democracy. Implicitly, and almost explicitly, he is calling for subjecting the CCP to periodic nationwide multiparty elections—which he implies the CCP could win if its policies are correct and truly "serve the people." What he, of course, does not say is what happens if the ruling party (PAP or CCP) fails to meet such popular expectations and is voted out of office.

During Mahathir bin Mohammad's time, Malaysia was seen by Chinese analysts as a somewhat different case, where the dominant party, the United Malays National Organization (UMNO) is an odd mix of strongman politics and decentralized constituencies where competing factions nominate candidates for office (although Mahathir selected the final slate, thus ensuring UMNO dominance of the political process and government).[45] Other sources of UMNO's longevity in power are said to include strong patriotic and moral education; dominance of government fiscal policy; and anti-American rhetoric.

Chinese analysts have also studied Japan's Liberal Democratic Party (LDP), though it also functions within a democratic system. Researchers at the Central Party School are impressed by the LDP's longevity of rule (except for a brief period in minority during the 1990s), its close links to the business sector, its strong rural base, and its close ties with government bureaucracy.[46] The triangular interrelationship of party, bureaucracy, and business is said to be a strength of the Japanese system. The authors are critical, however, of money politics in the LDP and the Japanese system, of factionalism within the party (*dangpai*), and of the fact that the LDP is an "elite, not a people's party."[47]

Needless to say, enormous efforts have been devoted to analyzing Taiwan politics and the political parties on the island. For analysts in China, there are multiple motivations for this. First, they want to constantly assess the potential for independence versus "reunification." Second, they want to know which individual politicians and factions within Taiwan's political parties might be susceptible to China's "united front" tactics. Third, however, they are interested in why the Kuomintang (KMT) failed as a ruling party and fell from power in 2000. Closely related, they are interested in what the post-KMT political transition on the island may mean for China's political future (this is also true of China's interest in studying the transition from authoritarianism to democracy in other states). Essentially, Chinese analysts blamed the KMT's loss of power on several factors: money politics ("black gold") and corruption, factional splits within the party, ineffectual leadership, the rise of nativist (*bentu*) Taiwanese identity and the KMT's traditional ties to mainlanders, and the machinations of Lee Teng-hui.[48]

Indonesia's Golkar and India's Congress Party have also been the object of Chinese study—because of both their longevity as ruling parties and also the factors that caused their falls from power. In the case of the Congress Party, six factors were identified as having caused its fall: personalization of party power in the Gandhi family, the domination of the government bureaucracy by the party (party = state = Congress), loss of support among traditional poor constituencies at the lower rungs of the caste system, factional struggles within the party, corruption within the party, and the difficulties of unifying such a large and diverse country.[49] In the case of Golkar, the principal blame for the loss of power was attributed to corruption within the Suharto family and ruling clique, but also to an intolerant party ideology that stimulated opposition across diverse sectors of society, rural poverty, the geographical dispersion of the nation and the difficulties of enforcing rule, factional infighting within the party, and the disloyalty of the military.[50]

The close links between the military and ruling parties in Asia were also seen as a source of single-party dominance (if not outright military rule) in South Korea, the Philippines, and Thailand. Concomitantly, the decline of military praetorianism in these countries was viewed as a crucial cause of democratization in each case.[51] In East Asia, as well as in Latin America, military rule is seen by Chinese analysts as inherently fragile, because such regimes never build social bases of support and usually do not form political parties.[52]

In other parts of the world, Chinese analysts have paid attention to states as diverse as Syria and Mexico where a single party is dominant. In the Syrian case, the ruling party's longevity is attributed to a combination of a strongman president (Hafez Assad and his son); a strong political role for the military, although the party exercises control over it; party penetration of all sectors of society; the formation of mass organizations; and party dominance of all local officials.[53]

In the case of Mexico and the Partido Revolucionario Institutional (PRI, Institutional Revolutionary Party, which ruled for seventy-one years), Chinese analysts are interested both in the sources of such lengthy rule as well as the causes of the PRI's loss of power. The PRI's power was attributed to a strong presidential-style system that played to the machismo political culture in Mexico, as well the PRI's ability to tap into a strong sense of nationalism, close identification with its rural base, and the implementation of economic policies that combined nationalization with marketization.[54] Though these methods were good enough to sustain the PRI in power for seven decades, Chinese analysts attributed their undoing to mistakes in economic policy, the pursuit of social democracy, an overly rigid party organization that could not undergo self-reform, corruption within the PRI, the impact of globalization and external pressures from the World Trade Organization and the North American Free Trade Agreement, U.S. support of opposition parties, and American diplomatic pressure.[55]

Chinese analysts have also evinced a strong interest in Latin American corporatist systems—particularly in Argentina, Brazil, and Chile. This is evident from the steadily rising number of delegations sent to, and received from, these countries by the CCP's International Department.[56] Interestingly, though, Chinese Latin Americanists have been slow to comment on the shift to the political left and election of anti-American socialists in Venezuela, Bolivia, Peru, and Chile in 2003–5—although there are some indications of Chinese irritation with the anti-American and anticapitalism rhetoric of President Hugo Chavez of Venezuela.[57] China's competition with Taiwan for diplomatic recognition in Latin America also influences its party-to-party relations. The People's Republic of China has made a concerted effort to develop party ties in countries which still recognize Taipei diplomatically. In the fourteen countries in Latin America with which the People's Republic does not have diplomatic relations, the International Department claims to have developed party relations in eleven.[58] Altogether, the International Department claims to have established relations with ninety-five political parties in twenty-nine Latin American countries.[59]

European social democratic parties and systems have also held strong appeal for Chinese analysts and the CCP.[60] This Chinese interest dates to the 1980s and was stimulated by three factors at the time: (1) China's Open Door policy, which permitted the first real and sustained interaction with European parties, governments, and nongovernmental entities; (2) China's more "liberal" reform period under Hu Yaobang and Zhao Ziyang, during which there was an interest in studying a variety of nonsocialist systems; and (3) particular interest in Europe's "capitalism with a human face" and social welfare policies.[61]

As a result of these stimuli, and the conclusion of numerous exchange agreements with European countries, China began to dispatch large numbers of delegations to Europe in the mid-1980s. Some were party-to-party exchanges that came under the auspices of the CCP International Department and were hosted by various European parties, whereas others came under academic and parliamentary exchange schemes. Before this time, the CCP had primarily restricted itself to dealing solely with communist and socialist parties (the only exception being a flurry of exchanges with far-right conservative parties during the late 1970s and early 1980s as part of China's united front work against Soviet expansionism). Another impediment was the CCP's ideologically rigid and dismissive view of social democracy, which dated to Leninist and Stalinist negative interpretations during the Second International.[62] But during the mid-1980s, with Deng Xiaoping in charge and a more progressive government in place, the CCP International Department began to quickly diversify its interactions with a wide range of political parties in Europe (and elsewhere),[63] and the CCP concluded that there might be some useful things to learn from social democratic systems.

Delegations fanned out across the United Kingdom and the European continent to study every conceivable aspect of how these governments and societies functioned.[64]

With respect to social democratic parties and systems, the Chinese learning passed through several stages. First, they had to familiarize themselves with the philosophical underpinnings of social democracy. One analysis, by Hua Qing of People's University, summarized the theoretical basis of democratic socialism as having six main roots:

- "moral socialism," based on Johann Wolfgang von Goethe's humanitarianism;
- Christianity;
- Marxism;
- French concepts of the social contract, separation of powers, liberty, equality, fraternity, human rights, sovereignty, and socially responsible democracy;
- Keynesian fiscal economics, particularly the role of government to stimulate consumption and investment; and
- organized labor.[65]

By the time the Chinese began to interact extensively with West European social democratic parties, they found many of them in a state of political crisis and in the midst of self-reflection and early stages of reform. Britain's Labor Party and Germany's Social Democratic Party, for example, had both experienced consecutive defeats at the polls in the face of staunchly conservative opposition parties. Much soul-searching was going on, and the Chinese observed it all with great interest. They witnessed the move away from the traditional base of support among trade unions and industrial workers, away from long-cherished beliefs about the nationalization of public services, away from beliefs about big government, away from traditional beliefs in the "welfare state," away from hostile views of market forces, away from views that fiscal interventionism should only stimulate production and not consumption, and so on.[66] They followed all these realizations and debates within West European social democratic parties with great interest. They were particularly interested in "New Labor" and the "Third Way" under Tony Blair in Britain.[67]

Chinese analysts watched closely as these parties progressively shed these vestiges of state socialism in favor of economic policies that shifted emphasis from social justice to economic efficiency; the reform of welfare systems; the privatization of public utilities and transportation; the devolution of government decisionmaking to more local levels; the recruitment into party membership of younger people, entrepreneurs, and business; the embrace of the high-technology revolution; the adoption of business-friendly policies; the adoption of more flexible labor laws; less state intervention in the economy and education; and other reforms.[68]

All these reforms were successful in overhauling European social democratic parties and returning many to office. As a study by the CCP International Department concluded, "Overall, the reform of West European social democratic parties has been very effective—marking the shift from traditional and ideological socialism to more modern, popular, and improved socialism. As a result, by 2000, thirteen European countries were again under the rule of social democratic parties."[69] In this process of social democratic reform, Chinese analysts have noted the increased marginalization of West European communist parties.[70] Chinese analysts have also carefully studied each European ruling political party, not just social democratic ones.[71] And they have closely examined the philosophical underpinnings of Western democratic theory and systems. For example, one textbook used for senior cadres at the Central Party School discusses at length the theories of people's sovereignty (Locke and Rosseau), separation of powers (Locke and Montesquieu), representative government (Mill), elite democracy (Weber and Schumpeter, Bell), pluralist democracy (Dahl), participatory democracy (Rosseau), and "third wave" democracy (Huntington).[72]

Finally, an analysis by the China Academy of Social Sciences Institute of European Studies offers an insightful contrast in comparing European and American political parties:

> European political parties have a more rigid structure to which its politicians are subject, while U.S. politicians are more loosely tied to their parties—coming together, more or less, only during election season. European countries operate under the parliamentary system, which gives less power to the chosen prime minister compared with the U.S. president, since the prime minister is more subject to the constraints of his or her own party. European elections are also more regulated by the government to ensure fairness in campaign financing, allowing for multiple parties to represent different sectors of society. In the U.S., corporate sponsorship is the key to a successful election, thus limiting power to the two major parties. The further integration also creates a regional government unlike anything the U.S. has experienced. Lobbyists are also much more

influential in Europe than in the U.S.; this is the result of the complexity of the European system and the vulnerability of the U.S. Congress. In addition, the monopolization of the major U.S. media outlets limits the differences of opinion that are disseminated to its citizens.[73]

The analysts at the Chinese Academy of Social Sciences also note some interesting differences in the relationship between the worldviews and foreign policies of Europe and the United States:

> The most characteristic philosophy in Europe is rationalism, while the most valued philosophy in the U.S. is pragmatism. The latter deals with the world task-by-task and does not tend to analyze situations deeply or systemically. While it is not irrational, it is a more simplistic and shallow worldview than rationalism. European rationalism considers situations more comprehensively and more deeply. As a result, Europe has a more mature outlook on the appropriate paths for global development. The philosophically shallower U.S., however, often has a hard time understanding the depth of European thinking and the extremely complex world. U.S. assessments of the global situation are often simplistic and biased, as exemplified by its belief that transforming the rest of the world in the mold of American-style democracy will guarantee world peace. Europeans once wanted to use religion and weapons to conquer the world, but their experiences with the tragedy of many wars have forced them to reexamine the nature of power. Americans are merely repeating the mistakes that Europeans have already learned from. European culture is actually more respectful of diversity of cultures. . . . The U.S. approach to global cultures is to try to conform other cultures to Western civilization. In contrast, Europe emphasizes the need for global cultural tolerance and dialogue.

Such perspectives are quite perceptive—offering insights into not only how China views Europe as a partner in world affairs but also concerning views of American political parties and politics.

Eclectic Borrowing

In this chapter, we have witnessed Chinese analyses of a wide range of political parties—communist, ex-communist, and noncommunist. The analytical effort devoted to such studies by the CCP and various research institutes, universities, and individual researchers is truly impressive (and goes well beyond the sources cited here). But, as in the study of communist party-states, it is not an abstract academic inquiry. It is being undertaken for very specific and practical reasons: to anticipate what generic challenges to the CCP may arise (based on these other cases) and to draw practical policy lessons about how to meet them in order to maintain the CCP in power. Maintaining the CCP in power is the bottom line. How to do so, while maintaining—and even improving—the party's legitimacy and "ruling capacity" (*zhizheng nengli*) is the principal challenge. To this end, studying and absorbing the experiences of other ruling parties—past and present—is a valuable tool for the CCP.

In such wide-ranging studies of other party-states and political systems, and the lessons derived therefrom, Chinese analyses have been remarkably eclectic. As in virtually every other area of China's reforms, in the political arena the CCP is certainly willing to search for useful characteristics abroad, so as to selectively borrow from them, adapt them, and graft them onto indigenous Chinese institutions and practices. I have referred to this very Chinese phenomenon elsewhere as China's "eclectic state."[74] Thus, in my view, the Chinese party-state is morphing and evolving into an eclectic entity—which comprises bits and pieces of the wide variety of systems discussed in this and the previous chapter. The following chapters show how these lessons have been absorbed and implemented by the CCP.

6

Rebuilding the Party:
The Ideological Dimension

Having reviewed what the Chinese Communist Party (CCP) learned from the cathartic events in the former communist world, as well as noncommunist systems, this and the next chapter turn to evaluating what the CCP is doing to implement these lessons and rejuvenate itself as a ruling party. The CCP's assessments triggered a range of inner-party initiatives, as well as reforms affecting other sectors of the state, society, and economy. While *reacting* to the events in former communist party-states, the CCP has been very *proactive* in instituting reforms within the party and within China. These reforms constitute the classic "adaptation" of a long-term ruling party that needs to relegitimate itself, strengthen its core capacities, expand its constituencies, and adjust its policies to new conditions.[1]

The CCP's adaptational reforms have been sweeping in scope and are intended to collectively strengthen its ruling capacity. The totality and efficacy of these reforms belies the general image in the West that there has been little or no political reform in China (at least since 1989) and that the Chinese political system remains an ossified Leninist state that will eventually succumb to the inevitable march of democracy.[2] It also belies the other accepted image that the CCP only sustains its rule on the twin pillars of economic growth and nationalism. To be sure, these are two key sources of its legitimacy—but they are far from sufficient explanations for its sustained ruling capacity.

Whether the reforms that the CCP is undertaking will prove sufficient for it to indefinitely sustain itself in power over the long-term is, of course, the big question (which is considered in the concluding chapter). Thus far, the reforms have been sufficient to sustain the party in power in the near-to-medium term, and even to strengthen its grip. The continued implementation of these reforms will help the party to further relegitimate itself and further consolidate its power and rule. Rather than withering away, stagnating, or facing an inevitable implosion, the CCP is taking measures to reinvent itself and sustain its rule indefinitely.

For the CCP, there is a premium placed on being adaptable and flexible. This is probably *the* single most important conclusion the CCP reached in its postmortem analysis of the collapse of the USSR—that a certain recipe for collapse is an ossified party-state that has a dogmatic ideology, entrenched elites, dormant party organizations, and a stagnant economy and that is isolated from the international community. Yet in its attempts to be flexible and adaptable, the CCP finds itself coping with a constant cycle of reform-readjust-reform-readjust, whereby each set of reforms triggers certain consequences (some expected, others unexpected) that in turn cause readjustments and further reforms. It is an inexorable dynamic in which the party is simultaneously proactive and reactive, and is only partially in control of its own fate.

This chapter sequentially examines what the party is doing to reform itself in the ideological (theoretical) sphere. The next chapter examines the organizational sphere, particularly institution (party) building and leadership reform. China's economic reform and foreign policy are important but auxiliary factors in strengthening party rule, but our focus remains on intraparty reforms.

Remolding Ideology

A strong case can be made that Marxist-Leninist ideology and its various Chinese permutations are irrelevant in today's China—or are an impediment to any real CCP reform. The logic of this argument is that, like socialism or communism as political-economic systems, Marxist-Leninist ideology has little analytical or policy relevance in the twenty-first-century world. Indeed, Marxism-Leninism is considered a hindrance to modernization and incapable of explaining contemporary phenomena like globalization.

The CCP, however, does not and *cannot* agree with this judgment—for the very reason that it is a communist party. As Wang Xuedong, director of the CCP Central Committee's Institute of World Socialism, observed: "We know there are those abroad who think we have a 'crisis of ideology,' but we do not agree."[3] To reject the underlying ideology is to reject the party's raison d'être itself (as Gorbachev did in favor of an alternative ideology of social democracy).

If the CCP cannot jettison its ideology, it is left with three alternatives: embrace the ideology and continue to try and build a socialist-communist future, ignore the ideology, or finesse and adapt the ideology to suit policy decisions taken on nonideological grounds. Since 1978 and the onset of Deng Xiaoping's reforms, the party has rejected the first option. It cannot really choose the second option, for that is tantamount to rejection. It must continue at least to pay lip service to the ideological canon. What it has done is to fully embrace the third option.

Ever since the 1978 "Practice Is the Sole Criterion of Truth" campaign, launched by Deng Xiaoping, the CCP has reversed the role that ideology plays in the Chinese policy process. Before that time, the relationship between ideology and policy was a deductive one. That is, policies were largely *derived from* a series of ideological principles and were thereby justified. Deng and his colleagues turned this relationship around. Thereafter, ideology became an inductive means for validating empirical realities. It became a post hoc rationalization device, while policy decisions were taken according to empirical criteria. This reversal of roles by no means jettisoned the role of ideology in the CCP or in China—rather, it deftly lessened its importance and reduced the role of ideology to that of a tool of post hoc rationalization. To be sure, ideological debates continued to be waged, ideological terminology (*tifa*) continued to be used as code words for internal policy debates, party cadres and (to a lesser extent) citizens continued to have to pay obeisance (or feign compliance) to ideological mantras, and a whole industry of "thought workers" continued to generate ideological explanations and justifications for CCP policies.[4]

Thus, ideology certainly did not die after the reforms began in 1978—but its nature and functions fundamentally changed. Ideology certainly has not remained stagnant over this period—indeed, as noted in chapter 4, this was one of the main conclusions drawn by the CCP about the role that ideology played in the collapse of the Soviet Union. Ideology there became stagnant, rigid, unimaginative, ossified, and disconnected from reality. Thus, it was not simply enough to justify contemporary policy with historical references to Marx, Engels, Lenin, Stalin, Mao, and the like. *New concepts* needed to be invented—those that were based on broad Marxist principles (however tenuous) but were derived from and respectful of local conditions, that is, ideology with "Chinese characteristics."

As the nature of ideology itself changed, so too did the means of inculcating it in the minds of society. The propaganda system is one of the fundamental instruments of party rule (along with party organizations and coercion), and it had to adapt to a new environment in which China was open to the outside world. Chinese citizens and party cadres now had access to a variety of sources of information not controlled by the CCP propaganda authorities. This has resulted in a repetitive cycle of loosening/tightening (*fang-shou*) of the propaganda apparatus since the 1980s.

The remainder of this section thus discusses these two phenomena: (1) the role of the propaganda system as part of the CCP's "atrophy and adaptation"; and (2) the most notable indigenous ideological campaigns of recent years—Jiang Zemin's "Three Represents," Hu Jintao's "Harmonious Society" and "Scientific Development Concept," and the party's "ruling capacity" campaigns.

The Propaganda Apparatus: Adaptation amid Atrophy

Few spheres better illustrate the CCP's simultaneous condition of atrophy and adaptation than the realm of information and ideology. The efficacy of China's propaganda system today has eroded considerably from its Orwellian Maoist past. Today it is being buffeted by the realities of the information revolution and globalization, yet it remains an effective instrument of the party-state to control most information that reaches the Chinese public and officialdom. In many ways, it thus epitomizes the broader processes of atrophy and adaptation that characterize the party's rule today.

The propaganda system (*xuanchuan xitong*) in China is a sprawling bureaucratic establishment, extending into virtually every medium concerned with the dissemination of information in China.[5] According to one CCP publication, the scope of propaganda oversight includes "newspaper offices, radio stations, television stations, publishing houses, magazines, and other news and media departments; universities, middle schools, primary schools, and other vocational education, specialized education, cadre training, and other educational organs; musical troupes, theatrical troupes, film production studios, film theaters, drama theaters, clubs, and other cultural organs; literature and art troupes, and cultural amusement parks; cultural palaces, libraries, remembrance halls, exhibition halls, museums, and other cultural facilities and commemoration exhibition facilities."[6]

This expansive definition means that virtually every conceivable medium that transmits and conveys information to the people of China falls under the bureaucratic purview of the CCP Propaganda Department (CCPPD). This includes all media organs, all schools and educational institutions, all literary and art organs, and all publishing outlets. In terms of channels of dissemination, the propaganda system encompasses an extensive range of media, publications, and other outlets. Official government sources report that, in 2003, this included 2,262 television stations (of which 2,248 are "local"), 2,119 newspapers, 9,074 periodicals, and 1,123 publishing houses that published 190,391 books.[7] In addition, hundreds of internal circulation papers and local gazetteers are published. There are also approximately 68 million Internet accounts with more than 100 million users, and more than 300 million mobile telephone users nationwide.[8]

The writ of the CCPPD has remained the same since the Maoist era, although its actual oversight and active censorship have changed considerably. Given the pluralization and marketization of media, art, and even education in China in recent years, it is simply impossible for the CCPPD and other censorship authorities to effectively police all these realms. A significant effort has been made to monitor the Internet (*yintewang*) with an estimated 30,000 personnel and a variety of sophisticated technological filters and devices,[9] but even this has had its limitations, given users' ability to circumvent firewalls. Globalization and the opening of the Chinese television market to satellite and cable broadcasts have also brought various foreign broadcast and print media directly into Chinese homes and work units.

Although the effectiveness of the CCPPD's ability to control the flow of information into and throughout China has relatively eroded over time, it continues to have the capacity to censor when and where it sees fit. Since 2004 in particular, under Hu Jintao's auspices and CCP directives, there have been a concerted crackdown on the media and a concomitant strengthening of the propaganda apparatus.[10] These cases of forced closure, investigations, intimidations, persecutions, arrests, prosecutions, imprisonments, and even deaths are well documented in a report by the exiled investigative journalist He Qinglian (herself an employee-turned-victim of the propaganda state).[11]

In addition to these active mechanisms, the CCPPD has a passive control capability in the form of *self-censorship,* rather than direct bureaucratic intervention. Perry Link has drawn attention to this phenomenon,[12] and numerous interviews confirm it. Creative intellectuals—whether they are journalists, professors, artists, or filmmakers—*know* the limits of the propaganda state, even if they are engaged in a process of constantly probing them. Not only do they have an innate sense of breaching established strictures and taboos, but interviews with scholars and journalists also indicate that mechanisms exist that specify the limits (elaborated below).

While the CCPPD's control and censorship abilities remain substantial, the propaganda authorities have lost much of their control in the face of technological modernization, social pluralization, economic marketization, and globalization. They are also losing influence due to public cynicism and skepticism. Given the range of information now available to Chinese citizens (particularly urbanites) and the growing awareness of the general population, people are much less willing to believe what they are told by the state media organs. The debacle of the attempted government cover-up of SARS in 2003 only fueled this public cynicism.[13]

This impression was also evidenced by an extraordinary diatribe against the CCPPD written by Jiao Guobiao, a Peking University professor, and published on the Internet in 2004.[14] Jiao's article was an unprecedented attack on the CCPPD, which charged it with being an impediment to modernization and called for its abolition. His broadside resulted in his dismissal and temporary exile abroad. The declining power and prestige of the CCPPD was similarly underscored in February 2006, when a group of party elders who had retired from the propaganda apparatus brazenly warned the CCP of the dangers of excessive media control. These elders included Mao Zedong's former secretary, Li Rui, the former CCPPD chief, Zhu Houze, the former editor of *People's Daily,* Hu Jiwei, and the former deputy director of the Xinhua News Agency, Li Pu. They warned in a (leaked) letter to the government that "at the turning point in our history from a totalitarian to a constitutional system, depriving the public of freedom of speech will bring disaster for our social and political transition and give rise to group confrontation and unrest. Experience has proved that allowing a free flow of ideas can improve stability and alleviate social problems."[15]

There is also an increasing tension between politics and commerce in the propaganda domain. The commercialization of the media is affecting the state's control of it. The commercial "bottom line" is increasingly undermining the "party line." The publishing industry in China today runs on business principles of profit and loss, sales and revenue.[16] Competition for readership and advertising revenue is fierce, and consumer preferences are now the driving force in many editorial decisions. For many publications, state subsidies have declined considerably if not disappeared altogether—

particularly for many state and party publications, which are having a hard time surviving without subsidies and guaranteed institutional subscribers. The printing and distribution of such staples as the CCP's flagship *People's Daily* have plummeted—from a circulation of 5 million paper copies per edition in the 1980s to an official figure of 1.8 million in 2004, although unofficial estimates run as low as 200,000.[17] Foreign investment in the Chinese media industry is also increasing rapidly, further eroding state control.

The shift from propaganda to profit means that journalists, broadcasters, publishers, and filmmakers must shift their thinking from being agents of the party-state to becoming commercially viable, which in turn means that their product must be appealing enough for people to pay for it. They must also become more professional in their training and daily practice of their profession. These new realities are occasionally reflected among the party-state's propaganda czars. Liu Binjie, deputy director of the powerful General Administration of Press and Publications, has admitted: "We cannot make all newspapers and periodicals the mouthpiece of the Party and country. On this, we have already changed our frame of reference. In the past (media) work units relied on the government and not the market. Now we have to liberate them and push them towards the market."[18]

Marketization also means the breakup of large media conglomerates (previously owned by party and state organs) into smaller, privately owned, and more competitive units. For example, *Beijing Youth Daily* (*Beijing Qingnian Bao*), a paper affiliated with the CCP Communist Youth League and part of China's second largest newspaper group, is preparing to list its noneditorial operations on the Hong Kong stock exchange with an initial public offering expected to raise approximately $300 million.[19] Various provincial media units, particularly in television broadcasting and cable operations, are beginning to be listed on domestic exchanges. Even China Central Television, CCTV, is considering an initial public offering for one of its subunits.[20]

These market-driven trends are only going to continue to gather force and propel China's media and publishing industry in new, and more open, directions. They will only continue to exacerbate the existing frictions between the party/government propaganda authorities and journalists and intellectuals. Publishers and editors are caught in the middle of the tug-of-war.

The to-and-fro between the propaganda authorities and the print media (to say nothing of the battle over cyberspace) occurs on an almost daily basis, with journalists and publications regularly probing the limits of control and the permissible.[21] This is colloquially referred to as "playing line balls" (*chabianqiu*).[22] Occasionally, in the classic Chinese deterrent method of "killing the chicken to scare the monkey," the propaganda authorities crack down and send a tough signal to the media or publishing industry about the boundaries of the permissible—such as when editors are fired, journalists are arrested, or publications are shut down. Nonetheless, on a daily basis, intellectuals and print journalists (television and radio broadcasters are far more circumscribed) probe the limits of the permissible.

Although investigative journalism has caught on in China, journalism remains a political profession in China and the price to be paid for violating the CCP's propaganda dictates can be harsh.[23] The international monitoring group the Committee to Protect Journalists reports that, at the end of 2004, forty-two journalists were imprisoned in China—more than any other nation in the world.[24] It is particularly apparent that propaganda and public security authorities are intent on controlling Internet access and blog discourse.[25] The international monitoring group Reporters Without Borders noted in its report *The Internet under Surveillance* that thirty-two journalists and sixty-one cyberdissidents remain imprisoned in China "for posting messages or articles on the Internet that were considered subversive."[26] Bulletin boards are monitored particularly closely.[27] As foreign companies—such as Yahoo, Google, and Microsoft—have entered the domestic Chinese market, they also have complied with government censorship regulations.[28]

The overall image one derives at present is that the propaganda system has atrophied considerably compared with its Maoist past yet remains a system still very capable of controlling the content of most information available to the Chinese public. It remains an important instrument in the party-state's toolbox of control. Yet it is also clear that the system is being buffeted by the forces of commerce, technology, globalization, public sophistication, and cynicism. Thus, the daily shadow boxing among propaganda authorities, media producers, public consumers, and commercial interests is intense in China today. This interplay is likely to only increase over time as the forces of commerce, technology, politics, and consumer preferences interact. These forces inexorably erode the party-state's control over the dissemination and content of available information, and cumulatively and progressively they undermine the system and the regime's ability to control the minds and beliefs of its citizenry.

The ultimate question remains whether the party-state can continue to effectively maintain its ideational influence in society when belief in its guiding ideology has eroded, and when the institutional mechanisms for controlling and disseminating information are growing weaker over time. To be sure, the party-state has many other means of control and influence—but if it is unable to substantially shape how people think and what they believe, it will have lost a key mechanism of its control and source of its legitimacy. If the party-state loses the battle for minds, losing the battle for hearts will not be far behind.

The New Ideology

How has the CCP been trying to win the minds of its members and the public? Four recent political campaigns are illustrative: Jiang Zemin's "Three Represents" campaign (launched in 2001), and Hu Jintao's "Scientific Development" and "Socialist Harmonious Society" campaigns (launched in 2003 and 2005 respectively), and a campaign launched in 2004–5 on the party's "Governing Capacity."

The "Three Represents"

The "important thought" (*zhongyao sixiang*) of the "Three Represents" (Sange Daibiao) was first enunciated by the CCP's general secretary, Jiang Zemin, in a series of speeches between February 2000 and a high-profile speech at the Central Party School commemorating the eightieth anniversary of the establishment of the CCP on July 1, 2001.[29] The originator of the concept was apparently Liu Ji, a theoretician who Jiang brought with him from Shanghai to Beijing.[30] Wang Huning, another key Jiang aide as head of the Central Committee Policy Research Office and former political scientist at Shanghai's Fudan University, is also said to have had a hand in formulating the Three Represents:[31]

1. The party should represent the advanced productive forces in society.
2. The party should represent advanced modern culture.
3. The party should represent the interests of the vast majority of the people.

Jiang's odd-sounding theory was quickly dismissed by most Western analysts (and ordinary Chinese alike) as yet another propagandistic cliché in the long liturgical litany of much-ballyhooed but quickly forgotten party mantras. Yet, upon closer examination, the Three Represents indicated an important, even radical, shift in party philosophy, party composition, and party orientation. At the Sixteenth Party Congress in 2002, the Three Represents was added to the CCP Constitution.

The main policy significance of the new ideological initiative at the time lay in the "first represent." This reflected an opening to recruit the so-called advanced productive forces into the party, for example, entrepreneurs and intellectuals from the private sector. Jiang first signaled this initiative in a speech during a May 2000 inspection tour of the lower Yangzi region. Cloaked in oblique Marxist language, Jiang put the party on notice that a major change in recruitment policy was forthcoming: "We must correctly understand and handle the relationship between emancipating and developing the social productive forces on the one hand and readjusting and perfecting the production relations on the other under new historical conditions, and *consciously reform and readjust those parts of the superstructure* that do not match the development of the economic foundation."[32]

This initiative was a demonstrable break with the eighty-year Marxist/Maoist emphasis on recruiting workers, farmers, and others of a traditionally proletarian background into the CCP. But, Jiang argued, the class composition of Chinese society and the proletariat had changed as a result of two decades of economic reform, and if the party was to remain the vanguard of the proletariat, it needed to become more inclusive of the newly emergent elements of the working class, particularly in the private sector. In so doing, Jiang echoed Deng Xiaoping's reclassification (at the 1978 National Science Conference) of intellectuals as members of the working class. But this was a very controversial move within the party, given its proletarian origins, identity, and ideology. Viewed more broadly, Jiang was also signaling that the CCP intended to go the way of many other ruling political parties in East Asia—to become a party of elites, including commercial elites.

Although the initial emphasis of the campaign was placed on this aspect of party recruitment, Jiang's speeches and exposition of the Three Represents also discussed other aspects of party reform: reforming the Communist Youth League; intensifying propaganda work; experimenting with new economic reforms; combating corruption; strengthening party cells and committees nationwide, but particularly at the local level; building a "political civilization" (*zhengzhi wenming*); and building a party of an "advanced nature."[33] These other facets of the Three Represents became clearer and were emphasized over the period 2002–5, following the Sixteenth Party Congress.

According to Zheng Bijian, then the executive vice president of the Central Party School and a Jiang adviser, the Three Represents theory was actually a comprehensive program for party reform that grew directly out of the CCP's assessment of the reasons for the failure and collapse of the Soviet Communist Party, as well as a three-year internal assessment of the CCP's own weaknesses.[34] In another interview with the Xinhua News Agency, Zheng emphasized that the Three Represents was an also a theoretical attempt to come to grips with three phenomena that were affecting China and the CCP: globalization and the advance of science and technology; the diversification of Chinese society, social organizations, and lifestyles; and lax party organizations and the need to improve the CCP rank and file.[35]

The promulgation of the Three Represents also clearly had to do with pushing forward economic reform. During the late 1990s, there had been intensive debate inside the CCP over the pace and scope of marketization and the system of ownership—particularly concerning the laggard state-owned industrial sector. A "leftist" faction within the party insisted that dismantling state ownership was tantamount to dismantling the socialist system, which in turn was the essence of the CCP. Jiang's Three Represents broke the logjam and resolved the debate in favor of essentially abandoning the public ownership system. This smashed the old "three major elements of socialism"—the planned economy, public ownership, and the distributional principle of "each according to his work"—and replaced it with the new principles sanctioning full marketization, private ownership, and the circulation of assets.[36]

Jiang developed a number of these themes in his July 2001 Central Party School speech. In the wake of his speech, a major national propaganda campaign was launched to publicize and propagate it. Special classes were convened at the Central Party School for Central Committee members,[37] study sessions were convened for party cadres across the country,[38] the media was filled with entreaties for the public to assiduously study the concept, and countless study guides were published to "explain" the concept to party members and the public alike.[39]

Like other ideological campaigns of the post-Mao era, however, Jiang's new theory was a codification of policies already under way. As Bruce Dickson's research demonstrates, the party had experimented with recruiting greater numbers of intellectuals and entrepreneurs over the previous decade.[40] Jane Duckett's research also demonstrates the cozy partnership between party committees, local government, and private business at the local urban level dating to the late 1980s.[41]

Having put the official stamp of approval on the new policy, CCP efforts to recruit from these sectors—but particularly from the private-sector entrepreneurial class—accelerated. Yet, interestingly, following Jiang's announcement of the new policy initiative, the recruitment of entrepreneurs into the party lagged substantially behind what the party envisioned.[42] This was probably due to the fact that in today's market economy, where the party no longer controls various goods and services, the incentives for joining it are substantially fewer. If anything, the party today represents a de facto "political protection racket" for those in private business. The CCP seeks to co-opt the entrepreneurial elites, while some in this newly emerging class seek the political "cover" of the party to more safely pursue their business interests.

Official figures, however, indicate that the party's attempts to recruit entrepreneurs and establish party cells in private-sector enterprises have been slow. By the end of 2003, 30 percent of private-sector entrepreneurs were party members—but, as Dickson points out, this number largely represents the widespread privatization of state firms and factories rather than the recruitment of *new* businesspeople into the CCP.[43] With this wave of privatizations, former firm managers and party secretaries could be counted officially as members of the "private sector." In 2004, by the CCP's own admission, of the 2.41 million new members admitted to the party, only 894 were private enterprise owners.[44] By mid-2006, perhaps in an attempt to fudge the failure to recruit significant numbers of entrepreneurs, the deputy director of the CCP Organization Department claimed that of the private companies "eligible" to have party committees established in them, 85 percent now had such committees.[45] Though initial efforts to recruit party members from the business sector lagged, more recent data and research by Dickson indicates that recruitment from this sector began to pick up starting in 2005.[46]

Unlike Jiang's emphasis on the recruitment of members of the "advanced productive forces" into the CCP, since coming to power in 2002 Hu Jintao has distinctly shifted the emphasis of the Three Represents to the *third* "represent": the interests of the vast majority of the people. This ideological reorientation was politically very astute. It not only indicated Hu's (and Premier Wen Jiabao's) appreciation of the widening and alarming gap in social stratification in China today, but also reflects their appreciation of the rising resentment in the interior of the country toward those in the coastal regions and major cities who have benefited most from the last decade's economic reforms—precisely the constituency catered to by Jiang. In many of their speeches and personal actions, Hu and Wen have shifted priorities away from Jiang's coastal constituency toward the interior (an actual shift in resources has been less apparent). By embracing the "third represent," Hu has adroitly changed the emphasis of the Three Represents campaign without jettisoning it. This tactical ploy is emblematic of Hu's savvy leadership style. While continuing the focus on the composition of party membership, the Hu-Wen leadership has also focused on rebuilding the party institutionally.

In addition to shifting the emphasis from the first to the third "represent," Hu Jintao also began to stress the need for "scientific development." There was a section on this in Jiang's 2001 Party School speech, but it was not a central feature of the speech or the Three Represents. Beginning with Hu's own Central Party School speech two years to the day later,[47] Hu began to develop the "Scientific Development Concept" (*Kexue Fazhanguan*). We will see below what Hu means by this concept, but it was another way that he subtly shifted the discourse on the Three Represents. At the end of his speech, he also listed various measures necessary to strengthen the party's "ruling capacity" (*zhizheng nengli*)—another key concept developed under his aegis (to be discussed below)—that varied from Jiang's policy priorities. In these ways, Hu astutely referenced and used Jiang's speech and the Three Represents yet adroitly shifted the emphasis on elements that Jiang underemphasized but Hu could develop and articulate as his own.

The "Socialist Harmonious Society"

Toward the end of his tenure in office, Jiang Zemin began to promote the overarching goal of building a comprehensively well-off society (*xiaokang shehui*). After succeeding Jiang, Hu Jintao began to modify and replace Jiang's vision with one of his own: building a "Socialist Harmonious Society" (*Shehuizhuyi de Hexie Shehui*). Hu's first major exposition of his concept came in a speech at the Central Party School in February 2005.[48] Hu defined his idea thus: "The socialist harmonious society we want to build should be a society featuring democracy, the rule of law, fairness, justice, sincerity, trustworthiness, amity, full vitality, stability, orderliness, and harmony between mankind and nature." Hu then elaborated on these components of his vision:

> Democracy and the rule of law mean that the socialist democracy should be fully developed, the general plan for running the country according to

law should be earnestly implemented and the positive factors of all social sectors should be extensively mobilized; fairness and justice mean that the relationship of interests between various social sectors should be properly coordinated, the contradictions among the people and other social contradictions should be correctly handled and social fairness and justice should be earnestly safeguarded and realized; sincerity, trustworthiness, and amity mean that members of society should help each other, be honest and keep their word, and all people should be equal and amiable and get along with each other harmoniously; full vitality means that all wishes for creation that is conducive to social progress should be respected, creative activities should be supported, creative ability should be brought into play and creative achievements should be affirmed; stability and orderliness mean that social organization mechanisms should be sound, social management should be perfected, social order should be good, the people should be able to live and work in peace and contentment, and the society should be able to maintain stability and unity; harmony between mankind and nature means that production should be developed, people should be able to live a prosperous life, and the ecology should be good.[49]

Though some may dismiss this as propaganda, it is nevertheless the vision articulated by China's paramount leader for his nation and society. It is a positive vision, rooted both in traditional Confucian concepts like *Datong* (Great Harmony) and in more contemporary socialist precepts.

However, Hu's vision also belies and illustrates some of the social problems that have developed in China—in particular, social stratification and inequity. Later in his speech, Hu stressed that "we must pay attention to social justice."[50] China now has among the world's fastest growing Gini coefficient ratings, a measure of the pace of income disparity and social stratification, as large numbers of the populace have been left behind as others have enriched themselves from the reforms. This disadvantaged and disenfranchised sector, known as *ruoshi tuanti,* has mushroomed over the past decade. During the Jiang era, economic policies disproportionately benefited the coastal areas to the neglect of the interior. The rural sector in particular experienced relative deprivation. According to Wang Weiguang, vice president of the Central Party School, in 2004 there were 49.77 million with an annual net income of between 669 and 924 renminbi (about $82 to $113), with an additional 26.1 million earning less than 668 renminbi ($81).[51]

Rising social inequities—particularly in the countryside—have led to rapidly rising incidents of social unrest. The minister of public security, Zhou

Yongkang, reported that there were 87,000 "public order disturbances" (i.e., demonstrations and riots) in China in 2005, a sizable increase over the 74,000 reported in 2004 and 58,000 in 2003.[52] To be sure, these protests are not only about income disparities—the vast majority are in response to the abuse of power by local cadres; ad hoc fees, taxes, and levies on peasants; arbitrary land seizures by local governments and companies; wage arrears; environmental pollution; factory working conditions; and systemic corruption. Most such protests are resolved peacefully, usually through cash payment to the protesters—but sometimes force is used by the police or People's Armed Police. The size of protests vary widely—ranging form several dozen to the 60,000 farmers in Huaxi, Zhejiang, who turned out against government indifference over the pollution caused by two chemical plants.[53] In October 2004, a clash between ethnic Han Chinese, Hui minorities, and the police left 100 people dead, including 15 police officers, with over 400 injured. In December 2005 in Dongzhou, Guangdong, the security forces opened fire, killing 20 villagers protesting the construction of a local power plant.

The priority attached to addressing the problems of income distribution and social stratification, and to building a "new socialist countryside," subsequently became hallmarks of the Eleventh Five-Year Program, submitted to the Fifth Plenum of the Sixteenth Central Committee of October 2005 and adopted at the 2006 National People's Congress. The State Council also enacted a series of policies aimed at improving the income distribution system and narrowing disparities.[54]

The main objectives of the Eleventh Five-Year Program, as submitted to the Fifth Plenum, were:[55]

1. doubling the 2000 gross domestic product per capita of 7,086 renminbi by 2010;
2. markedly improving efficiency in utilizing resources, including energy consumption per unit of gross domestic product by 20 percent by 2010;
3. developing a number of major enterprises into internationally competitive companies with well-known brands;
4. improving the market economic system and achieving a basic equilibrium in the balance of international payments;
5. universalizing and consolidating nine-year compulsory education and developing a sound social security system;
6. improving the income levels and the quality of life for urban and rural residents and keeping the overall price level stable;

7. significantly improving living, transportation, educational, cultural, health, and environmental conditions for the population;
8. making progress in building socialist democracy, legal institutions, and spiritual civilization; and
9. further advancing social order and production safety and making progress in building a socialist harmonious society.

The 2006 annual session of the National People's Congress amended the draft plan presented at the plenum and formally adopted it as the *Outline of Eleventh Five-Year Program for National Economic and Social Development.*[56]

In addition to the above, the final program document also stressed a number of specific social goals, for example: stabilizing the low birthrate, enhancing services for the elderly, safeguarding the interests of women and children, protecting orphans, improving services for the handicapped and disabled, comprehensively raising living standards and ameliorating income gaps, introducing a proactive and coordinated national employment policy, enlarging basic pension insurance coverage in urban areas, increasing poverty relief, improving nutrition, providing economical and low-rent housing, raising health standards and providing comprehensive universal health provision and coverage, controlling the spread of infectious diseases, strengthening workplace safety, ensuring food and drug standards, and controlling crime.[57] These and other policy priorities associated with the "Socialist Harmonious Society" were officially approved by the Central Committee at the Sixth Plenum of the Sixteenth Congress in October 2006. The plenum communiqué noted that

> there are quite a lot of contradictions and issues that impair social harmony [in China today]. We must place more attention on developing social services and push forward economic and social development in a coordinated way. Social equity and justice is a basic condition of social harmony, while a sound system provides the fundamental guarantee to social equity and justice. We must accelerate construction of the system that ensures social equity and justice to guarantee people's rights and interests in political, economic, cultural, and social fields and guide our citizens to exercise their rights and fulfill their obligations according to the law.[58]

These are admirable goals, and they represent a dramatic shift away from the growth-at-all-costs agenda of the Jiang era. The Hu-Wen administration is to be commended for identifying and enunciating such a humanist policy agenda. This is the right agenda on which to focus, and it certainly resonates among the populace. In many cases, they are also attainable goals. However, in many others, it will not be so easy to turn around some chronic systemic problems.

The "Scientific Development Concept"

A central feature, perhaps *the* central feature, of Hu Jintao's goal of creating a harmonious society is his "Scientific Development Concept" (*Kexue Fazhanguan*). As noted above, early in his tenure as party and state leader, he began to discuss "scientific development" in the context of the Three Represents, but it became quickly clear that it was not science per se that he had in mind. Over time, during the period 2003–4, he began to further develop his thinking on the subject.

An inspection trip to Jiangxi Province in September 2003 was apparently the first time that Hu elevated his terminology to the "Scientific Development Concept." Over the next month, he began to elaborate his thinking. Two elements emerged as the core of the concept: "taking people as the basis" (*yi ren weiben*) and "comprehensive development" (*zonghe fazhan*). Both seemed to be deft but substantial modifications of Jiang's priorities. The former contrasted with Jiang's emphasis on commercial and social elites (although, to be fair to Jiang, his third represent spoke about the broad masses), while the latter was an implicit criticism of the unbalanced growth that had favored the coastal provinces, neglected the interior and agriculture, and damaged the environment. Hu was thus subtly, but substantially, shifting the party's reform agenda, and at the same time giving evidence of his own attentiveness and concern for the downtrodden. The Politburo formally endorsed Hu's Scientific Development Concept at its November 24, 2003, meeting.[59] The Central Party School was given the research task of fleshing out the concept and developing it theoretically.[60]

During the period 2004–5, the Central Party School, the CCP's propaganda organs, and Hu himself began to develop and elaborate the Scientific Development Concept, and in so doing they turned it into an umbrella theory—under which numerous policies could be encompassed. For example, by December 2005, Hu was able to give a lengthy speech that embraced all the following topics (and more) under the rubric of the Scientific Development Concept: improving the rural situation; accelerating economic growth; overcoming energy bottlenecks; efficiently using resources; fostering competitiveness and a culture of innovation; reforming the administrative system; improving government transparency and introducing e-government; continuing the transformation of state-owned enterprises without allowing state asset stripping; breaking up pricing and production monopolies; controlling pollution and environmental degradation; continue opening to the global economy; developing high-quality talent (*rencai*); improving public health and safety; increasing employment, job retraining, and reemployment; opening up the labor market; solving the internal migration problem; constructing new social security systems for basic services and pensions; improving tertiary and secondary education, particularly in rural areas; deepening poverty relief programs; improving workplace safety standards; dealing more effectively with social unrest; improving relations with ethnic minorities; and undertaking a series of measures to strengthen the party apparatus from top to bottom. Hu's lecture in Qinghai was a remarkably comprehensive policy blueprint—all in the name of the "Scientific Development Concept"![61]

Another important element of Hu's Scientific Development Concept concerned personnel policy. In December 2003, he gave an important speech on the need to improve the quality of party and state cadres,[62] a theme that would become a key component of another new political campaign to be carried out in 2005–6. Thereafter, the Scientific Development Concept became inextricably intertwined with the campaigns to improve the party's "governing capacity" (*zhizheng nengli*) and "advanced nature" (*xianjianxing*).[63] As the party leader Hu observed in a speech commemorating the eighty-fifth anniversary of the CCP in 2006, "Building up the Party's governing ability and construction of the Party's advanced nature are two closely related things that supplement and enhance each other. They should run through the Party's ideological construction, organizational construction, improvement of work style, and institutional construction."[64]

Democracy with Chinese Characteristics

We are willing to practice the policy of opening up, study all advanced achievements of civilizations in the world, integrate them with our own realities, and take the path of Chinese democracy.[65]

We must base ourselves on our national condition, and actively explore in practice the laws of building *democratic politics with Chinese characteristics* (emphasis added).[66]

—Premier Wen Jiabao, 2007

We must continue to expand orderly participation of our citizens, perfect the democratic system, enrich the form of democracy, and broaden the democratic channel; we must press on with our efforts to make decision making more scientific and democratic, perfect decisionmaking information, and intellectual support systems; we must develop grassroots democracy and ensure that the people can exercise their democratic rights directly and in accordance with the law.[67]

—General Secretary Hu Jintao, 2007

The "D Word" (democracy) has more fully entered the CCP lexicon during the Hu Jintao–Wen Jiabao era. While the CCP has spoken of building "socialist democracy" in the past, various ideas and terminology about democracy have been put forward by CCP theorists and officials since 2004. To be sure, what is mainly being discussed is *intraparty* democracy (*dangnei minzhu*). This particular concept, with which Hu has closely associated himself, is discussed at greater length in the next chapter. In this section, we survey some of the concepts for building democracy put forward by leading CCP theorists and the premier himself.

Although some of these ideas are fresh and have the potential to alter the ways in which the party operates, it is important to note here that very few of these theorists advocate empowering and enfranchising the population with democratic rights. It is highly doubtful that the CCP would embrace such a move. Rather, much of the discourse on democracy inside the CCP refers largely to *within-system* (*tizhinei*) democracy, that is, enlivening intraparty norms and channels of freer discussion and collective decision-making. This is classic CCP discourse, with precedents dating back to the Yanan era in the early 1960s under Deng Xiaoping and Liu Shaoqi, and to the mid-1980s under Hu Yaobang. However, some argue that the extension of democracy should be a two-stage process—first within the party and then outside. As Liu Ji, the originator of the "Three Represents" theory, put it: "We will first achieve democracy within the CCP and then extend it to the whole population."[68]

This kind of reasoning is a long-standing Chinese view dating back to Sun Yat-sen, based on concepts of tutelage and the elitist idea that the Chinese masses are not "ready" for democracy. Echoes of this reasoning are heard in Yu Keping's notion of "incremental democracy." Yu is the deputy director of the Central Committee's Compilation and Translation Bureau and is a close adviser to Hu on political reform. In his writing, Yu emphasizes incremental democracy to uphold stability, which remains paramount, but not what he calls "static stability." Rather, he calls for "dynamic stability," whereby the government expands the net of citizen participation progressively.[69] He also refers to the concept of "orderly democracy" (*yongxu minzhu*), which he sees as a kind of twin of incremental democracy, whereby he says that the "political participation of citizens must be legalized, organized and orderly."[70] He articulates an ever-widening circle of citizen participation in China, what he calls the "three roads to democracy in China": from local to higher levels; from inner-party to society; and from less competition to more competition.[71] Expanding citizen participation is central to his thinking. In one of a pair of serialized articles in the Central Party School's *Study Times,* based on his provocatively titled book *Democracy Is a Good Thing,* he argues that citizen participation has five principal benefits:[72]

1. Citizen participation is a basic way to realize civil rights.
2. Citizen participation can effectively prevent the abuse of public power.
3. Citizen participation can ensure that public policies are made in a more scientific and democratic way.
4. Citizen participation can promote the harmony and stability of social life.
5. Citizen participation itself embodies citizens' values and virtues.

There is little doubt that Yu's thinking is progressive within the Chinese context in general and within the CCP in particular. How much resonance it has with Hu and other senior party officials is unclear, but he certainly has important channels within the party for articulating his views.

Another leading party theorist is Li Junru, who is now vice president of the Central Party School. His contribution to the democracy discourse has mainly been his concept of "consultative democracy" (*xieshang minzhu*).[73] In one interview in 2006, he expanded on his views:

There are three types of democracies in the world: (1) direct democracy by voting, where the majority rule and the minority follows; (2) democracy by means of negotiation, where competing interests are negotiated in an adversarial environment, and coalitions sometimes formed; and (3) deliberative, consultative democracy, where consensus is built via consultation. Chinese-style democracy is the third way, although we also use elections. The United States wants us to adopt multiparty democracy, but our national conditions are different. We cannot copy any country's model of democracy—we must develop our own form. Consultative democracy is our contribution.[74]

In another interview in 2007, Li again emphasized electoral and consultative democracy and claimed that he had written a report on it, which was accepted by the Center (*Zhongyang*) and incorporated into Central Document No. 5 (2007). He also made a strong case for promoting professional competence and ethics in Chinese officials, and he downplayed the notion that elected officials are necessarily the best officials: "Those who win the most votes may not have good ethics. The exercise of electoral democracy cannot control corruption. There are corrupt officials who can buy votes and trick people. Elections do not guarantee competence."

Premier Wen Jiabao also weighed in on the democracy discourse active in China during the run-up to the Seventeenth Party Congress in 2007. The premier published an article under his name in the *People's Daily* in February 2007, which seemed aimed at the percolating democracy discourse in the party and country at the time. In it, Wen sent two messages. The first was unmistakable—those requesting or expecting more rapid moves toward democracy would have to wait a long time. He gave a standard recitation of the "primary stage of socialism lasting 100 or more years," China being a large and underdeveloped country with complex conditions, and the goal "to build a rich, strong, *democratic* [emphasis added], civilized, and harmonious modern socialist state in a big country with a population of over 1 billion is an unprecedented creation in human history and is also a long-term and arduous historical task."[75] Yet, later in the article, Wen wrote: "China must follow its own path of in building democratic politics. We have always held the view that the socialist system and democratic politics are not mutually exclusive, and a high degree of democracy and perfect legal system are precisely the important hallmarks of a mature socialist system. It is completely possible for us to build a democratic country with the rule of law under socialist conditions."[76]

When asked about his published article and views of democracy at the annual (2007) National People's Congress press conference, Premier Wen further elaborated:

That recent article of mine expounded the argument that socialism is not in conflict with democracy and the rule of law. I said that democracy, the rule of law, freedom, human rights, equality, and fraternity are not something peculiar to capitalism. . . . I have to say clearly that socialist democracy is, in the final analysis, to let the people be the masters of the country. We must guarantee the people's rights to democratic election, democratic policy decisionmaking, democratic management, and democratic supervision. We must create the conditions for the people to supervise and criticize the government. We must allow everybody to develop in an all-round manner in an environment marked by equality, impartiality, and freedom. We must give full play to the people's creative spirit and their ability to think independently. We must practice governing the country according to law, perfect the system of governing according to law, and build a law-governed country.[77]

The premier's words about democracy are the most forthright of any CCP leader since the purge of Zhao Ziyang in 1989 (Wen used to be an aide to Zhao). Whether it is a bellwether of protodemocratic changes to come will have to be seen. As usual, foreign observers are skeptical.[78]

Strengthening the Party's Governing Capability

At the Fourth Plenum of the Sixteenth Party Congress in September 2004, the CCP Central Committee adopted an important *Decision on the Enhancement of the Party's Governing Capacity* (Zhonggong Zhongyang Guanyu Jiaqiang Dangde Zhizheng Nengli Jianshe de Jueding).[79] This is probably the most important party meeting and document to be published since the critical Third Plenum of 1978. Though the *Decision* itself had been drafted and redrafted over the course of the previous year, under the direction of a high-level group headed by Zeng Qinghong, the contents of the document reflect many more years of the CCP's self-reflection and examination. It also reflects the culmination and closure of the intensive inner-party discourse on the causes of the collapse of the former Soviet Union and other communist party-states (discussed in chapter 4). As the *Decision* noted: "We must develop a stronger sense of crisis, draw experience and lessons from the success and failure of other ruling parties in the world, and enhance our governance capability in a more earnest and conscientious manner."[80]

Not only is the *Decision* a reflective and cumulative statement of policy, but it was also a surprisingly candid and objective one. It explicitly identified, rather than glossed over, problems faced by the party. It was also quite straightforward about the stakes and consequences of the challenges facing the CCP. As it notes at the outset, "Vigorously enhancing the Party's governing capabilities is a major strategic subject with a bearing on the future and destiny of the Chinese nation, the life and death of the Party, as well as the lasting stability and prosperity of the country."[81] Elsewhere it says:

- "The problem of corruption remains quite serious in some areas, department and units. The fight against corruption is a life and death issue for the Party."
- "Some leading party members do not have a strong sense of responsibility, personal integrity, a down-to-earth style of work or a close connection with the general public."
- "Some Party organizations at the grassroots level are weak and slack, while some Party members have failed to play an exemplary role."
- "Weak, slack, and impotent Party committees must be frequently reshuffled and unqualified Party members must be severely dealt with."[82]

If one compares the "lessons" and conclusions of the CCP's postmortem on the USSR with the organization and content of the *Decision on the Enhancement of the Party's Governing Capacity,* they are remarkably similar. Virtually all the major "lessons" are incorporated into this document:

- Place priority on economic, material, and social development.
- Pay attention to ideology, and make it flexible and adaptable to national conditions.
- Combat corruption and strengthen party discipline.
- Rotate, retire, and change leading personnel.
- Promote inner-party democracy and extraparty consultation.
- Reform and reinvigorate local party branches.
- Improve cadre competence and recruitment into the party.
- Combat Western attempts at subversion and "peaceful evolution."
- Pay attention to a range of social development problems.
- Pursue a foreign policy of openness and integration into the international community.

Following the Fourth Plenum and the adoption of the *Decision,* a major national campaign was launched to propagate and implement the document's recommendations. Zeng Qinghong—vice president, Politburo Standing Committee member, Central Committee Secretariat chairman, and Central Party School president—led the way with a lengthy and widely publicized speech on October 8, 2004.[83] The CCP general secretary, Hu, had put Zeng in charge of the drafting committee for the *Decision* (an astute move to test and co-opt Zeng's political allegiance).

In his speech, Zeng went much further than simply reiterating (often verbatim) the content of the document (which is normally the case during the implementation phase of such campaigns). For example, he provided a candid connection between the lessons learned from the collapse of the Soviet Union and the *Decision:*

> We can gain profound enlightenment from the painful lesson of the loss of power by the communist parties of the Soviet Union and Eastern Europe. A number of old and big parties throughout the world lost power one after the other in the late 1980s and early 1990s. The Soviet Union used to be the world's Number 1 socialist country, but overnight the country broke up and political power collapsed. The Communist Party of the Soviet Union was a big party with an 88-year history and 15 million members, yet it was disbanded. Communist parties in the Soviet Union and Eastern Europe lost their status as parties in power. Although many factors were involved, one important reason was that in their long time in power their system of governing became rigid, their ability to govern declined, people were dissatisfied with what the officials accomplished while in charge, and they became seriously isolated from the masses of the people.
>
> The *Decision* asserts that it is not easy for a proletarian political party to gain power, and even harder to exercise political power well, especially when it is held for a long time, and the Party's status as a party in power does not necessarily last as long as the Party does, nor is it something once achieved never lost. These incisive judgments in the *Decision* drew profoundly from the lesson of the experience of the rise and fall, success and defeat, of foreign political parties—including the Communist Parties of the Soviet Union and East European countries. The intent [of the *Decision*] is to get all the Party's comrades, and especially leading cadres at all levels of the Party, to wake up, think of danger in times of peace, heighten their sense of hardship and their sense of governing, and earnestly strengthen the Party's ability to govern.[84]

Zeng then proceeds to elaborate, embellish, and interpret at considerable length the content of the *Decision,* often going beyond—in tone and content—the original document. He soberly concludes that "if our Party does not undertake to correct our ways and implement the *Decision,* our Party might even lose its governing status!"[85] Following Zeng's hard-hitting speech, a vigorous national campaign unfolded to promote and implement the *Decision.* This was done through the publication of multiple study volumes,[86] the dispatch of central-level teams to provincial and local levels to explain the *Decision,* and the convening of countless study sessions from the top to the bottom of the national party apparatus. Unlike most such campaigns, however, this one did not fizzle out after a few months, and there was no fixed timetable for concluding it. In this sense, the *Decision* was more of an open-ended, indefinite, and wide-ranging program of party adaptation and improvement.

From Theory to Practice

These ideological initiatives have served as the theoretical underpinning for a series of practical efforts by the CCP to strengthen its organizational apparat and capabilities. Because the essence of a Leninist party is its organizational penetration and domination of society, the CCP has accordingly undertaken a number of initiatives to strengthen and rebuild the party apparatus from top to bottom. We examine many of these efforts in the next chapter.

7

Rebuilding the Party:
The Organizational Dimension

As a result of its study of foreign political parties and systems, as well as its own intensive self-examination, the Chinese Communist Party (CCP) has been implementing a series of new policies and programs aimed at reinvigorating and strengthening its organizational apparatus from top to bottom. The ideological/theoretical rationale for these initiatives was outlined in the previous chapter. Though some of these reforms predated 2002, most of the initiatives have occurred since the Sixteenth Party Congress, and in particular since the adoption of the *Decision on the Enhancement of the Party's Governing Capacity* adopted at the Fourth Plenum of September 2004. This chapter summarizes a number of these efforts.

Maintain the Advanced Nature of the Party

As part of the "Party's Governing Capacity" program, the CCP launched a special campaign aimed at "maintaining the advanced nature of CCP members" (*baochi dangyuan de xianjianxing*). After two years of pilot studies, the Central Committee fully endorsed the campaign at the Fifth Plenum of the Sixteenth Party Congress, and it commenced in January 2005. As Qi Yu, a senior CCP Organization Department official and deputy director in charge of overseeing the campaign implementation, reflected:

> Today's cadres must be familiar with many new challenges. But we have some shortfalls in our work—so we decided to carry out the *xianjianxing* campaign. Since I was so personally involved, I have three observations about its outcome. First, it was a good opportunity for all CCP

members to receive Marxist education. Second, it consolidated party organizations at lower levels—every party member, party committee, and party group went through it. Third, the campaign helped the general population experiencing difficulties in their lives.[1]

The campaign was first launched in the pages of the *People's Daily,* the official CCP paper, in a series of articles in late December 2004 and early January 2005.[2] A few days after the editorials, the Xinhua News Agency released the "Opinions of the CCP Central Committee" on the campaign, which elaborated the reasons for the campaign and what it sought to accomplish.[3] These "Opinions" echoed the content of the aforementioned *Decision,* but they particularly focused on the issues of strengthening party committees at all levels, increasing party members' awareness of Marxism, improving inner-party democracy, and combating inner-party corruption and laxity.

At first, many party cadres thought it was just another pro forma ideological campaign that would include several study sessions and then wither away.[4] But this proved not to be so. It quickly became clear that this was an old-fashioned "rectification" campaign (*zhengfeng yundong*), a particularly intrusive type of witch hunt aimed at interrogating party members, exposing them to criticism and self-criticism, and penalizing or expelling those found to be lacking. "This is an old-style [rectification] campaign, the first since 1983, and it reminds us of Mao and the Cultural Revolution," said one party member.[5]

The campaign unfolded in three distinct phases over an eighteen-month period, culminating in the summer of 2006.[6] The first phase was carried out among central, provincial, and municipal-level party committees. The second phase was for party committees at and above the county level. The third phase was for party committees and members below the county level. These three phases overlapped:[7]

- Phase 1: Three months of organized group study of relevant party documents (some original Marxist-Leninist texts, some of Mao Zedong's writings, a number of Jiang Zemin's and Hu Jintao's speeches, a number of CCP "Decisions" adopted at various party meetings, and special study documents prepared for the campaign[8]), followed by three months of "self-reflection" (*fanci*) and individual study.
- Phase 2: Three months of writing a "self-criticism" (*ziwo piping*), followed by three months of circulating it to colleagues for feedback.

- Phase 3: Three months of criticism by colleagues, followed by three months of revising one's "self-criticism." After this is accepted, it goes into one's party personnel dossier (*dang'an*).

Party members were subjected to wave upon wave of propaganda materials.[9] Study sessions were mandatory. Party members were not allowed to leave the country during phase 1.[10] Following intensive study, the campaign transitioned into the criticism/self-criticism phases.

By July 2006, the eighteen-month campaign had come to a conclusion. According to a media briefing by Ouyang Song, deputy head of the Central Leading Group for Advanced Nature Education and concurrently deputy director of the CCP Organization Department, the campaign was concluded in full and on schedule.[11] All 70.8 million party members, including 3.5 million "party grassroots organizations," participated. Over the course of the eighteen months, 130,000 new party organizations were created, while 156,000 "weak or nonfunctional local level party organizations were rectified" and required to improve their work. A total of 2.919 million heads of party organizations received special intensive training on how to improve their work, and the Central Committee allocated 1.75 billion renminbi ($21.8 billion) to help villages build 164,000 places for conducting party activities. It was also discovered during the campaign that approximately 3.4 million party members had disappeared into the national "floating population" of migrants,[12] estimated to be as high as 180 million nationwide.[13]

Of those party members who were deemed "unqualified," 44,738 were expelled from the party. Since 2002, it was found that between 2.1 and 2.47 million new members had joined the party each year. In 2005, for example, 17 million applied for membership, with 2.47 million granted admission as new members, of which 2 million were under the age of thirty-five years. By the end of 2004, the party had 12.96 million female members (18.6 percent of the total) and 4.41 million members from ethnic minority groups (6.3 percent of the total). In terms of education, 56.6 percent of party members had received a senior middle school education, and 27.3 percent had a college education or above.[14] The percentage of women and minorities in the party has held quite steady at these levels over time. According to Wang Tingda, the director of the Central Committee Organization Department Party Building Institute, the current recruitment criteria emphasize two sectors: "Right now we are targeting youth and workers in the frontline of production [read: private and collective enterprises] and have no quotas for admitting women, minorities, and the like."[15]

The CCP has not only concentrated on vetting and improving its membership. It has also concentrated attention on institution (re)building.

Strengthening Party Building

Another key determination made by the CCP about the reasons for collapse of the Communist Party of the Soviet Union and the USSR was that the Soviet Communist Party had allowed its organizational capacity to atrophy. Subsequent surveys by the CCP during the 1990s of its own party committees and party members were showing similar signs of deterioration. Party committees in the countryside, below the county level, and in state enterprises were found to be in a particularly bad state. Given this deteriorating state of affairs, during Jiang Zemin's and Hu Jintao's tenure, the CCP undertook a series of systematic and comprehensive programs intended to "(re)build the party" (*dang jian*), improve "party life" (*dang de shenghuo*), improve the "party's ruling capacity" (*dang de zhizheng nengli*), improve the "party's advanced nature" (*dang de xianjianxing*), and "improve inner-party democracy" (*dang nei minzhu*). The remainder of this section reviews six distinct but complementary sets of reforms—each aimed at addressing different aspects of the party's overall program to strengthen itself and overcome its vulnerabilities.

Fighting Corruption and Improving Party Discipline

Maintaining party discipline, both for individual party members and as an organization, is vital for a Leninist party. If party members and party organizations disobey or disregard the dictates and policies of the party leadership, or if they contravene established procedures, the entire party apparatus quickly breaks down. Inner-party corruption is a manifestation or example of such indiscipline and disobedience.

Clearly, corruption is one of the principal challenges facing the CCP and Chinese society, because it permeates both. Jiang Zemin and Hu Jintao have both referred to the problem as a "life and death" issue for the party. No doubt the CCP leaders know the role that corruption played in bringing down Kuomintang rule on the Chinese mainland in the 1930s and 1940s and on Taiwan in the 1990s, and they are aware of the role it played in the Soviet and East European cases. In a 2003 interview with the deputy director of the Central Discipline Inspection Commission of the Central Committee (Jilu Jiancha Weiyuanhui, or CDIC), Liu Fengyan explicitly linked his organization to the CCP's ability to survive the collapse of the USSR: "I must stress that our party members willingly accept our inspection and supervision—this is why we have survived the collapse of the former Soviet Union. The CCP has survived the collapse of the USSR and East European states exactly because we have strict discipline."[16] Thus, maintaining discipline and combating corruption are among the party's highest priorities.

The principal CCP body responsible for maintaining party discipline and norms, as well as ferreting out corruption within the party ranks, is the CDIC.[17] The CDIC dates to the early years of the People's Republic, and the CCP (like the Qing and Republican governments before it) has always believed that it is capable of policing itself and, concomitantly, that there is no need for extraparty mechanisms of supervision. However, as is discussed below, when considering the new movement to increase intraparty democracy and extraparty consultation, the CCP may have recently come to believe that there should be a limited role for mechanisms other than the CDIC in supervising party discipline. As Hu Jintao put it in 2006: "We must intensify the supervision over leading party bodies and leading party cadres; closely combine the inner-party supervision with the supervision of the people's congresses, supervision by special government bodies, democratic supervision by people's political consultative committees, supervision by democratic parties, supervision by judicial authorities, supervision by the masses, and supervision by the media—so as to create a supervisory force and improve the effectiveness of supervision."[18] We will explore some of these proposals below, but it is a significant development for the CCP to recognize the need to strengthen—albeit relatively—these consultative and supervisory mechanisms.

Notwithstanding these initiatives, the CDIC remains the party's watchdog on discipline and corruption. In 1993, the CDIC and the State Council's Ministry of Supervision were effectively merged, although bureaucratically the latter still exists under the State Council. Since then, they have both occupied the same mammoth compound on Ping'an Boulevard in central Beijing, exemplifying the Chinese bureaucratic tradition of "one organization, two signs" (*yige jigou, liang kuai paizi*). After the merger, the organization was reduced in size in keeping with the State Council directive to streamline and reduce bureaucratic redundancies.[19] An interview with the CDIC staff in 2003 revealed that the internal organization of the merged organs has 23 functional departments with 1,400 personnel working in the headquarters compound (several thousand more work throughout the country).[20] The Ministry of Supervision (MOS) has a staff of 800, divided into twenty-one functional departments, at the headquarters in Beijing.[21] Despite the merger, there is still a strict division of labor whereby the CDIC polices the party while the MOS does the same in State Council organs; a separate CDIC system exists within the military.[22] The CDIC penetrates the party apparatus from top to bottom (subcounty level) and practices the "dual leadership system" (*shuangtong lingdao zhidu*), whereby at each level there is a parallel discipline inspection committee or office, as well as discipline inspection officers working within ordinary party committees.[23] Thus the CDIC enjoys the simultaneous status of both being embedded within the party committees themselves yet also enjoying autonomous supervisory powers.[24] In a meeting with the author in 2007, the CDIC and MOS said they were undertaking to establish a new National Bureau of Corruption Prevention (Guojia Zhufang Fubai Ju). The new bureau will be a separate State Council organ, but it will be bureaucratically under the MOS and headed by an MOS ministerial level official.[25]

At its 2006 plenary session, the CDIC reported that from November 2004 to December 2005, it had investigated 147,539 cases of violations of party discipline regulations.[26] Of those, 143,391 cases were resolved—resulting in the expulsion of 24,188 members from the party. A total of 115,143 party members were punished for breaches of party discipline, accounting for 1.7 per 1,000 party members. Of these punished members, 15,177 were handed over to judicial departments for suspected involvement in criminal activity. The statistics for 2006, provided during an interview at the CDIC, revealed a slight drop in the total number of party officials punished (97,260) and in officials punished for administrative breaches of discipline (37,775, including 8 ministerial-level officials).[27] The CDIC claimed that party members punished had been 1.7 per 1,000 in 2004, rose to 1.8 per 1,000 in 2005, but had fallen to 1.4 per 1,000 in 2006.[28] In 2006, the CDIC investigated 21,889 cases of business bribery, of which 4,772 involved public servants (21.8 percent of all cases).[29]

Over the longer period between October 1997 and September 2002, CDIC organs nationwide punished 846,760 members for breaching party discipline, of which 137,711 were stripped of their party membership.[30] This included the high-profile Dangjiang and Xiamen smuggling cases, as well as the execution of the governor of Jiangxi Province (Fu Qiangxing), the vice chairman of the National People's Congress (Chen Kejie), the vice minister of public security (Bi Jizhou), and the mayor of Shenyang (Mu Juxing).[31] The Beijing mayor, Chen Xitong, and the Shanghai party secretary, Chen Liangyu, were also removed on corruption charges.[32]

Despite these reported cases of investigating and prosecuting corruption in the CCP, the problem remains both systemic and endemic. As the Central Party School's former executive vice president, Yu Yunyao, observed: "To the party as a whole, the longer it is in power, the greater the danger of its being divorced from the masses and the grimmer the test of fighting corruption. With regard to leading cadres, the higher his position, the greater his power, and the longer he assumes leadership, the larger the number of seductions and the greater the possibility of his being corrupted."[33]

At its Sixth Plenum in January 2006, the CDIC adopted a number of new measures to combat corruption, including the systematic reform of discipline inspection committees at all levels, increasing the attention paid to unauthorized fee charging, increasing random audits of enterprises and party committees, investigating dereliction of duty by cadres endangering public safety and the environment, and creating roving inspection teams at the county and subcounty levels.[34] The CDIC has also set up a series of "masses' accusation centers" (*renmin qunzhong zhubao zhongxin*), where members of the public can file anonymous complaints against party and state cadres.[35] The CCP Organization Department has also established a confidential hotline telephone number (12380) for the public to comment on the selection of party and government officials.[36]

Thus, despite the difficulties of coming to grips with corruption, the CCP is not sitting idly by while it spreads like an infectious cancer throughout society. Despite its efforts, however, party indiscipline and corruption are likely to continue as a festering fact of life for the CCP.

Rebuilding the Local Party Apparatus

In 2007, the CCP possessed approximately 73.36 million members and 3.6 million local-level party organizations across the People's Republic of China.[37] The CCP must, therefore, be thought of primarily as an enormous vertical organization that penetrates state and society from top to bottom. This is the essence of Leninism: penetrating into localities, social and professional organs, and establishing party cells within them. The twin problems for the CCP have been that new social and professional groups have proliferated rapidly across China, and existing party committees have lost much of their relevance and appeal at the local level.[38] In 2005, there were about 310,000 civic organizations at the county level and above across China.[39] The CCP's Organization Department has been particularly concerned about the atrophying of party committees in rural villages and state-owned enterprises, as well as the admitted difficulty of establishing party cells in private-sector enterprises.[40]

Thus, the CCP has undertaken a significant effort since the mid-1990s to try to strengthen and enliven existing party committees and cells, while establishing new ones in newly emerging entities. The effort has not only been to strengthen local party committees to make them more responsive to higher-level dictates but also to make local party committees more responsive and relevant to local interests. This has been done in three principal ways: holding elections for party committee heads, increasing "intraparty democracy," and rebuilding the party committees themselves. The first of these two methods is discussed separately below, but let us consider the process of reconstituting party committees.

To find out the real situation of local party committees and the degree to which they had decayed or become dysfunctional, beginning in 2001 the CCP Organization Department undertook a series of investigations (*kaocha*) and formal surveys. They were published in internally circulated (*neibu*) volumes issued by the Organization Department's publishing house. These revealed a number of anomalies in party committee performance, but they also identified a number of new socioeconomic developments that the party needed to accommodate and reflect.

One survey of 4,000 party members in Jilin Province rated the work of party committees there as good (45.8 percent), average (37.5 percent), and poor or bad (16.7 percent).[41] When further asked to identify the reasons for the low ratings, several defects were identified: 34.7 percent found the party committees to be "weak and passive"; 40.4 percent found cadres to have "insufficient ideological liberalization" (code words for ideological dogmatism); 47.2 percent identified an arbitrary work style and patronage as problems; 52 percent said there was "insufficient democracy"; 55 percent said there was "insufficient scientific decisionmaking"; 40.3 percent of cadres were deemed to be "corrupt"; 69.9 percent said that party cadres used public funds for personal consumption; and a shocking 80.2 percent reported that cadres had extracted illegitimate fees from the public (rent seeking).[42] Dogmatism, formalism, obstructionism, and arbitrariness were all cited as common characteristics of party cadres. Many complaints surfaced about the so-called *yibashou*—literally the "number one leader"—but a euphemism for overzealous rent-seeking local officials. The investigation also found that a large number of party committees in state-owned enterprises had ceased to function.[43]

Another nationwide investigation undertaken in 2000 noted the rapidly changing composition of the socioeconomic structure and the need for the party to target the newly emergent private commercial sector and "new social associations" (*xin shehui shetuan*). It found that while the private sector was expanding rapidly, only 1.9 percent (464,000) of party members came from this dynamic sector.[44] A total of 82 percent of private enterprises were found to have no party organizations at all. In Guangdong, of the 7,301 social associations identified, only 1.7 percent had party organizations in them. Of the 10,380 social associations identified in Sichuan, only 3 percent had party organs in them. Another investigation by the CCP Organization Department a year later examined the formation of social groups outside the business world—in educational, cultural, medical, scientific, and technological circles—and found party organs to be wholly lacking in these sectors.[45] Such findings no doubt fed into and fueled the Three Represents initiative to establish party organs in these new social groups—particularly private enterprises—and to recruit new party members from them.

Faced with these types of problems, the CCP responded with four principal measures. First, it began a systematic effort to establish party committees in these newly emergent social, professional, and commercial entities. Second, the party launched a national effort to intensify the midcareer training of party cadres (see below). Third, special efforts were made to investigate and rebuild party committees in rural areas.[46] And, fourth, it launched the eighteen-month-long systematic campaign to evaluate every party member and every party committee nationwide as part of the "party's advanced nature" program (see above).

The CCP has also made some new efforts to improve the transparency of decisionmaking. In March 2005, the Central Committee and State Council jointly adopted the document *Opinion Concerning the Further Promotion of Open Information on Governmental Affairs*. Accordingly, Politburo and Standing Committee meetings are now routinely reported in the press, and efforts have been made to do the same at provincial and municipal levels. For example, the CCP is experimenting at the local level with a "*gongshi zhidu*" (public notice system), whereby the local government committee calls for public feedback on major expenditure projects or the local Party Committee (Organization Department) calls for public feedback on its intention to appoint a cadre to a leading position.[47] In April 2007, the State Council announced new *Regulations on Publicizing Government Information,* in a further step toward increasing the transparency of governance. Though such steps are unprecedented in China and are to be welcomed, China remains a very long way from having open and accountable government.

Improving Extraparty Consultation and Supervision

Another related reform effort has been to improve "multiparty cooperation" (*duo dang hezuo*). The idea is to strengthen the eight "democratic parties" and the legislative body in which they participate, the Chinese People's Political Consultative Congress (CPPCC).

In February 2005, the Central Committee issued the important document "Opinions of the CCP Central Committee on Further Strengthening the Building of the System of Multi-Party Cooperation and Consultation under the Leadership of the CCP."[48] Under this initiative, the CCP is to consult more closely with these noncommunist parties, to submit major policy programs to the CPPCC for feedback before adoption, and to better respect their views. In 2007, leading CPPCC (non-CCP) members have been appointed to top posts in the State Council (minister of health and minister of science and technology).

Altogether, there were only 720,000 CPPCC members nationwide in 2007, but this number is expected to grow to 1 million by 2010.[49] Sixty percent of members are noncommunist, and 40 percent are CCP members (the fact that the CPPCC includes CCP members belies its professed autonomy and is another example of Leninist penetration).[50] The CPPCC operates at the national, provincial, municipal, and township levels.

Previously, the CCP viewed these parties and the CPPCC as mere tools in a united front mobilization strategy to win over these noncommunist constituencies to support the CCP. Though this remains the case to some extent, nowadays the emphasis is on strengthening these parties in their own right, consulting more closely with them, and creating new mechanisms for their involvement in the national policy process. To some extent, these efforts have accelerated since Hu Jintao became the CCP general secretary.[51] A member of the CPPCC reported in 2005 that, as a result of this new initiative, the noncommunist parties and CPPCC were being more systematically brought into the CCP policymaking process by being shown drafts of various policy initiatives, party and state documents, and being asked for feedback on them.[52] According to the State Council's 2005 White Paper *Building Political Democracy in China,* thirty-six such forums and briefings were convened in 2003–4 by CCP leaders with the noncommunist "democratic parties" (thirteen of which were presided over personally by Hu).[53] In 2006, the CCP Politburo met twenty-three times with members of the CPPCC, while CCP general secretary Hu did so eight times.[54] Party publications are also replete with figures of dramatic growth in membership in the eight "democratic parties," with the majority being added in the nonstate sector.[55]

Thus there appears to be an evolution in the way that the CCP thinks about the CPPCC and the noncommunist parties—moving gradually away from viewing them as united front tools and toward more systematic and respectful consultation with them. To be sure, one should not place too much stock in this initiative, but it is an important part of a broader package of reforms outlined in this chapter—all aimed at building extraparty devices to supervise and improve the governance of the CCP.

Increasing Inner-Party Democracy

In addition to increasing extraparty consultation, the CCP has launched a major initiative to improve what it describes as "inner-party democracy" (*dang nei minzhu*). Although discussion began in earnest at the Sixteenth Party Congress,[56] it accelerated in 2005–6. Hu has made a particularly strong case for enlivening party committees at all levels—from the village to the Politburo Standing Committee—with freer discussion.[57] Various other party speeches and documents, as well as training handbooks,[58] reveal that this initiative has five main components:

1. experimenting with multiple candidate elections for party committees,
2. exposing party committees to input and criticism from local citizens,
3. encouraging intraparty criticisms of policies,
4. increasing the transparency of decisionmaking and improving accountability, and
5. increasing the responsiveness of party decisions to critiques from the "democratic parties" (see above).

These reforms are all inspired by CCP assessments of the causes of collapse of the Soviet Communist Party in the Soviet Union.[59] Had the Soviet party apparatus not been top heavy, dogmatic, rigid, and routinely suppressed contrary views expressed within the party, Chinese analysts argue, the Soviet Communist Party would have been more adaptable and could have saved itself and survived. Paradoxically, this is one thing Mikhail

Gorbachev was attempting to do—but it was too little and too late. As a result, it was determined that the CCP needed to be enlivened from the bottom up. Divergent viewpoints and feedback were to be encouraged both inside and outside the party.[60] For "democratic centralism" to succeed, there has to be greater emphasis placed on the former and less on the latter, although inner-party discourse continues to stress the ultimate need to uphold centralism and party discipline.[61]

For several years now, the CCP has experimented with elections to village and township government committees, but in the last few years the party has begun to experiment with similar contested elections for local-level party committees.[62] By one estimate, 20 percent of village party committees now hold multicandidate elections—while 70 percent of village governments now are contested in this way.[63] Zheng Bijian, the former chairman of the China Reform Forum and adviser to Jiang Zemin and Hu Jintao, claims that 99 percent of village governments now hold elections (although other estimates do not corroborate this figure).[64] These elections have proven effective and popular because they expose local party cadres to accountability and responsiveness to local interests and needs.[65] Sometimes the party candidates are defeated at the ballot box.[66]

At the same time as experiments are proceeding with local elections, party committees at all levels of the system have been encouraged to improve their consultation with the public as well as debate within party committees. This is meant to encourage horizontal consultation and debate within a vertical system. Thus far, it is this normative dimension of inner-party democracy—freer discourse and greater consultation—that has received emphasis.

Of course, such "democratic" reforms are all to occur *within* the one-party system (*tizhinei*) and within well-defined political and intellectual boundaries. Though such dissenting opinions are being encouraged within the party, the CCP has zero tolerance for organized opposition outside the party. Where the CCP's experiments with democracy will ultimately lead remains unclear. Various CCP leaders have repeatedly ruled out the adoption of a multiparty system. For example, in 2004, Hu Jintao explicitly stated: "History indicates that indiscriminately copying Western political systems is a blind alley for China."[67] Despite Hu's dismissal, the party continues to experiment with pseudodemocratic elections at the local level. Over time, these elections will likely spread up to the county level, while the election of delegates to local party congresses are increasingly contested.[68] The Central Party School researcher Zhou Tianyong argues that

China needs a thirty-to-sixty-year period to make the "transition (*guodu*) to full democracy," and that the socioeconomic conditions will be ripe in 2020 to begin this process.[69] Ultimately, one could envision a day when the CCP felt comfortable enough about its own popularity and legitimacy to subject itself to contested direct elections at the national level—as is the case with the ruling People's Action Party in Singapore.

Improving Cadre Competence

Another key component of the party-building effort has been to improve the qualifications and competence of cadres in the CCP, but also in the state apparatus. Zeng Qinghong has been at the forefront of this effort, both during his time as director of the Central Organization Department (1999–2002) and subsequently as president of the Central Party School (2002–). In a speech to the 2005–6 incoming class of the Central Party School, Zeng declared that "we must assemble outstanding personnel in all areas and use them in party and state causes."[70] He then elaborated the qualities to be looked for and trained in cadres:

> To judge a person, we should judge his real nature, his attitude in handling important matters, his mainstream mentality, his development potential, his political character, his work performance, and people's views of him. By no means should we permit those who do hard work without complaint and who never advertise their good work go unacknowledged; and by no means should we permit those who go after fame and benefits, who are opportunistic and who play tricks to become powerful and influential. While the people we use must be morally acceptable and professionally competent, we must not expect them to be absolutely flawless; while we must follow the set criteria, we must not stick to any one pattern; and while we should pay attention to using people with different talents, we should also recommend those who have unique skills. The objective is one where everyone can bring his or her talents into full play, talents can be fully used, everybody can put his strengths into play, and each is in his proper place.[71]

Improvement of the cadre corps has taken a number of forms. The 2005–6 *xianjianxing* campaign, described above, was one systematic attempt to examine every single party member. This resulted in weeding out about 45,000 cadres deemed unfit for the party, but the review process also identified those who had vulnerabilities and were in need of further training. Increasing and improving midcareer training has been a second main method for improving the cadre corps. This has principally been carried out through the extensive party school system. A third measure has been to strengthen the vetting and approval process by the CCP Organization Department for the appointment and promotion of cadres at all ranks. Let us examine each of these latter two methods at greater length.

The party's Organization Department is one of the, if not *the,* most important organs in the CCP. It is the institutional heart of a Leninist party system. It controls all 70-plus million party personnel and all personnel assignments throughout the national system. There are three main categories of party personnel assignments: the *nomenklatura* system; the *bianzhi* system; and ordinary party committee assignments.

The *nomenklatura* system was inherited from the Soviet Communist Party. It is a list of *positions* for approximately 2,500 party officials at the rank of minister in central-level organs or governor and party secretary in China's thirty-one provinces and four centrally administered municipalities (Beijing, Tianjin, Shanghai, Chongqing), and an additional 39,000 officials at the bureau level whose appointment must be reported to the Central Committee.[72] Within the *nomenklatura* list, there is a more select group (truly the elite within the elite) known as the Zhongyang Ganbu Mulu (Central Cadres List), which in 2003 included about 1,000 in total.[73] The *bianzhi* list is different from the *nomenklatura* list. The *bianzhi* system is a State Council administrative office, whereas the *nomenklatura* system is administered by the CCP Organization Department. The *bianzhi* is a list of the authorized number of personnel and defines their duties and functions in government administrative organs (*guanli jiguan*), state enterprises (*guoying qiye*), and service organizations (*shiye danwei*).[74] The *bianzhi* covers all those employed in these organizations, while the *nomenklatura* only applies to leadership positions. According to recent statistics (2004), the *bianzhi* system amounts to 33.76 million personnel![75] The last category of personnel managed by the CCP Organization Department are those in leading positions of the 168,000 party committees nationwide (out of a total of 3,445,000 total party organs nationwide).[76] Through these three personnel control systems, the Organization Department manages its cadre corps—and through them the 70-plus million party membership.

Between 2001 and 2004, a torrent of regulations were adopted by the Central Committee and State Council, aimed at improving the quality of party and state cadres and the methods for selecting them, including *2001–2005*

National Cadre Education and Training Plan (2001);[77] *Regulations on the Selection and Appointment of Party and Government Leading Cadres* (2002); *Measures to Supervise and Examine the Recruitment and Appointment of Party and Government Leading Cadres* (2003); *Provisional Regulations on the Work of Openly Selecting Party and Government Leading Cadres* (2004); and the *Provisional Regulations on the Work of Openly Selecting Party and Government Leading Cadres* (2004).[78]

Since the promulgation of the *Regulations on the Selection and Appointment of Party and Government Leading Cadres* in July 2002,[79] the Organization Department has stepped up its evaluation of all party cadres. All party personnel now have annual appraisal reviews, according to three criteria: professional merit and moral integrity, one's professional achievements, and whether they are accepted by the "masses" (i.e., the public).[80] According to the new norms, a ten-day public notification period must be given for public comment prior to the appointment of a party or government official at the local level. The methods used by the Organization Department for appraisal include individual interviews, questionnaires and opinion surveys, "democratic assessment by the masses" (a recent addition since 2002), on-the-spot investigations (*kaocha*), examinations, and the evaluation of personnel records.[81] In some cases, cadres are also judged on a "GDP index," that is, how much gross domestic product, or GDP, grew annually during their tenure in their region. It is also interesting that several of the criteria used in cadre appraisals use terminology reminiscent of the Confucian personnel system of imperial times: *de* (morality), *neng* (capability), *qing* (diligence), *ji* (achievement), and *lian* (uncorrupt).[82] The overall goal, according to many official documents, is to create a cadre corps composed of talented people (*rencai*), another Confucian concept.

The adoption of new appraisal methods and criteria after 2002 came not only in response to the need to rectify inefficient party committees but also to open up the evaluation process—which had previously been deemed to be

- too secretive,
- carried out by a narrow circle of party committee evaluators (who were often susceptible to payoffs for filing positive evaluations),
- using nonstandardized, meritocratic criteria, and
- having no input from one's colleagues or from the general public.[83]

The new appraisal and appointment guidelines are intended to rectify all these deficiencies. In 2005, the CCP issued a more comprehensive and systematic set of regulations to guide the appraisal process, which specify in great detail how personnel appraisals should be conducted and according to which criteria, what merits promotion, and how problem cases should be handled.[84]

Midcareer Training

Midcareer cadre training (*ganbu peixun*) has also been an increasingly important method to improve governance and competence in the party, government, and military sectors. As CCP general secretary Hu Jintao stated in 2000 (when he was president of the Central Party School): "The Central Committee of the Party has made it very clear that Party School education is the main channel of regular and rotational training for Party cadres at various levels."[85] According to a 2006 CCP Directive, all cadres must have a minimum of three months' training every five years.[86] Such "executive training" is done principally through the extensive nationwide networks of cadre management schools (*ganbu guanli xuexiao*) and administrative management schools (*xingzheng guanli xuexiao*) administered by a combination of local and provincial governments, the party school system, and other specialized vocational training programs.

By the end of 2001, of the 6,932,000 party cadres nationwide (as distinct from the total of 40,510,000 party and state cadres nationwide), roughly half (3,078,000) had received one or more of these forms of midcareer cadre training.[87] Of these, 989,000 had been trained in party schools, 195,000 at administrative schools, 225,000 at managerial cadre schools, and 1,669,000 in other vocational training programs.[88] From its reopening in March 1977 (following the Cultural Revolution) through September 2000, the Central Party School (CPS) trained more than 4 million personnel, including 2.3 million high-level and middle-level cadres, 4,500 "young reserve cadres," 3,000 national minority cadres, and 7,300 propaganda cadres and CPS faculty.[89] From 1981 to 2006, the CPS graduated 266 Ph.D. and 1,126 M.A. students.[90] Another CPS source indicates that there are 70,000 party cadres at the central (*zhongyang*) level, and because the CPS can only train 5,000 people a year, it takes fourteen years to matriculate each one—but that is the goal.[91]

The Party School System

The nationwide system of CCP party schools is a critically important organizational device through which the CCP maintains control over its 40 million cadres in the party and state systems. These cadres are the backbone of the CCP and are central to the party's Leninist character and its ability to maintain political authority and control throughout the vast People's Republic of China. If one wants to know *how* the CCP rules China, one *must* understand how the party's Central Committee Organization Department functions and controls personnel throughout the party and state apparat. The national party school system (*dangxiao xitong*) is a core element of the Organization Department's personnel control system.

Through the national party school system, its parallel public administration school system (for state cadres), and Colleges of Socialism (Shehuizhuyi Xueyuan) run by the CCP United Front Department, these schools fulfill several key functions through a variety of midcareer training programs:

- training in Marxist-Leninist ideology and the latest party policy documents;
- training in mechanisms and methods of party organizational control;
- training in administration, management, and leadership science; and
- training in broader fields of basic education, for example, economics, accounting, history, international relations, and philosophy.

Every single individual of the 70-plus million (2006) members of the CCP who passes through one of the approximately 2,700 party schools in China receives training in these four fields.[92] In addition, the party school system—and particularly the CPS in Beijing—serves an important role as *think tank* and incubator of reform ideas and policies. Over the years, many key reform ideas have germinated within and then emerged from the CPS. Provincial and subprovincial-level party schools have also generated similar reform ideas customized to more local conditions, while similarly serving as conduits to test out proto-reforms developed at the central level.

Following the Fifteenth Party Congress in 1997, the Central Committee adopted another important document concerning the CPS, the "Decision on Accelerating the Reformation of Party School Work Towards the 21st Century." Since that time, the CPS has substantially expanded its curriculum beyond ideological indoctrination (although this remains a core function) to a considerably wider field of instruction; it has trained increasingly large numbers of party and state cadres, military officers, intellectuals, and even (since 2001) businesspeople; it has dramatically expanded its staff size and its physical plant; it has opened its doors to large numbers of foreign visitors and has engaged in collaboration with foreign institutions; it has significantly strengthened its research capacity and served as a "brain trust" for the party; and it oversees the nationwide network of party schools at lower levels.

The CCP Central Directive No. 10 of 2000, "Central Committee Decision on Comprehensively Accelerating and Advancing Party School Work in the 21st Century," and the "2001–2005 National Cadre Training Program Plan" listed nine categories of cadres to be targeted for party school training:[93]

1. leading cadres of the party and government;
2. experienced cadres;
3. government civil servants (*guojia gongwuyuan*) and working-level cadres in party organs;
4. managers of state-owned enterprises;
5. specialized technicians (*zhuanye jishu renyuan*);
6. court personnel, procuracy personnel, police personnel, and other political-legal work cadres;
7. local-level cadres;
8. national minority cadres, female cadres; and
9. cadres from western areas.

The CCP maintains (at great expense) an enormous network of party schools nationwide, which totaled no fewer than between 2,600 and 2,700.[94] They range in number per province. For example, in 1996 Hebei had 165 party schools, Sichuan 160, Jiangsu and Jiangxi each 100, Shandong 126, and Xinjiang 46, while Hainan only had 5.[95] Most provinces have, on average, 70 to 80 party schools. At the provincial and subprovincial levels, they are often coterminous and colocated on a joint campus with the Provincial School of Administration (Xingzheng Xueyuan), which ostensibly trains nonparty cadres, and frequently also together with the Colleges of Socialism (Shehuizhuyi Xueyuan) run by the CCP United Front Department. The vast majority of midcareer cadre training takes place in the vast network of provincial and subprovincial party schools throughout the nation.

Although the CPS trains cadres at the ministerial and provincial levels (*sheng bu ji*), provincial-level party schools train cadres at the municipality and provincial department (*shi ting ji*) levels, while subprovincial-level party schools train cadres at the county and municipal department (*xian chu ji*) and township department levels (*ke ji*). Subprovincial party schools exist at the municipality (*shi*), county (*xian*), and township (*xiang*) levels.[96] Provincial party schools are administratively directly under the provincial party committee (*sheng dangwei*), while the provincial schools of administration (often coterminous with the party schools) are under the provincial government (*sheng zhengfu*).

There are basically three types of training courses in these provincial party schools: *zhutiban* (principal classes), of which there are two subtypes—*yanjiuban* (advanced training class) and *peixunban* (regular training class); correspondence courses (*hanshou jiaoyu*); and degree (M.A. or Ph.D.) education. A survey of textbooks recently used in these schools emphasizes the "Three Basics" (*San Jiben*) and "Five Contemporaries" (*Wuge Dangdai*). The Three Basics are Marxism-Leninism, Mao Zedong's thought, and Deng Xiaoping's theory. The Five Contemporaries are the contemporary world economy, world science and technology, the world legal system, the world military and China's national defense, and world ideational trends.

Although provincial party schools train large numbers of local-level cadres and have revamped and professionalized their curricula in recent years, the overall quality of such training remains uneven. There has also been a problem in some schools of forged attendance data and fraudulent degrees. To some extent, this malfeasance has been driven by the pressure for revenue in these schools (although they are heavily subsidized by party and government organs). Some now charge tuition fees, which is a kind of in-kind lateral transfer scheme from one party or state organ (employers) to another part of the system (party schools). In one reported case, the Hainan Party School was found to be running a diploma-for-fee scheme. The school charged 7,000 yuan tuition and additional fees of about 1,000 yuan for each of 500 students enrolled per year ($487,804). An investigation found that, in 2001, school administrators pocketed at least 1.7 million yuan ($207,317) from the B.A. program alone, that truancy was high (the attendance rate was only 20 percent), and that nearly 70 percent of the degree recipients had not completed the required coursework.[97]

Another indication that all is not on the straight-and-narrow in China's party schools comes from the Hebei Party School in Baoding, where the vice president, Geng Sude, was fired and stripped of her party membership for organizing Bible study sessions in the school's tenth-floor auditorium. Police raided and broke up one meeting on New Year's Day 2007 and detained 500 Christian attendees for questioning, including lawyers, professors, writers, journalists, and artists. When interviewed by Reuters, Geng indicated that "it never occurred to me that the authorities would regard this seriously," adding that she decided to host the event in the party school auditorium because it was rarely used. "The Bible study session was aimed at helping to build a harmonious society [as the party seeks], the party should ease, not create contradictions. Class struggle is no longer the party culture—the party should be more forgiving and tolerant," said the third-generation Christian.[98]

Despite such occasional instances of malfeasance, the party school system is often the first postsecondary education many local cadres receive. It thus provides some basic training in key administrative skills, as well as ideological indoctrination and adherence to party directives. Though party schools are not the cadres' only source of postsecondary education, figure 7.1 shows the results of a recent survey (based on Ministry of Civil Affairs data) of 268 government department heads at the county level, which found that 56.6 percent of those who received postsecondary training did so at party schools (21 percent at the CPS, 27.6 percent at provincial party schools, and 8 percent at subprovincial party schools).

Thus, despite the attention usually paid to the Central Party School, one must be cognizant of this much more extensive provincial party school system. Without it, local cadres would have little contact with the central CCP organization, ideology, recent policies, and the like. But, equally important, party schools at this level provide real training in concrete practical skills

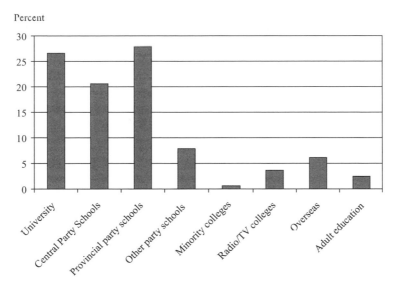

Figure 7.1. County-Level Cadre Postsecondary Education

Source: Ian Seckington, "County Leadership in China: A Baseline Survey," unpublished paper; this graph is used with permission from the author.

that local cadres can use on the job—thus improving the efficiency and skill sets so critical to functional and responsive governance in any society, but particularly important in a society as large and complex as China's.

Cadre Training Academies

Another key set of institutions in the party school system are the three new "cadre training academies," whose establishment in 2005 was a manifestation of the CCP's campaign to improve the "party's governing capacity" (*dang de zhizheng nengli*), which unfolded in the wake of the Sixteenth Party Congress. The creation of all three academies was the brainchild of Politburo member Zeng Qinghong (China's vice president and president of the CPS). In establishing these academies, Zeng's intent was to create a "cadre production line."[99] The choice of these three locations had to do with CCP revolutionary history (Jingganshan and Yan'an) and its reform and opening to the world (Shanghai/Pudong), as well as representing three different economic development regions. Preparations for the three academies began in 2003, with personnel directly transferred from the CCP's Organization Department and CPS.[100] The division of labor among the three academies is that the Jinggangshan and Yan'an academies are to emphasize the history of the revolution, the "national situation," and the interior of the country—while the Pudong Academy is to emphasize innovation in system reform (*xitong chuanxin*), human resource management, and leadership methods.[101] By the end of 2006, the Pudong Academy had graduated more than 4,000 cadres from its training programs, while the Jingganshan and Yan'an academies had each graduated more than 2,000.[102]

The China Pudong Cadre Academy (Zhongguo Pudong Ganbu Xueyuan)—or the China Executive Leadership Academy Pudong (CELAP), as it is known in English—opened on March 18, 2005, with Hu Jintao, the CCP's general secretary and People's Republic president, presiding over the ceremony.[103] Situated on an extremely modern campus of 41.2 acres in Pudong, CELAP offers graduate degrees in public administration (MPA) and business administration (MBA). The campus itself is architecturally extraordinary, with a futuristic main building in the shape of a giant girder, with reflecting pools, beautiful landscaping, and dormitory (exclusive apartments) housing.[104]

The Pudong Academy enrolls 800 to 1,200 "students" at any time. There are 160 full-time faculty and staff. The CCP Central Committee Organization Department director, He Guoqiang, is the president, although really only in name. Training courses are offered for different durations for "leading cadres" (*lingdao ganbu*) from the central and provincial-level party and state organs, with a few managers of the largest 165 state-owned enterprises and some representatives of civil society. Most are above the bureau level (*ju yishang*). The CCP's Central Organization Department selects the cadres to be trained, while the General Political Department selects the few military officers that attend. The majority of courses are three to four weeks in duration, although there is also a three-month module.

CELAP's faculty and coursework are divided into four main divisions: economics, public administration and management, leadership studies, and civil law. CELAP claims that, "in contrast to the Party School's emphasis on political theory, CELAP's courses are less theoretical and more practical, focusing more on the economy and associated issues. The Central Government really wants us to take advantage of our location and resources, so we emphasize on-site visits, case studies and scenario modeling, and practical lectures (one-third each). Frequently, leading cadres go through a three-stage sequence of training first at the CPS, then come to CELAP, and finally to either Jinggangshan or Yan'an."[105] Finally, CELAP is developing extensive ties with counterparts aboard and hosts distinguished foreign lecturers.

The Central Party School

At the national level, the Central Party School in Beijing remains the most important institution in the whole midcareer training system. The CPS runs a variety of courses throughout the year.[106] These are for five types of cadres:

- ministerial and provincial leaders (with a short specialized course of seven to ten days, or courses of three to six months or one year);
- mayors of large cities and prefectures (four and a half months);
- select county party secretaries (four and a half months);[107]
- cadres involved in ethnic work (six months, one year, or two years); and
- young cadres at the central level before promotion to vice ministerial or the equivalent level (various periods).

In addition, there are specialized training classes for cadres from the central and western provinces; state-owned-enterprise cadres; united front work cadres; and cadres involved in theoretical work. Every semester there are on average 1,600 cadres (students) in residence enrolled in these various training courses. The CPS administration has 1,360 staff members, including 600 faculty members (with 168 full and 159 associate professors). A total of 70 faculty members are qualified to supervise Ph.D. students. The CPS now has six Ph.D. and fourteen M.A. state-certified degree programs. Since 1981, 266 Ph.D.s and 1,126 M.A.s have been conferred.

In terms of curriculum, the CPS offers a number of required courses that students take in sequence during their training periods, but there are also a number of electives available. The CPS describes several "newly designed courses," including Basic Issues of Marxism-Leninism, Basic Issues of Mao Zedong's Thought, Basic Issues of Deng Xiaoping's Theory, Basic Issues of "Three Representatives" Thought, Contemporary World Economy, Contemporary World Science and Technology, Contemporary World Legal Systems, Contemporary World Militaries and China's National Defense, Contemporary Ethnicity and Religion in the World and China, and Contemporary World Thought.[108] M.A. and Ph.D. students follow a somewhat different curriculum from the cadre training classes.

Since Jiang Zemin's July 2001 "Three Represents" speech, which put the imprimatur on inducting entrepreneurs and businesspeople into the party, the CPS has hosted week-long seminars and three-week nondegree courses for party members in this sector.[109] These courses are allegedly very popular, attracting 80 entrepreneurs per session, with a claimed total of 10,000 having participated in such courses since 2001.[110] CPS "students" from the business sector are charged around 6,800 renminbi ($829) for the course and a diploma, and many consider it a good deal. Said one: "For less than 7,000 yuan—including airfare and accommodation—you can get a diploma from the party's premier training academy and the chance to meet former senior officials."[111] Such attendance at the CPS and connections with the party are a form of political protection for the business elite—just as they are a method of political co-optation by the CCP.[112]

In addition to training cadres, another key role played by the CPS is as a think tank for party reform policies.[113] In many cases, major theoretical/ideological/policy initiatives *originate* in the CPS, but CPS theoreticians usually play the role of explicating them. "*All* the preparation work for the Fourteenth, Fifteenth, and Sixteenth party congresses, and the general secretary's speeches to the congresses, were prepared here," boasted CPS vice president Wang Weiguang in an interview with the author.[114] No doubt the same is currently the case with preparations for the Seventeenth Party Congress to be held in late 2007. The CPS has similarly been a prominent location for the CCP general secretary to launch new initiatives. Jiang Zemin launched his theory of "Three Represents" there on July 1, 2001,[115] and Hu

Jintao launched his theory of the "Socialist Harmonious Society" there in February 2005.

The now-retired CPS theorist Yu Yunyao was a major contributor to JiangZemin's "Three Represents" theory and is said to be the originator of Wen Jiabao's "Taking People as the Center" concept, as well as Hu Jintao's "Scientific Development Concept."[116] Pang Yuanzheng, Dong Deguang, Wang Huanchao, and other CPS theorists have further elaborated the "Scientific Development Concept." Zheng Bijian—the former CPS executive vice president and chairman of the China Reform Forum (which is closely affiliated with the CPS)—was the originator of the "China's Peaceful Rise" theory.[117]

Concerning political reform, as discussed in chapter 7, CPS vice president Li Junru is a leading theorist who masterminded the currently popular "consultative democracy" concept and contributed to the "Three Represents" theory. Li and others, such as Cheng Shu, have contributed much to the post–Sixteenth Party Congress campaign to improve "intraparty democracy" (*dangnei minzhu*). Zhuang Congsheng has also been a significant contributor to the "consultative democracy" concept (which is very popular at present and likely to find its way into the Seventeenth Party Congress documents). Zhou Tianyong, Shi Taifeng, and Li Liangdong have been consistent advocates of political system reform (*zhengzhi tizhi gaige*). Hou Shaowen has written a lot about strengthening the People's Congress system. Xie Chuntao has written a lot on the relationship between the party and the government. Wang Changjiang has pioneered the idea of "issue politics" (*wenti zhengzhi*), and has written extensively about the "Control of Cadres in a Scientific Manner" (*dangguan ganbu de kexue fangfa*), that is, meritocratic personnel evaluation. Several CPS theoreticians have contributed to the campaign to "Improve the Party's Governing Capacity" since it was launched in 2004. The current CPS president, Zeng Qinghong, is said to have been the mastermind behind the "Party's Advanced Nature" (Dang de Xianjianxing) campaign begun in December 2004. CPS theorists, such as Zhu Fu'en and Zhang Xixian, fleshed out the concept in a series of publications. CPS vice president Wang Weiguang has contributed much to Hu Jintao's "Socialist Harmonious Society" concept, particularly regarding social equity issues, while various CPS theorists (Yan Shuhan, Wu Zhongmin, Xie Zhiqiang, and others) have all contributed to explicating the policy. Finally, CPS staff members played a major role in the heated and protracted internal debates over the causes of the USSR's collapse.

Transforming the Party Leadership

A central Chinese critique of the Soviet Union was its ossified leadership and bureaucracy. This critique emerged well before the collapse of the USSR. Indeed, Deng Xiaoping made the rejuvenation of the Chinese leadership a priority immediately after garnering power in 1978. Thereafter, Deng initiated the transition from the "first" to the "second" generation of CCP leadership, notably bringing Hu Yaobang, Zhao Ziyang, and Li Peng into the Politburo Standing Committee. Deng also had to work hard, throughout much of the 1980s, to retire the first generation old guard—instituting, for the first time in the CCP's history, formal retirement regulations and transitioning many party elders on to the newly created (and now defunct) Central Advisory Commission.[118] Though there certainly is some irony in the fact that an octogenarian introduced the retirement norm into the CCP, Deng's initiatives were an important starting point for leadership reform in the party.

New Generations of Leaders

In the aftermath of 1989, Deng again saw a need to engineer a leadership transition, this time to the "third generation." Jiang Zemin was promoted as the "core" of this new generation of leadership. At the Fourteenth and Fifteenth CCP congresses, in 1992 and 1997 respectively, a wholesale transition to civilian and military elites took place. In the party, this new leadership reflected four main features: "technocratic" backgrounds and outlooks; training in the Soviet Union during the 1950s; work in the intraparty apparatus at the provincial and central levels; and suspicion of the United States and the West.[119] As time passed during the 1990s, this leadership began to exhibit one other notable feature: ties to Shanghai, particularly during Jiang's tenure there. A "Shanghai bang" (Shanghai clique) became dominant in elite politics.

At the Sixteenth Party Congress (October 2002) and Tenth National People's Congress (March 2003), the civilian party leadership was overhauled again (a similar turnover occurred in the People's Liberation Army).[120] Strict retirement norms were enforced—over 61 percent of the Central Committee were sent into retirement, with thirteen of twenty-one Politburo members also retiring. As table 7.1 shows, this turnover rate was in line with the previous four congresses.

Table 7.1. Central Committee Turnover
Rates at Party Congresses (percent)

Party Congress	Turnover Rate
Sixteenth	61
Fifteenth	63
Fourteenth	57
Thirteenth	68
Twelfth	60

Source: The author is indebted to Li Cheng for these
tabulations.

A new 198-member Sixteenth Central Committee (plus 158 alternates) was elected in their place, headed by Hu Jintao as the new general secretary of the CCP. As a result of the personnel changes, 16 of the Politburo's 25 members were new to the body; 6 of the 9 members of the Politburo Standing Committee were new; 7 of the 8 members of the Party Secretariat were new; all the 5 main Central Committee departments (Organization, United Front, Discipline Inspection, International, and Propaganda) were new; 4 of the 5 State Council vice premiers and all 5 of the state councilors were new; 18 of 28 State Council ministers were new; 3 of 8 Central Military Commission members were new; and 11 of 31 provincial party secretaries and 15 of 31 provincial governors were newly appointed.[121] In sum, this was the largest, most thorough turnover of the party elite since it came to power in 1949. The fact that it occurred peacefully and according to institutional procedures, absent a purge, is also a noteworthy indication of the institutionalization and regularization of inner-party norms.

Although this "fourth generation" also exhibited the predominant characteristic of coming from "technocratic" (i.e., engineering and industrial management) backgrounds, seven other attributes characterized the new party leadership. First, this was the post-Sino-Soviet split generation, who came of age (actuarially and politically) in the aftermath of the 1960 rupture between Moscow and Beijing—thus one assumes that their affinity for Russia is less than their predecessors'. Second, the vast majority had backgrounds of party work in the provinces—many, like Hu Jintao and Premier Wen Jiabao, in poor interior provinces. Hu had spent fourteen years in Gansu, three years in Guizhou, and four years in Tibet, while Wen had spent fourteen years in Gansu. Third, though the majority came from engineering, industrial, and party work backgrounds, for the first time one sees a growing cohort that possess backgrounds in finance, economics, and law. Fourth, they were substantially younger than the previous Central Committee (55.4 years old). Fifth, they were the best-educated leadership in CCP history; fully 99 percent of the Sixteenth Central Committee had attended university (as compared with a much lower 23 percent for the entire CCP membership). Sixth, the fourth generation leadership is the "Cultural Revolution generation"—but not all experienced the Cultural Revolution in the same ways. Some, like Hu Jintao, graduated from university on the eve of the event (1965) whereas others had their educations interrupted by the movement. Many participated in the Cultural Revolution as Red Guards or "sent-down youth" (to the countryside). Last, given their backgrounds, when they assumed office, this generation of CCP leaders was quite inexperienced in international affairs, were very insular in their backgrounds, were not educated overseas and had not traveled much abroad, and therefore did not possess any strong foreign leanings (like the Soviet Union for the third generation and the West for the successor fifth generation). There are a number of good studies of the Sixteenth Party Congress and its new leadership that further profile the fourth-generation leadership,[122] but these are their essential features.

In terms of factional alignments, the twin congresses sent mixed signals. On the one hand, Jiang Zemin did his best to orchestrate the succession to benefit his supporters, his policies, his power base, and himself. He even refused to hand over to Hu his portfolio as chairman of the Central Military Commission until September 2004. On the other hand, the new Politburo lineup evinced a few individuals whose career paths had paralleled or intersected with Hu's, as well as some evidence that Hu was creating his own "factions," drawing on his network of colleagues from Qinghua University and the Communist Youth League (CYL).

Jiang was able to have several of his allies from the Shanghai bang elevated to senior positions. His trusted aide, Zeng Qinghong, was elevated to the Politburo Standing Committee, became vice president of the People's Republic and head of the Party Secretariat, and replaced Hu as president of the Central Party School—but Zeng was notably not given a position on the Central Military Commission. Four other Shanghai allies—Wu Bangguo, Huang Ju, Zeng Peiyan, and Chen Liangyu—were promoted, respectively, to the positions of chairman of the National People's Congress, vice premiers of the State Council (Huang and Zeng), and mayor and party secretary of Shanghai. Other Jiang allies (although not from Shanghai)—Jiang Qinglin,

Wu Guanzheng, and Li Changchun—all were promoted to the Politburo Standing Committee. The Central Military Commission (CMC) was also loaded with generals promoted by, and presumably loyal to, Jiang.[123] Thus, all these key central political organs were effectively "stacked" with Jiang allies.

For Hu's part, the first thing to note is that he had *not* cultivated a web of patron-client ties and did not seem eager to supplant Jiang's network. Even if he had, he was substantially outnumbered. Over the next few years, it was interesting to watch how Hu set about trying to co-opt, rather than undermine or supplant, Jiang's lieutenants. Hu's style was much more one of consensus and coalition building.[124] He was also smart not to try and challenge straight-on a dominant leadership faction, but rather to bide his time and work progressively to increase his own influence and insert his own people into positions of power, progressively modifying the party's national policy agenda.

After the twin congresses in 2002–3, those few individuals promoted to positions in the central party apparatus who did have ties to Hu came from diverse backgrounds but had careers that had intersected with Hu's—rather than having been affiliated with Hu in faction-like relationships over time. Premier Wen Jiabao must be considered in this group, as he and Hu worked together in Gansu. The Secretariat member and head of the CCP Propaganda Department, Liu Yunshan, also had ties to Hu dating to their tenures as provincial party secretaries. From 1987 to 1991, Liu was the secretary of the Inner Mongolia Autonomous Region Party Committee, while Hu served in the Tibetan Autonomous Region.[125] The two apparently interacted fairly regularly in provincial party forums and meetings concerning ethnic minority work, and both had ties to former CCP general secretary and Youth League chief Hu Yaobang.[126] Hu similarly had ties to General Liao Xilong dating to these years, when Liao was deputy commander of the Chengdu Military Region (and responsible in part for the 1989 Lhasa suppression). Liao was promoted to the CMC and simultaneously as director of the People's Liberation Army General Logistics Department. Other than these three, however, Hu Jintao was notable for his *lack* of factional or patronage ties in the Central Party apparatus. However, when provincial-level officials are examined, a greater number share ties with Hu through the CYL. The Liaoning party secretary, Li Keqiang, the Shanxi party secretary, Zhang Baoshun, and the Jiangsu party secretary, Li Yuanchao, all served under Hu when he was secretary of the CYL from 1982 to 1984. The CCP's United

Front Work Department head, Liu Yandong, the minister of civil affairs, Li Xueju, and the minister of supervision, Li Zhilun also overlapped in the CYL during Hu's tenure.[127]

After the Sixteenth Party Congress and Tenth National People's Congress, this leadership balance did not change a great deal. While Jiang himself did relinquish his last post as CMC chairman in 2004, his network of Shanghai and other allies remained largely in place. Nor has Hu done much to promote individuals associated with his past. Rather, his favored strategy has been to push his populist policy agenda forward and thereby attempt to co-opt Jiang's clients and other officials to it—thus forging a broad coalition that is much more issue based than personality or faction based.

What Hu has astutely done is to set items on the national agenda and then launch a political campaign in support of each component. In each case, he has turned to different key officials to implement the campaigns, thereby "testing" their loyalty and in effect co-opting them into compliance. He first did this with the Jiang stalwart and Politburo Standing Committee member Zeng Qinghong, who was put in charge of drafting and implementing the important program to improve the "party's ruling capacity" (*zhizheng nengli*) at and after the Fourth Plenum of September 2004. He did this with CCP Propaganda Department director Liu Yunshan during the SARS crisis and when he subtly shifted the orientation of the Three Represents campaign in the spring of 2003. He did this with CCP Organization Department director He Guoqiang during the "Party's Advanced Nature" campaign during 2005 and 2006. And he did it to Wen Jiabao and others in the State Council when he succeeded in smuggling his "Socialist Harmonious Society" theory and the "Scientific Development Concept" into the Eleventh Five-Year Program in 2005. These were all very astute moves by a politician playing a weaker hand. Of course, Hu did benefit from the fact that he had become the primus inter pares—if not the outright party, state, and military leader. In China, power does flow to the position and not just the individual—and Hu has used his seniority and authority very effectively.

The China leadership specialist Cheng Li argues that Hu has been able to forge an unprecedented "bipartisanship" between the two dominant policy coalitions—the Jiang Zemin/Zeng Qinghong coalition and the Hu Jintao / Wen Jiabao coalition.[128] Rather than pushing alternative competing policy agendas (and thus aggravating factional cleavages), the genius of Hu's approach has been to generate and shift the policy agenda toward three components that have proven very popular inside and outside the party:[129]

- more balanced regional economic development,
- increased concern for social justice and social harmony, and
- greater party and state transparency and institutionalization.

Thus, the days of CCP factional politics and strongman rule—so characteristic of the Mao, Deng, and Jiang eras—seem to have passed. More institutionalized, consensus-based, and coalitional elite politics is emerging instead. Though these characteristics do seem to be taking hold, the party's history of "winner take all" and "tiger eat tiger" elite factional politics cannot be quickly dismissed. Such factional differences may simply be submerged and suppressed and could quickly reappear under conditions of a serious crisis or emergency. As Li Cheng's research has also shown, factional ties in contemporary Chinese politics have more to do with the type of university education (engineering, finance, law, etc.); networks developed in college or vocational training (including midcareer training in the party school, civil servant, and military staff college systems); cliques forged among leaders' assistants (*mishu*); generational cohorts; and "princeling (*taizi*) networks.[130] Yet, all the multiple elements of party institutionalization described in the previous section on party building have had their effect on weakening factional ties—as did the searing impact of the split in the leadership around the time of June 4, 1989. The CCP leaders today seem to have adopted the dictum that they must hang together or they will hang separately.

The Hu-Wen Leadership Five Years On

Five years after coming to power, the Hu-Wen leadership appears to be very stable. Hu and Premier Wen Jiabao have proven a very capable team, who work very well together without encroaching on each other's bureaucratic or policy turf. Hu Jintao has moved gradually and deliberately to consolidate his power base—both within the leadership and the party apparatus more broadly. Just as important, predictions of a rivalry between Hu and the Jiang Zemin protégé Zeng Qinghong (the No. 5 ranking Politburo member and People's Republic vice president) have not become manifest,[131] and Hu has proven able to work with other leaders promoted under Jiang. Meanwhile, Jiang himself has remained in the background, with little evidence of his trying to set or manipulate the policy agenda from behind the scenes. The only real public and intraparty attention he has received since his retirement occurred with the publication in September 2006 of his three-volume *Selected Works,* which was accorded a national publicity campaign and immediately became compulsory reading for party members.

In terms of policy, there have been some important new emphases—although the broad priorities of "reform and opening" remain. The more interior-oriented and populist agenda is certainly an important shift, but many policies begun under Jiang's tenure have continued. They have pushed ahead with various market-oriented reforms, particularly in the state industrial and banking sectors. These are the two least reformed sectors of the economy, but significant strides have been made in each case since 2002. Further overhauls of these two chronic sectors can be expected. New reforms have also been introduced in the agricultural sector in an effort to boost decade-long declines in rural incomes.[132] Generally speaking, with the exception of the realm of intellectual property rights, the government has pushed ahead in complying with China's accession commitments to the World Trade Organization. Though one would have expected the Hu-Wen leadership to more strongly push forward the "Open the West" (Xi Bu Kaifa) economic and infrastructure campaign, there has, in fact, been notable inattention in this policy area. At the same time, there has been a rhetorical drop-off in support for coastal-led growth with greater attention paid to the north-central and northeastern provinces.

Of particular importance, other than the SARS crisis in the spring of 2003, the current leadership has not had to confront any major internal or external crises (notwithstanding the periodic high temperature on the Taiwan issue). The eruption of such a crisis could trigger resurgent factionalism and test the leadership's coherence and mettle.

Politically, the Hu-Wen leadership has done nothing to loosen coercive controls on dissent, the Internet, or other potential challenges to CCP rule.[133] To the contrary, those who hoped that Hu might be a Gorbachev-in-waiting have been sorely disappointed.[134] Since 2005, the security apparatus has tightened controls over the media and Internet, and a general chill has once again affected the intellectual climate.[135] Publicly, Hu's rhetoric has been reformist and moderate in tone, but in inner-party speeches, he has railed against "hostile Western forces" and "bourgeois liberalization" that seek to "split and Westernize China" *(fenhua, Xihua).*[136] This crackdown has been accompanied by a CCP-wide indoctrination campaign for party members, as discussed above. This side of Hu is entirely consistent with his background as a party apparatchik. As such,

Hu's training has been in the traditional Leninist tools of ideology, organization, and propaganda.[137] These are the principal approaches evident in his rule.

The adroit manner in which the Hu-Wen leadership managed the passing and memorial for the disgraced party leader Zhao Ziyang in January and February 2005 was also indicative of their conservative instincts. Given the lingering shadow of Zhao's liberal legacy and the 1989 suppression of the Tiananmen Square demonstrators, his death had the potential to trigger discontent and unrest both inside and outside the party. After an initial period of indecisiveness, Hu forged a consensus within the Politburo on sponsoring a low-keyed memorial service at Baobaoshan Cemetery.[138] This defused the situation.

Hu also approved a posthumous political rehabilitation of the former and semidisgraced party leader Hu Yaobang on the occasion of his ninetieth birthday on November 18, 2005, and adroitly dispatched Zeng Qinghong to give the official commemorative address.[139] This, too, had the potential to resurrect memories of the more liberal Hu Yaobang (no relation to Hu Jintao), who was purged in 1987. It was his sudden death (from a heart attack in a Politburo meeting) that triggered the 1989 popular protests that resulted in the infamous military suppression. For Hu Jintao to approve such a move should be interpreted more as a sop to the reformist wing of the party, and particularly the CYL faction within the CCP (previously headed by both Hu) than any new and genuine embrace of the kind of liberal policies that Hu Yaobang (and Zhao Ziyang) advocated during the 1980s.

Such cautiousness does not mean, however, that Hu, Wen, and other party leaders are paralyzed and afraid to undertake any political reforms. Quite to the contrary, as indicated above, the Hu-Wen leadership (and in this area, we have to include Zeng Qinghong) has focused on strengthening and rejuvenating the party apparatus from top to bottom. As this chapter has detailed, their focus has been *institutional* in nature, and a number of CCP organizational reforms have been launched. Some of these reforms continue those begun under Jiang Zemin's "second term" (since the Fifteenth Party Congress), whereas others are new initiatives.

Thus, it is apparent that Hu Jintao and Wen Jiabao enjoy a potent partnership and have moved quite quickly to consolidate their positions, authority, and rule. The Central Committee and senior leadership elected at the Seventeenth Party Congress in 2007 also reflect a number of new faces who have worked their way up the party and state apparatuses under Hu's and Wen's tenure. With this Congress, Hu's and Wen's power base is fully consolidated, and they can then enjoy four more years in charge, while also laying the groundwork for their expected succession and full installation of the "fifth-generation" leadership at the Eighteenth Party Congress in 2012 and Twelfth National People's Congress in 2013.

8

Staying Alive:
Can the Chinese Communist Party Survive?

The central argument (and subtitle) of this book has been that the Chinese Communist Party (CCP) is in the simultaneous state of *atrophy and adaptation*. Chapters 6 and 7 elaborated many of these dimensions—the degree of atrophy and the attempts to forge adaptive procedures and policies to strengthen the CCP's institutional character. Many of these adaptive measures grew out of the CCP's assessments of ex-communist and noncommunist party-states described in chapters 4 and 5. This concluding chapter thus seeks to answer the natural, but difficult, question of whether the CCP can survive. Will adaptation win out over atrophy? What is the relative balance between atrophy and adaptation?

Atrophy and Adaptation: The Balance Sheet

These are large and difficult questions to answer, but they are central to the principal question of this study: How can the CCP remain relevant to an increasingly diverse and demanding society? One's ability to "answer" these questions depends in part on the level of analysis and variables one examines.

One metric is comparative. Table 8.1 catalogues nearly seventy factors that contributed to the collapse of the Soviet and East European party-states, and it asks whether these conditions are present in today's China. Though China is certainly different from these other nations, many of the systemic conditions are present in the People's Republic and are thus comparable.

When seen in this comparative light, the number of factors that were present in the former USSR and Eastern Europe that are present in China

Table 8.1. Factors in the Collapse of Communist Power: China in Comparison

Category	Factor	Present in China (X = present; O = not present; N.A. = not applicable)
Economic	Economic stagnation	O
	Consumer deprivation	O
	Overspending on the military and resulting distortion of central government expenditures	O
	"Second economy" and black markets	O
	Nonintegration into international trade and financial systems	O
	Little inbound foreign direct investment (or foreign direct investment as an agent of change)	O
	Inflation in some countries	O
	Nonconvertible currencies	X
	Insolvent banking sector and debt overhang ("triangular debt")	X/O
	Laggard agriculture	O
	Inefficiencies of central planning	O
	Party intervention in planning process	O
	Undeveloped and retarded market mechanisms	O
	Price distortions	X/O
	Subsidies and "soft budget constraints"	X/O
	Erosion of state monopoly on property rights	X
	Little revenue sharing by central governments with localities, but reduced local government dependence on higher-level allocations due to extrabudgetary revenue	O
	Increasing government budget deficits	X
	Perestroika in the Soviet Union and market reforms in Hungary and Yugoslavia	X
	Path dependence once economic reforms had begun, due to new vested interests of local cadres and empowered citizens	X
	New sources of revenue available to local party and state organs (military too), and the resulting rise of governmental "rent seeking"	X
Political	A transformative reformist leader like Gorbachev	O
	Glasnost in the Soviet Union	O
	Formation of autonomous trade unions (Poland)	O
	Linkages between reformist elites and civil society	O
	Delegitimization of Marxist-Leninist ideology	X
	Official corruption and party privileges	X
	Declining ability of party to enforce discipline within its ranks	O
	New political elites emerge at the local level outside of party structure	X
	Cadres (at all levels) gain a vested interest in the "new economy"	O
	Bureaucratic unresponsiveness and inefficiency	O

Table 8.1. Continued

Category	Factor	Present in China (X = present; O = not present; N.A. = not applicable)
	Decreased writ of the *nomenklatura*	O
	Despite transition to "technocracy," increasing incompetence and inability of cadres and bureaucrats to perform meritocratically	O
	Corrosion and disappearance of local party cells in work units	X
	Disobedience of central party and government directives and/or feigned compliance	X/O
	Declining state capacity in provision of publics goods	X
Social	Rise of semiautonomous or autonomous civic organizations (civil society)	X
	Alienation from the workplace and the state	X
	Rising corruption	X
	Increased labor mobility and alternative employment opportunities	X
	Decline in peer monitoring and surveillance	X
	(Frustrated) desires for foreign travel and ability to make foreign comparisons	O
	Decoupling of political loyalty and tangible rewards in the enterprise (declining "neotraditional" dependency structures)	X
	Increasingly tense labor-management relations	O
	Sporadic social protests, strikes, and slowdowns	X
	Extrajudicial "taxes," levies, and fees administered by local state	X
	Pressures build to establish legitimate channels of interest articulation	O
Cultural	Moral vacuum and public cynicism toward regime and its ideology	X
	Alienation from socialist culture and rewritten history—search for the past	X
	Increasingly noncompliant media	O
	Globalization affects popular culture	X
	Declining appeal of moral incentives	X
	Ethnic tensions and seeking secessionist regions/states	X/O
	Increasing nationalist identity (as distinct from socialist identity)	X
	Increasing appeal of religion	X
Coercive	Decline of the "party-army"—rise of professional militaries	X/O
	Uncertain loyalty of paramilitary and security services to ruling party	O

continued

Table 8.1. Continued

Category	Factor	Present in China (X = present; O = not present; N.A. = not applicable)
	Corruption in coercive apparatus	X
	Decline in use of mass terror and intimidation tactics	X
	Increased sensitivity to human rights concerns	X
International	"Imperial overstretch" (USSR)	O
	Collapse of the "Brezhnev Doctrine"	N.A.
	Ostpolitik between East and West Germany	X (Mainland-Taiwan)
	Increasingly independent (from Moscow) foreign policies of East European states	N.A.
	Imposed party-states from without (by USSR)	N.A.
	Globalization	X

today are truly striking. Table 8.1 shows that China shares more factors (thirty-six) than distinguish them (thirty), with three variables not applicable. In general, China does not share the economic or international variables but does possess the majority of the political, social, cultural, and coercive characteristics found in these former communist party-states. By these criteria, *this is evidence of party atrophy.* But there are also some important dissimilarities—particularly in the economic realm, owing to China's hugely successful reforms. Also, many of the international factors that were peculiar to the Soviet Union under Brezhnev and Gorbachev are not relevant to China. And the CCP is undertaking a wide variety of *political* reforms aimed at shoring up its base and power. Yet, when one examines these categories—political, social, cultural, and coercive—it is striking just how many of the intrinsic and systemic factors that led to the implosion of these former communist states *are present* in China today.

Although these are large generalizations and variables, they are nonetheless suggestive and provide a comparative metric to measure the CCP's degrees of atrophy and adaptation. It provides a sober reminder of the party's vulnerabilities. Yet it is precisely these vulnerabilities of which the CCP is so conscious and has sought to address.

For example, if one focuses at the level of senior CCP leadership, it can be concluded that elite succession has been handled quite successfully since 1989. By the end of 2007, four party congresses have occurred with a comprehensive turnover of leadership. The "third generation" has transitioned to the "fifth generation." Elite factionalism and conflict have been kept to a minimum, and elite turnover has, by and large, been predictable and smooth (the ouster of Qiao Shi and the Yang brothers being exceptions to the rule). Similar elite circulation has occurred throughout the party, state, and military systems nationwide.[1] Moreover, the competence and training of these officials has improved dramatically. Not only are younger officials and new recruits being brought into the party-state apparatus (and also the military), but we have noted (chapter 7) the various programs for midcareer training to improve both tangible skills and party allegiance.

If one examines the CCP's macro-level relations with the other two legs of the Chinese Communist triad of power—the government and the military—the CCP does not seem to be in danger. It has paradoxically loosened its grip over both, and thereby has strengthened it. That is, both the government and the military have been given considerably increased scope for running their own affairs without interference from the party, and a kind of Faustian bargain has been struck with each: The party provides political protection and resources in exchange for corporatist professionalism and allegiance. Though some elements of this increased independence are consistent with Zhao Ziyang's policy of "party-state separation" (*dang-zheng fenkai*) during the late 1980s, it is also the case that the CCP has been very wary of going too far in this area, as a result of witnessing what happened in the Soviet Union when Gorbachev tried to truly remove the Soviet Communist Party controls from the government and military.

In the case of the People's Liberation Army (PLA), it is still loyal to the CCP and remains a "party-army" in significant respects, but one that enjoys relative professional corporate autonomy.[2] The "interlocking directorate" of military officials in the upper echelons of the party has been virtually eliminated, and senior PLA officers play little if any role in national policymaking outside the national security domain. There are no PLA officers on the Standing Committee of the party Politburo. The PLA also spends considerably less time in ideological study of party political campaigns. What has really emerged is a triangular relationship between party, PLA, and State Council—rather than simply a party-army relationship. The State Council now exercises authority over the military's finances,[3] and it has legal oversight (via the 1997 National Defense Law) over a wide variety of military activities.

If one takes a different level of analysis   party membership and organization—the picture is more mixed. It is certainly true that the party faces major problems with corruption, cronyism, and nepotism—although, as the research of Lu Xiaobo and of Melanie Manion illustrates, these have been perennial problems in the CCP.[4]

Part of the corruption problem owes to the party's "neotraditional" methods of garnering and distributing prized resources to its members and their families,[5] although the party's ability to dole out resources to its members has eroded in the face of the marketplace. Part of the problem relates to the predatory tendency of rent seeking by local cadres who no longer have a monopoly over these key resources. Part of the cause of this corruption is sociologically rooted in the *guanxi* culture of China. Part of it is related to the lack of the rule of law, while part of it is the result of the flood of cash in the economy and the new opportunities for graft, embezzlement, and profiteering.

Whatever the sources of corruption, the party recognizes it to be a threat of the gravest nature—a matter of "life and death," according to Jiang Zemin and Hu Jintao—and it is dealing with it in increasingly direct and harsh terms. Yet these new efforts, no matter how serious, are never likely to come to grips with the essence or extent of the corruption epidemic in China. At bottom, the corruption problem is directly related to the nature of the political system—particularly the party's insistence that it can police itself effectively (via the Central Discipline Inspection Commission of the Central Committee), its refusal to empower nonparty institutions or the media to expose corruption, and the judiciary's lack of independence. Unless and until the CCP recognizes and addresses these three systemic flaws, corruption will continue to flourish in China.

Similarly, if one examines party committees at the local level, one sees various signs of atrophy and adaptation. It is evident that local party officials in urban areas are increasingly entrepreneurial and perform a range of non-Leninist roles—time spent promoting business is time not spent promoting politics. As discussed in chapter 7, the party has found it difficult to embed itself in the plethora of newly emergent professional associations and private sector of the economy. In the countryside, many party cells and committees had simply ceased to function—or feigned compliance with higher-level authorities at best. Public apathy and cynicism toward politics have also contributed to the erosion. As a consequence, the presence and control by party committees nationwide atrophied badly during the 1990s.

Sensing this atrophy, and witnessing its impact in the former Soviet Union, since 2002 the CCP has set about systematically trying to strengthen the party apparatus (discussed in chapters 6 and 7). Considerable effort and resources have been devoted to this drive, and some progress seems apparent—but its net lasting effect remains uncertain. However, the twin campaigns of the "Increasing the Party's Ruling Capacity" and "Promoting the Party's Advanced Nature" have been two of the most intense political efforts undertaken in China in many years and have no doubt had some salutary effect.

The declining appeal of ideology and the growing moral vacuum in society have been other signs of the fraying Leninist party-state, as described in chapter 6. The CCP has therefore increasingly substituted nationalism for Marxist ideology, but it has also unleashed a wave of pseudo-ideological campaigns in the name of "socialism with Chinese characteristics." But, it must be said, this traditionally Leninist instrument is perhaps the most glaring example of party atrophy. One must only ask: If people do not believe the message, when will they begin to question the messenger? Without a persuasive or convincing message (or underlying vision), the party has to fall back on more traditional instruments of control.

When one looks at the capacity of key party organs, such as the Propaganda Department and Organization Department, a mixed picture also emerges. The CCP Propaganda Department no longer possesses anywhere near the control and influence it enjoyed during the Maoist era and is being buffeted by the triple forces of commercialism, cynicism, and globalization. As elaborated in chapter 6, the propaganda system is something of a microcosm of the party's broader atrophy and adaptation.[6] Yet it remains capable of significant censorship and media manipulation. The CCP Organization Department is stronger and has been strengthened in recent years. It continues to control the *nomenklatura* and *bianzhi* personnel systems nationwide and, as described in chapter 7, has introduced a variety of new regulations and procedures aimed at upgrading the quality of officials in the party and state systems. The party itself has also become much more selective in its recruitment policies—expelling large numbers of those who do not fit the targeted profile, while expanding recruitment of the "new productive forces."

Thus, if one examines the party as an institution, there is mixed evidence of atrophy and adaptation. Yet, if one looks at a third level of the party's role—vis-à-vis society—there is reason to conclude that there is far more atrophy than adaptation. This can be seen on a number of levels.

First, as Samuel Huntington's typology predicted, China—and the CCP—have entered into a qualitatively new phase of development. This phase is characterized by the revolution of rising expectations and rising public demands for an improved quality of life. The citizenry's increased demands for improved welfare, health care, education, environment, social order, public infrastructure, communications, and good government all are rising. This is to be expected, because it follows a more generic pattern evident in other newly industrialized countries. Once the citizenry reaches a threshold where essential material needs are satisfied and lifestyles have diversified and improved to the point that they have today in much of China, people begin to expect improvement in these other areas of life (including spiritual). With these demands comes different, but raised, expectations for the regime to address. Not only do citizens expect the demands to be addressed, but they require adequate political channels to articulate the demands in the first place.

In both respects, responsive government and transparency of policymaking are important. It is apparent that the government (at all levels) is attempting to address the increasing demands for an improved quality of life and to strengthen its governance capacity. A major study on China's governance by the Organization for Economic Cooperation and Development (OECD) judges that important improvements and progress are being made.[7] Studies by Dali Yang and Barry Naughton concur, although other studies—such as those by Hu Angang, Wang Shaoguang, and Minxin Pei—lament the decline of public services, deteriorating state capacity, and poor governance.

Although the government is attempting to improve its governance capacity (and this is disputed), it is equally evident that the CCP is also addressing the need to create better channels for interest articulation. Perhaps this reflects a slight shift away from the zero-sum view of political power and a neuralgic negative reaction to the enfranchisement and empowerment of civil society the CCP leadership has held since 1989. One of the principal "lessons" that the party leadership seems to have drawn from the uprisings in Eastern Europe in 1989 was that enfranchising labor unions, autonomous churches, and other civic organizations is a slippery slope to enfranchising a political opposition. Instead, the CCP has responded with a mixture of suppression and co-optation of such social groups and nongovernmental organizations.

The other related problem confronting the party and its popular and political legitimacy is its lack of a convincing vision of the direction in which it seeks to lead the nation. A Marxist-Leninist future certainly seems out of the question, for this theology has been diluted beyond recognition. Yet no persuasive alternative vision has been substituted and offered by the party. Jiang Zemin's "Three Represents" or Hu Jintao's "Socialist Harmonious Society" do not seem to stir the nation (even if they are de rigueur propaganda). Nor do the party's calls to build a "socialist spiritual civilization" or "socialism with Chinese characteristics."

Aside from these propagandistic clichés, what the party has consistently advocated is really little different from the core themes that all Chinese rulers since the Self-Strengtheners of the 1870s have advocated: attaining wealth and power (*fu-qiang*); enhancing nationalism and international dignity; and preserving unity and preventing chaos. In these respects, contemporary Chinese leaders are no different than Deng Xiaoping, Mao Zedong, Chiang Kai-shek, Yuan Shikai, and Li Hongzhang. Though not original, these core visions do resonate deeply in China and do lend the current party leadership legitimacy and continuity with the past. This said, it is also true that the Hu Jintao–Wen Jiabao leadership has deviated from this long-standing emphasis on attaining wealth and power by addressing a broad array of social concerns and putting forward a less nationalistic and more people-friendly agenda. In his 2007 Work Report to the National People's Congress, for example, Premier Wen emphasized programs that address the poor, the rural sector, the environment, balanced regional development, energy consumption, social services, public spending, corruption, and state-owned enterprise reform.[8] These are precisely the major issues of current public concern—so one cannot say that the current CCP regime is "out of touch" with people's concerns and livelihood.

These public concerns are completely commensurate with the experiences of other nations that have transitioned from being developing to newly industrialized societies—the phase of development that China has now entered. Responding to the revolution of rising expectations is, however, going to be an ongoing and real challenge for the CCP party-state, because it essentially requires a responsive and proactive party-state. The Hu regime seems to be moving in this direction. In this regard, if managed carefully, the CCP can adapt and respond effectively to the rising demands placed upon it by society. There is no guarantee that it will be able to do so, for it requires altering its zero-sum thinking about civil society, among other things. To offer a convincing vision for the future of the nation entails a party-state that has a sound sense of its own institutional identity. Leadership presupposes such a vision. To lead is to be proactive and convincing in message and direction. The CCP needs to be more of a transformational than a transactional party.[9] The central challenge for the fourth- and fifth-generation leadership is not only how to remain relevant to society as a ruling party but also how to inspire and lead the nation in new directions.

Nonetheless, the Hu-Wen policy agenda does evince a programmatic vision that seems much more in touch with the needs of the nation than that of their predecessors. It is a populist agenda that recognizes and emphasizes the various disparities and inequities in society—particularly in the country's rural areas and deep interior. Yet it is also an agenda that emphasizes strengthening all aspects of CCP control. Bruce Dickson aptly describes these twin, and somewhat contradictory, policy emphases as "populist authoritarianism."[10]

Predicting the Future

China specialists would be well advised to heed Yogi Berra's admonition: "Prediction is difficult, especially about the future!" The variables at play are so complex, the nation is so large, its history is so long, and the consequences of modernization are so far-reaching for so many people that China watchers should tread carefully before hazarding predictions about the future of CCP rule. The Sinological landscape is littered with predictive casualties. It should also be remembered that the CCP is a ruling party of almost nine decades that clings tenaciously to its power and has repeatedly proven its willingness to use coercion and force to remain in power. The events of 1989 were no aberration. The party may be threatened, but it likely will not go quietly.

The complexities and tenaciousness of the party have, however, not deterred some China specialists from outlining a range of scenarios for China's political future. We examined some of these in chapter 3, but consider the following prognostications offered by six leading specialists.

Sinological Prognostications

In 1993, the veteran Asia and China specialist Robert Scalapino of the University of California, Berkeley, outlined four plausible probabilities, assigning them a rough order of probability.[11] The first he labeled "continuance of the status quo" (circa 1993). The features of this scenario included:

> On the political front, Leninism would continue to prevail, albeit with certain special features. Nationalism would supplement but not supplant Marxism–Leninism–Mao–Deng Thought. The dictatorship of the proletariat would continue, although the leadership would be more collective.

Tight control over freedom would be maintained, although leaders would listen to the "voices of the people" when serious grievances erupted. Some type of federal system would preserve China's unity while accepting a sizable degree of decentralization as a necessary part of modernization. The military would grow more powerful in its capacity to handle domestic strife and to reach beyond China, but it would remain subordinate to Party control. Economic contradictions between the socialist and market elements would continue to trouble administrators, but accommodations would be sufficient to keep overall growth high.[12]

Scalapino's second scenario was one in which China was divided into parts—either through political-military strife or in an evolutionary fashion, "with politics following the natural course of economics." His third scenario envisioned the possibility of "the relatively rapid emergence of a new nation in which political pluralism and a market economy were joined—not necessarily in the fashion of the West, but patterned after Japan and the NIE [newly industrializing economies] models." Fourth, Scalapino depicted a scenario labeled "authoritarianism-pluralism," which possessed the following features:

> Politics would be authoritarian, with restraints on freedom and the preservation of a single or dominant party system. Yet Leninism would give way to a more flexible political order, one subject to a loosening, depending upon conditions. The frontiers of permissibility would be constantly tested. Retreats as well as advances in political openness would take place, but in general ideology would occupy a decreasing position and the legitimacy of the government would depend upon performance as well as the persuasive capacities of leaders, playing strongly upon patriotic and developmental themes. Meanwhile, in the social and economic spheres, pluralism would prevail. The many difficulties confronting the economy would not be totally resolved, but on balance rapid economic progress would continue. A federal system balancing power at various levels would evolve and civilian control would be maintained, with the military a cohesive, modern force—willing to respond loyally when requested both at home and abroad on behalf of perceived national interests.[13]

Of these four alternatives, Scalapino deemed the "authoritarian-pluralist scenario" as having the greatest likelihood of being realized, although he noted "it is a flexible, non-permanent, experimental order."[14]

In 1996, Richard Baum of the University of California, Los Angeles, posited seven scenarios for China's political future, with variations on two:[15]

1. Cautious "muddling through."
2. Neoconservatism.
3. Neoauthoritarianism.
4. Political fission (immobilism, regional fragmentation, and chaos).
5. Praetorian military intervention.
6. Democratization (either introduced from above or revolution from be-low).
7. Neo-Maoist revival.

Baum was (wisely) loathe to predict which scenario would prevail. Rather, he clustered the alternatives into three groups and "handicapped" the relative odds for each.[16] The "more likely" alternatives were neoconservatism (with odds of 3–1), neoauthoritarianism (4–1), and muddling through (6–1). The "less likely" possibilities were immobilism (8–1), praetorian military intervention (10–1), democratic revolution from above (12–1), and regional fragmentation (15–1). Baum's "least likely" scenarios were democratic mass movement from below (20–1), chaos (25–1), and neo-Maoist revival (50–1).

In 2004, the Stanford University professor Andrew Walder envisioned three alternatives for political change.[17] The first "is that the regime itself will internally generate creative solutions to governance problems that involve gradual organization and constitutional change." This alternative envisions the leadership "generating creative solutions to political governance problems in much the same way that it has generated creative solutions to economic reform over the last 20 years." Walder's second alternative is similar to the first, but it envisions regional political elites—instead of those in Beijing—"pioneering experiments in changing political organization well in advance of the rest of the country . . . in a gradual and piecemeal fashion similar to what we have observed in the economy in past decades." Third, he raises the specter of "a political crisis or challenge from some social group outside the Party." Should such an event occur, the regime, he argues, could respond in one of two ways: (1) "Use massive force and halt the process of political change," or (2) "respond in a spirit of accommodation and compromise [which] is more likely to implement creative changes that promise greater future stability." He implies that all three alternatives are plausible (although he dismisses the possibility of a massive use of force), perhaps in tandem. Yet he concludes that the *most plausible* political scenario is the emergence of Hong Kong–like model:

> This would imply a gradual expansion of political participation under rules that guarantee the Party's overall control for an indefinite period. This would logically begin with inner-Party elections (or elections by a selectorate chosen from the Party membership), or with functional constituencies (labor, education, civil service) along the Hong Kong pattern. This could gradually evolve into a multi-Party system with relatively heated political competition (as in South Korea), but an evolution into a stable system dominated by a single party (as in Japan or Singapore) is much more likely.[18]

In 2005, the Harvard University professor Tony Saich offered six scenarios for political change:[19]

1. China breaks apart.
2. Collapse of central political rule, leading to a takeover by the military.
3. Collapse of the political system.
4. The emergence of "fascistoid" rule following systemic collapse (the emergence of new authoritarian elites backed by the military).
5. "Soft authoritarianism" followed by a democratic breakthrough.
6. Continuation of "muddling through" (defined as "an essentially technocratic approach where the leadership tries to maintain an authoritarian political structure combined with growing economic liberalization").

Saich ruled out options 1, 2, 3, and 5. He assigned some plausibility to option 4, but concludes that option 6 is the most likely course.

In 2006, the George Washington University professor Bruce Dickson posited four alternative futures for China's polity:[20]

1. Regime continuity and continued CCP rule.
2. Unconsolidated or illiberal democracy.
3. Successful democratization.
4. Military regime.

Dickson weighed the possibilities for each and finds options 2 through 4 least likely, although leaving the door open for option 3. He concluded:

The CCP is not in imminent danger of collapse, either due to internal decay or external pressure. Although it faces a host of serious problems, it has repeatedly proved itself to be adaptable and resilient enough to survive. It has not fully resolved these problems, and some, such as corruption and public protest, continue to escalate, but it has been able to cope with them. The renewed emphasis on enhancing the CCP's governing capacity suggests the fourth generation of leaders intends to pursue this strategy of survival without undertaking fundamental reforms of the political system.[21]

In 2007, the Brookings Institution scholar Cheng Li offered three political scenarios for China in 2020:

- The emergence of a democratic China.
- Prolonged chaos.
- A resilient, authoritarian China.

Li is optimistic and argues that democracy has a chance to evolve out of the existing political system in China. He thinks that the current political system is characterized by a "bipartisan" alliance of two main factions—elitists and populists—and that this system will evolve to "make political lobbying more transparent, factional politics more legitimate, and elections more regular and genuine. If so, it is not difficult to imagine that the CCP will split along the lines of an elitist coalition and a populist coalition after ten or fifteen more years of this inner-party bipartisanship. In 2020 elections and competition within the CCP may extend to general elections in the country and, consequently, inner-party democracy will transform into a constitutional democracy."[22]

The Author's Perspective

So, how does this observer see the CCP and China's political system evolving? I share many of my colleagues' inclinations. First, I concur that several alternatives can essentially be ruled out.

I deeply doubt that Western-style democracy is going to come to China—either as a result of elite-led tutelage or via mass demands from below. I also have serious doubts about Cheng Li's prediction that inner-party "bipartisanship" can evolve into contested elections by rival factions. However, as discussed below, this is not to rule out the possibility of the creation of competitive constituencies *within a one-party system*—along the lines of the Singaporean or Hong Kong models. This is consistent with a corporatist system. The fifth-generation leadership, some of whom have been trained in the West, may be more amenable to such pseudodemocratic competition. The fourth generation is already experimenting with limited intraparty elections and increasingly widespread village government elections. I do not, however, think that the adoption of a Japan-style system, which legitimates competitive factions (as Li's model envisions) would be amenable to a Leninist party that has spent its entire institutional life trying to eliminate intraparty factionalism. There exists a profound normative predilection against legitimating factionalism, although it may be in the political DNA of the nation.

More likely than the advent of some form of democracy is the further development of greater consultation with nonparty groups—such as with the Chinese People's Political Consultative Congress (CPPCC)—or greater empowerment of the National People's Congress. This is what Baum describes as "Consultative Leninism." To be sure, such consultation has long been more feigned than real—consistent with the united front approach of co-optation—but the CCP has been emphasizing this approach and could take a number of steps (outlined below) to give these bodies greater credibility.

Another far-fetched scenario is systemic collapse (I disagree with Gordon Chang on this point). Despite the various stresses and strains on the party-state, particularly in rural areas, the chances of system meltdown and regime collapse seem remote. Nor is China poised at a "tipping point" awaiting revolution from below or democratic breakthrough from above (I disagree with Bruce Gilley and the other "pessimists" on this point). Nor is the state stagnating (I disagree with Minxin Pei on this point). Nor is the CCP a fragile institution (I disagree with Rod MacFarquhar and Susan Shirk on this point).

As argued in this book, the CCP *has atrophied* over time and its Leninist instruments of control are not as sharp as in the past, but its tools of rule are far from blunt—*and they are being restrengthened.* The party remains a nationwide organization of considerable authority and power. It is the only political game in town. Through its monopoly on personnel management (through the *nomenklatura* and *bianzhi* systems), the party effectively controls not only the government at all levels but also a wide variety of professional institutions, corporations and enterprises, universities and research institutes, and service organizations. It also controls the military and all coercive institutions (People's Armed Police, People's Militia, Ministry of State Security, and Ministry of Public Security). It also controls much of the media and flow of information to and within society. The party certainly does not intend to relinquish these instruments of control—quite to the contrary, it has been doing much to strengthen them. It also brooks no opposition, and it quickly suppresses any sign of organized political activity.

Thus, despite its atrophy, I see the CCP as a reasonably strong and resilient institution (I agree with Andrew Nathan's characterization of the CCP's "authoritarian resilience"). To be sure, it has its problems and challenges, but none present the real possibility of systemic collapse.

Systemic political breakdown followed by the territorial fragmentation of China seems even more improbable, because no Chinese government could tolerate or would grant independence to peripheral provinces. Similarly, the notion that China could dissolve into competing "warlord" fiefdoms or that the PLA could fragment into rival armies is thoroughly inconsistent with the PLA's current unitary character. If anything, the Chinese military has become more of a national military—defending the nation's and state's interests—and *relatively* less of a classic party-army.[23] Recognizing this, the PLA can still be counted on to uphold the ruling position and power of the CCP and obey the national command structure—which runs directly from the CCP Politburo Standing Committee to the Party's Central Military Commission. Also for these reasons, a coup d'état is not a possibility. As witnessed in 1989, army units might disobey orders in a crisis, but the possibility of a group of dissatisfied officers mounting a coup or dominating the party leadership (as occurred during the Cultural Revolution) is difficult to imagine and completely inconsistent with the symbiotic ties of party and army. All military officers above the rank of colonel are, after all, party members.

Prolonged stagnation is neither a valid description of China today nor, in my view, a prediction of China tomorrow (I disagree with Minxin Pei on this point). China is not Nigeria or Indonesia. It is certainly not a "failed state" like North Korea or the Taliban's Afghanistan. Nor is it wallowing in poverty like Bangladesh or Sudan. It has the world's fastest-growing economy, with the largest inflow of foreign direct investment, a booming international trade profile, an unprecedented explosion of infrastructure construction, a competent government that does a good job (given the size of the population) delivering basic public goods to the population, and a positive international profile. This is not a state or nation in stagnation.

Devolution into a fascist-type system is also highly unlikely (I disagree with Arthur Waldron on this point). Among other reasons, it would require the regime to rebuild the totalitarian state that has been dismantled over the past three decades. It is also an ideology that does not resonate among ordinary Chinese. Some intellectuals flirt with so-called neoconservatism (*xin baoshouzhuyi*), which embodies fascistic-like characteristics, but it has not gained wide appeal.

Similarly, a return to the Maoist system can also be ruled out. Again, though there are some neo-Maoists among party stalwarts and disaffected intellectuals, Maoism (as distinct from Mao Zedong) has been discredited in the eyes of the citizenry and the CCP itself. The idea that China could roll back its market reforms, recentralize and restore the planned economy, reinstitute communes and collectivized agriculture, get the population to dutifully implement a barrage of political campaigns, and resurrect all the other vestiges of the Maoist system is fantasy.

If these alternatives can be effectively ruled out for China's political future, what *is* likely? Where is China headed politically?

Not surprisingly, the answer/prediction to the question of whether the CCP can survive is not as straightforward as the question itself. It is not simply a matter of "yes" or "no." Unfortunately, the multitude of variables and the complexity of the political system in a nation the size of China just do not lend themselves to such straight-line projections, simplistic descriptions, or confident predictions. Nor is it a zero-sum situation, because it is most likely that the existing situation of *atrophy plus adaptation* will coexist and be sustained indefinitely. Thus, the answer to the party survival question is neither "yes" nor "no" but "both." This may not satisfy those who seek clear-cut black/white predictions, but reality often lies in the "gray zone," and such is the case with China. Indeed, though each policy adaptation addresses some element of the existing atrophy, each adaptive measure stimulates new expectations and problems—which, in turn, require further adaptational measures. Just as atrophy is not an inexorable process leading to ultimate collapse, neither does adaptation lead to the happy land of political stability and sustainability. Neither is a static phenomenon—both are dynamic and interactive processes.

One thing that does seem certain—both from the China case but also from the former Soviet Union—is that stasis, nonadaptability, and inattention to change by the ruling party are a recipe for accelerated atrophy and likely regime collapse. In this regard, Kenneth Lieberthal offers the useful distinction between *dynamic stability* and *static stability*.[24] The latter is a system whereby the leadership is either frightened into inaction or is self-satisfied with the status quo, and thus undertakes no adaptation. It produces the illusion of stability but is really reflective of a rotting system. Such was the case in the pre-Gorbachev Soviet Union or in North Korea today. Dynamic stability, conversely, recognizes the need to constantly adapt and change—and thereby produces a kind of stability.

This study has shown how the post-1992 Chinese leadership overcame its post-1989 paralysis to (1) intensively analyze its ruling capacity in light of collapsed communist party-states elsewhere and its own institutional (party) capacity; and (2) to institute a wide range of reforms aimed at strengthening the Chinese party-state. This shows that, in Lieberthal's terms, the CCP accepts that "dynamic stability" is the only way forward. Indeed, as we have noted, the static nature of the Soviet ancien regime was identified by CCP analysts as probably the *greatest* vulnerability of the Communist Party of the Soviet Union. The lesson is clear: Adapt and survive—or atrophy and die. The CCP has clearly chosen the former option and, at least for the time being, is enjoying "authoritarian resilience" (Nathan's term).

Yet it cannot be assumed that, ipso facto, adaptation can rescue an atrophying regime to provide indefinite political life. At least four things could go wrong. First, the piecemeal adaptive reforms could be insufficient to the totality of illnesses afflicting the system. Second, the adaptive reforms themselves could trigger new problems that would overwhelm the party-state. Third, new challenges could arise in the natural course of the developmental process that a neo-Leninist party-state like the CCP, no matter how flexible and adaptive, would be ill equipped to handle. Or, fourth, the CCP could morph into some new kind of hybrid party-state.

If the fourth possibility were to occur, the CCP might need, over the next five to ten years, to institute greater political competition within the system. The party could stay in power *without* opening up the system, but—like other single party-states—it might conclude that increasing political pluralism is in its long-term interests. There are some indications (examined in chapters 6 and 7) that the Hu Jintao–Wen Jiabao regime recognizes this and is incrementally expanding the "democratic space" between state and society. However, this needs to be done within parameters and boundaries so as not undermine or challenge the CCP as the single ruling party, empower institutionalized opposition groups, legitimate factions, or enfranchise civil society. This will not be easy, and examples from other ruling parties in Asia and Latin America suggest that enfranchising any kind of outer-party opposition groups (*dangwai*) can lead to undermining single-party rule. The People's Action Party in Singapore and the United Malays National Organization in Malaysia succeeded in such a limited opening, but the counterexamples of single ruling parties that tried to broaden political enfranchisement without losing control *but failed* are far more numerous. Yet, as Walder has suggested, there already exists a good precedent for enfranchising and legitimating nonparty functional constituencies and allowing them to compete and participate in the legislative and political process, while still maintaining executive-led government and one-party control. This is the example of Hong Kong.

In China, creating limited political competition and increasing checks and balances on the CCP could conceivably be done in at least two ways, which are not mutually exclusive and which would each create a new kind of hybrid party-state. The first would be to significantly strengthen the authority and autonomy of the National People's Congress (NPC) vis-à-vis the CCP (at present, the NPC remains a puppet legislature that essentially rubber-stamps party policies), thus creating some checks and balances within the system. Several other moves to empower the NPC are also feasible.[25] For example, the NPC could sit in year-long session (with appropriate holidays) and become an active legislature. There could also be a prohibition on CCP, state, and military officials from serving as NPC deputies—instead creating an autonomous geographic and functional constituency-based system (as Walder and the Hong Kong model suggests). Creating NPC "member districts" or functional constituencies would immediately create a constituency-legislator relationship and increase the voice of citizens in making public policy. Most important, the NPC could assume an active oversight role in relation to the State Council and military, with standing oversight committees empowered to take testimony from sitting officials, review budget allocations and expenditures, and look out for the public interest. This could be done without subjecting the CCP to such direct oversight and would still be a major step forward in improved governance. The NPC could also assume an oversight role for government ethics violations and corruption—thus leaving the Central Discipline Inspection Commission to focus on intraparty discipline and anticorruption measures.

A second method might be to give greater authority and autonomy to the eight "democratic parties," which could contest elections nationally, possibly merge the CPPCC into the NPC (thus creating a true national legislature), and create further checks and balances on the CCP. If this were to occur, China could possibly make the transition to a parliamentary-style system, whereby parliamentary coalitions would be forged and the executive level of government would be formed by the majority coalition. Short of contested elections between the CCP and the noncommunist parties, the CCP is already experimenting with broadening consultation with non-CCP elites and citizens. A small threshold of this nature was crossed in April 2007, when a member of the CPPCC and the Zhi Gong Party (Wan Gang) was appointed as minister of science and technology.

These options are privately discussed among some intellectuals and CCP members in China (and occasionally with foreigners). Though the CCP is definitely attempting to adapt to new circumstances, "change with the times," and reform itself institutionally, until Hu Jintao and Wen Jiabao came to office the reforms had concentrated on making the existing vertical Leninist system function more effectively rather than subjecting the CCP to increased supervision from nonparty elements. Hu and Wen are not opening the system to *competition,* but they are definitely attempting to increase *consultation.* Still, it is all *tizhinei* (intrasystem) reform, with no real *tizhiwai* (extrasystem) checks and balances. Thus the CCP *is* attempting to improve communication and consultation inside and outside its apparatus, but within very prescribed and proscribed boundaries. This may help to improve the party's popular legitimacy in the near term, but over the longer term more competitive dynamics need to be introduced into the system.

The catalysts for more competitive initiatives would likely arise from the need for greater accountability and transparency, and the need to improve governance and the delivery of public services. These forces for change already exist and are only going to become more intense over time. This is as close to a "law" of political development as exists—when a nation makes the transition from developing country to newly industrialized country, the pressures from society on the state to effectively govern rise.

The ruling party-state has essentially only two options once this process begins: Stifle or suppress the demands, *or* open channels to accommodate the demands. The Jiang Zemin regime (1989–2002) essentially opted for the former tactic, whereas the Hu Jintao (2002–) regime shows signs of adopting the second strategy. Only time will tell if such a limited opening will work—or whether it will stimulate broader demands for citizen empowerment. The current CCP leadership is keenly aware of the consequences in the former Soviet Union when Mikhail Gorbachev opened the system with glasnost. As described in chapter 4, the CCP's assessment is that the conditions were not ripe for such a limited political opening, that Gorbachev did it too quickly, and that he institutionally empowered competitive parties. The current CCP leaders certainly do not envision empowering truly competitive parties at this stage (if ever), even if they may envision giving fuller scope to the roles of the eight "democratic parties" over time.

Just as in its experience with economic reform, the CCP is most likely to pursue political reform *incrementally:* experimenting with new methods here and there, expanding them gradually horizontally and vertically within the country, embracing those that work while rejecting those that do not. In this cautious and incremental process, a new kind of party-state is being born: China's *eclectic state.*[26] Just as in the economy, society, and other areas of development in rapidly changing China, contemporary Chinese politics will reflect a variety of foreign and indigenous practices grafted together into a new kind of political hybrid.

Notes

Notes to Chapter 1

1. "The Chinese Communist Party," or "CCP," is the conventional usage abroad, although the official name is "the Communist Party of China," or "CPC."

2. See James Mann, *The China Fantasy: How Our Leaders Explain Away Chinese Repression* (New York: Viking, 2007).

3. See, e.g., "A Dragon Out of Puff," *The Economist* (Special Survey of China), June 15, 2002; and "China: What Could Go Wrong," *Barron's,* July 31, 2006.

4. See Francis Fukuyama, *The End of History and the Last Man* (New York: Free Press, 2002).

5. Lucian Pye, *The Mandarin and the Cadre: China's Political Culture* (Ann Arbor: University of Michigan Center for Chinese Studies, 1988).

6. See "Introduction: The Evolving and Eclectic Modern Chinese State," in *The Modern Chinese State,* ed. David Shambaugh (Cambridge: Cambridge University Press, 2000).

7. George J. Gilboy and Eric Heginbotham, "The Latin Americanization of China?" *Current History,* September 2004, 256–67.

8. See Minxin Pei, *China's Trapped Transition: The Limits of Developmental Autocracy* (Cambridge, Mass.: Harvard University Press, 2006); and Susan Shirk, *China: Fragile Superpower* (Oxford: Oxford University Press, 2007).

Notes to Chapter 2

1. The American Council of Learned Societies even established a Committee on Comparative Communist Studies.

2. During the 1990s, following the collapse of many communist states and the "transition" to postcommunist regimes, *Problems of Communism* was appropriately renamed *Problems of Post-Communism* and *Studies of Comparative Communism* became *Communist and Post-Communist Studies.*

3. Frances Stonor Saunders, *The Cultural Cold War: The CIA and the World of Arts*

and Letters (New York: New Press, 2000); Volker Berghahn, *America and the Intellectual Cold Wars in Europe* (Princeton, N.J.: Princeton University Press, 2001).

4. Among the many monographic studies, see Gilbert Rozman, ed., *Dismantling Communism: Common Causes and Regional Variations* (Washington, D.C., and Baltimore: Woodrow Wilson Center Press and Johns Hopkins University Press, 1992); Daniel Chirot, ed., *The Crisis of Leninism and the Decline of the Left: The Revolutions of 1989* (Seattle: University of Washington Press); Gale Stokes, *The Walls Come Tumbling Down: The Collapse of Communism in Eastern Europe* (Oxford: Oxford University Press, 1993); Michael Dobbs, *Down with Big Brother: The Fall of the Soviet Empire* (New York: Vintage Books, 1996); Renee de Nevers, *Comrades No More: The Seeds of Change in Eastern Europe* (Cambridge, Mass.: MIT Press, 2003); Bartlomiej Kaminski, *The Collapse of State Socialism* (Princeton, N.J.: Princeton University Press, 1991); Robert Strayer, *Why Did the Soviet Union Collapse?* (Armonk, N.Y.: M. E. Sharpe, 1998); Leslie Holmes, *Post-Communism: An Introduction* (Cambridge: Polity Press, 1997); Timothy Garton Ash, *The Magic Lantern: The Revolution of '89 Witnessed in Warsaw, Budapest, Berlin, and Prague* (New York: Random House, 1993); John Gaddis, *We Now Know: Rethinking the Cold War* (Oxford: Oxford University Press, 1998). and Peter Rutland, "Sovietology: Notes for a Post-Mortem," *The National Interest* 31 (Spring 1993): 109–23.

5. Benjamin B. Fischer, ed., *At Cold War's End: U.S. Intelligence on the Soviet Union and Eastern Europe, 1989–1991* (Langley, Va.: Central Intelligence Agency, 1999). For a sharp critique of this volume and the argument that the CIA had accurately forecast the collapse of the Soviet Union, see Melvin A. Goodman, "The Politics of Getting It Wrong," *Harper's,* November 2000, 74–80. The author contends that the Central Intelligence Agency "cooked the books" through the partial and selective release of documents in this volume, so as to improve the agency's image post hoc.

6. See National Intelligence Council, *Tracking the Dragon: National Intelligence Estimates on China During the Era of Mao, 1948–1976* (Washington, D.C.: U.S. Government Printing Office, 2004); and "ESAU Documents" and "POLO Documents," available at http://www.foia.cia.gov/cpe.asp.

7. See Francis Fukuyama, "The End of History?" *The National Interest,* no. 16 (1989): 3–18; Francis Fukuyama, *The End of History and the Last Man* (New York: Free Press, 1992); and Charles Krauthammer, "The Unipolar Moment," *Foreign Affairs* 70, no. 1 (1991): 23–33.

8. See, e.g., Jack Gladstone, "Predicting Revolutions: Why We Could (and Should) Have Foreseen the Revolutions of 1989–1991 in the USSR and Eastern Europe," *Contention* 2, no. 2 (Winter 1993): 127–52.

9. See Brzezinski's masterful and prescient study, *The Grand Failure* (New York: Charles Scribner's Sons, 1989). Though not explicitly predicting the collapse of the Soviet Union, in August 1989 Peter Reddaway analyzed the "insoluble crisis of authority" in the former USSR and predicted an inexorable "drift towards anarchy as the authority of the government continues to decline and the social and the social and ethnic groups go on pressing their claims." For other Sovietologists who focused on the fragilities of the Soviet system, see the writings of Marshall Goldman (over many years) and Peter Reddaway, "Is the Soviet Union Drifting Towards Anarchy?" *Radio Liberty Report on the USSR* 1, no. 34 (August 25, 1989).

10. See, e.g., the September–October 1991 and November–December 1991 issues

of *Problems of Communism.* Also see Daniel Orlovsky, ed., *Beyond Soviet Studies* (Washington, D.C. Woodrow Wilson Center Press, 1995).

11. See Kenneth Jowitt, *New World Disorder: The Leninist Extinction* (Berkeley: University of California Press, 1992); and Andrew Janos, "Social Science, Communism, and the Dynamics of Political Change," *World Politics,* October 1991, 81–112.

12. See Larry Diamond and Marc F. Plattner, eds., *Democracy after Communism* (Baltimore: Johns Hopkins University Press, 2002); John S. Dryzek and Leslie Holmes, *Post-Communist Democratization* (Cambridge: Cambridge University Press, 2002); Michael McFaul, Nikolai Petrov, and Andrei Ryabov, *Between Dictatorships and Democracy: Russian Post-Communist Political Reform* (Washington, D.C.: Carnegie Endowment for International Peace, 2004); Tomáš Kostelecky, *Political Parties after Communism: Developments in East-Central Europe* (Washington, D.C., and Baltimore: Woodrow Wilson Center Press and Johns Hopkins University Press, 2002); and Juan J. Linz and Alfred Stepan, *Problems of Democratic Transition and Consolidation: Southern Europe, South America, and Post-Communist Europe* (Baltimore: Johns Hopkins University Press, 1996).

13. Anna M. Grzmala-Busse, *Redeeming the Communist Past: The Regeneration of Communist Parties in East-Central Europe* (Cambridge: Cambridge University Press, 2002); Luke March, *The Communist Party in Post-Soviet Russia* (Manchester: Manchester University Press, 2002); Marina Ottaway, *Democracy Challenged: The Rise of Semi-Authoritarianism* (Washington, D.C.: Carnegie Endowment for International Peace, 2003).

14. Richard Lowenthal, "Development vs. Utopia in Communist Policy," in *Change in Communist Systems,* ed. Chalmers Johnson (Stanford, Calif.: Stanford University Press, 1970), 33–116.

15. Richard Lowenthal, "The Ruling Party in a Mature Society," in *Social Consequences of Modernization in Communist Societies,* ed. Mark G. Field (Baltimore: Johns Hopkins University Press, 1976), 81–120.

16. Chalmers Johnson, "Comparing Communist Nations," in *Change in Communist Systems,* ed. Johnson, 1–32.

17. Robert C. Tucker, "The Dictator and Totalitarianism," *World Politics* 17, no. 4 (July 1965): 560. Also see Allen Kassof, "The Administered Society: Totalitarianism Without Terror," *World Politics* 16, no. 4 (July 1964): 573.

18. Samuel P. Huntington, "Social and Institutional Dynamics of One-Party Systems," in *Authoritarian Politics in Modern Society: The Dynamics of Established One-Party Systems,* ed. Samuel P. Huntington and Clement H. Moore (New York: Basic Books, 1970), 23–40.

19. Zbigniew Brzezinski, *The Grand Failure: The Birth and Death of Communism in the Twentieth Century* (New York: Charles Scribner's Sons, 1989), 255.

20. See ibid., esp. chap. 24.

21. Brzezinski raised this possibility as early as 1956 in his classic work, with Carl Friedrich, *Totalitarian Dictatorship and Autocracy* (Cambridge, Mass.: Harvard University Press, 1956). A decade later, he raised the possibility again in his "The Soviet Political System: Transformation or Disintegration?" *Problems of Communism* 15, no. 1 (January–February 1966): 1–15.

22. In Eastern Europe, these include Yugoslavia (later to include Slovenia, Croatia, Bosnia-Herzegovina, and Macedonia), Bulgaria, Hungary, Romania, Albania, East Ger-

many, Czechoslovakia, and Poland. In Asia, there are the cases of Mongolia, Laos, and Cambodia (Kampuchea). The Soviet Union split into the Russian Federation, Ukraine, Belarus, Georgia, Armenia, Moldova, Azerbaijan, Latvia, Estonia, Lithuania, Uzbekistan, Turkmenistan, Tajikistan, Kazakhstan, and Kyrgyzstan.

23. These categories are suggested in Steven Saxonberg, *The Fall: A Comparative Study of the End of Communism in Czechoslovakia, East Germany, Hungary and Poland* (Amsterdam: Harwood Academic Publishers, 2001), 14.

24. See Juan Linz and Alfred Stepan, "Post-Communism's Pre-Histories," in *Problems of Democratic Transition and Consolidation,* chap. 15.

25. This point is noted by Andrew Walder in "The Quiet Revolution from Within: Economic Reform as a Source of Political Decline," in *The Waning of the Communist State,* ed. Andrew Walder (Berkeley: University of California Press, 1995).

26. For an excellent discussion of this issue, see Andrew Walder, "The Decline of Communist Power: Elements of a Theory of Institutional Change," *Theory & Society* 23 (1994): 297–323.

27. John O. Koehler, *Stasi: The Untold Story of the East German Secret Police* (Boulder, Colo.: Westview Press, 1999); Markus Wolf, *Man without a Face* (New York: Public Affairs, 1997).

28. See Mike Dennis, *The Rise and Fall of the German Democratic Republic, 1945–1990* (Harlow, U.K.: Longman, 2000), chap. 13.

29. Corey Ross, *The East German Dictatorship* (New York: Oxford University Press, 2002), 147.

30. See David Childs, *The Fall of the GDR* (Harlow, U.K.: Longman, 2001).

31. This point is well developed in Saxonberg, *The Fall.*

32. The classic work on the subject (although it is drawn from the China case study) is *Communist Neo-Traditionalism: Work and Authority in Chinese Industry,* by Andrew G. Walder (Berkeley: University of California Press, 1986).

33. Seymour Martin Lipset and Gyorgy Bence, "Anticipations of the Failure of Communism," *Theory & Society* 23 (1994): 170.

34. Gale Stokes, "Lessons of the East European Revolutions of 1989," *Problems of Communism,* September–October 1991, 20.

35. There is a large literature here, but see, e.g., Dale Herspring and Ivan Volges, eds., *Civil-Military Relations in Communist Systems* (Boulder, Colo.: Westview Press, 1978); William Odom, *The Collapse of the Soviet Military* (New Haven, Conn.: Yale University Press, 1998); Timothy Colton and Thane Gustafson, eds., *Soldiers and the Soviet State* (Princeton, N.J.: Princeton University Press, 1990); Jonathan Adelman, *Communist Armies in Politics* (Boulder, Colo.: Westview Press, 1982); Dale Herspring, *Russian Civil-Military Relations* (Bloomington: Indiana University Press, 1996); and Kenneth M. Currie, *Soviet Military Politics* (New York: Paragon Press, 1991).

36. See Linz and Stepan, *Problems of Democratic Transition and Consolidation.*

37. See Ivan Szelenyi and Balazs Szelenyi, "Why Socialism Failed: Toward a Theory of System Breakdown: Causes of Disintegration of East European State Socialism," *Theory & Society* 23 (1994): 211–31; Janos, "Social Science, Communism, and the Dynamics of Political Change"; Holmes, *Post-Communism;* Kenneth Jowitt, "The Leninist Extinction," in *The Crisis of Leninism and the Decline of the Left,* ed. Daniel Chirot (Seattle: University of Washington Press, 1991); Daniel Chirot, "What Happened in Eastern Europe in 1989?" in *Crisis of Leninism,* ed. Chirot; Minxin Pei, *From Reform to Revolution: The Demise of Communism in China and the Soviet Union* (Cambridge,

Mass.: Harvard University Press, 1994); Saxonberg, *The Fall;* and Gladstone, "Predicting Revolutions."

Notes to Chapter 3

1. See Edwin Winkler, ed., *Transitions from Communism in China: Institutional and Comparative Analyses* (Boulder, Colo.: Lynne Rienner, 1999); Barrett L. McCormick and Jonathan Unger, eds., *China after Socialism: In the Footsteps of Eastern Europe or East Asia?* (Armonk, N.Y.: M. E. Sharpe, 1996); and Edward Friedman and Barrett L. McCormick, eds., *What if China Doesn't Democratize?* (Armonk, N.Y.: M. E. Sharpe, 2000).

2. See the state-of-the-field assessments in *China Watching: Perspectives from Europe, Japan & the United States,* ed. Robert Ash, David Shambaugh, and Seiichiro Takagi (London: Routledge, 2006); Bruce Dickson, ed., *Trends in China Watching: Observing the PRC at Fifty* (Washington, D.C.: Sigur Center for Asian Studies, 1999); and David Shambaugh, ed., *American Studies of Contemporary China* (Washington, D.C., and Armonk, N.Y.: Woodrow Wilson Center Press and M. E. Sharpe, 1993);

3. See, e.g., Roderick MacFarquhar, "The Anatomy of Collapse," *New York Review of Books,* September 26, 1991, 5–9.

4. Very few academic China specialists cross the internal-external divide—and as a result, they are really two separate communities of political scientists studying China (in the United States). Among those who do study China's domestic politics, there is a further differentiation between the majority who study one or another specific aspect of domestic politics and the minority who focus on the whole macro national situation.

5. Susan L. Shirk, *China: Fragile Superpower* (Oxford: Oxford University Press, 2007).

6. David M. Lampton, "Paradigm Lost: The Demise of 'Weak China,'" *The National Interest,* Fall 2005, 73–80.

7. Roderick MacFarquhar, "Why Leadership Analysis Counts," speech at the conference "Behind the Bamboo Curtain: Leadership, Politics, and Policy," Carnegie Endowment for International Peace, Washington, November 22, 2005. Transcript from Federal News Service, quotation on p. 12.

8. Roderick MacFarquhar, "China's Political System: Implications for U.S. Policy," in *U.S.-China Relations: Fourth Conference* (Aspen Institute) 17, no. 3 (2002): 15.

9. "Debate #1: Is Communist Party Rule Sustainable in China? Remarks by Roderick MacFarquhar, Harvard University," in *Reframing China Policy: The Carnegie Debates,* Library of Congress, October 5, 2006, http://www.carnegieendowment.org/events/index.cfm?fa=eventDetail&id=916&&prog=zch.

10. Ibid.

11. Shirk, *China,* 6–7.

12. Richard Baum, "China's Road to "Soft Authoritarian Reform," *U.S.-China Relations and China's Integration with the World* (Aspen Institute) 19, no. 1 (2004): 15–20.

13. Gordon G. Chang, *The Coming Collapse of China* (New York: Random House, 2001).

14. Ibid., 284–85.

15. Gordon G. Chang, "Halfway to China's Collapse," *Far Eastern Economic Review* 169, no. 5 (June 2006): 25.

16. Ibid., 28.

17. Ibid.

18. See, e.g., Arthur Waldron, "The Chinese Sickness," *Commentary,* July 2003, 36–42; Arthur Waldron, "A Free and Democratic China?" *Commentary,* November 2000, 27–32; Arthur Waldron, "China's Coming People Power," *Washington Post,* October 11, 2005; Arthur Waldron, "The End of Communism," *Journal of Democracy* 9, no. 1 (1998): 41–47; Arthur Waldron, "Cracks in the Middle Kingdom," *Journal of Democracy* 13, no. 2 (2002): 171–79; Arthur Waldron, "Watching China" *Commentary,* October 2003, 20–23; and Arthur Waldron, "After Deng, the Deluge," *Foreign Affairs,* September–October 1995, 148–53.

19. See, e.g., Jeffrey Wasserstrom, "Beijing's New Legitimacy Crisis," *Far Eastern Economic Review,* December 2004, 25–30; and Jeffrey Wasserstrom, "Will the Party Never End," *Australian Financial Weekend Review,* June 11, 2004. Also see Vivenne Shue, "Legitimacy Crisis in China?" in *State and Society in 21st Century China,* ed. Stanley Rosen and Peter Gries (London: Routledge, 2004).

20. Merle Goldman, "The Phrase 'Democracy and China' Are Not a Contradiction," in *China and Democracy: A Contradiction in Terms?* Asia Program Special Report, ed. Mark Mohr (Washington, D.C.: Woodrow Wilson International Center for Scholars, 2006).

21. See Bruce Gilley, *China's Democratic Future: How It Will Happen and Where It Will Lead* (New York: Columbia University Press, 2004); Bruce Gilley, "The Year China Started to Decline," *Far Eastern Economic Review,* September 2005, 32–35; and Bruce Gilley, "Should We Try to Predict Transitions to Democracy? Lessons from China," *Whitehead Journal of Diplomacy and International Relations,* Winter–Spring 2005, 113–28.

22. Will Hutton, *The Writing on the Wall* (New York: Free Press, 2006), 11, 87.

23. Ibid., 113.

24. Ibid., 134.

25. Zheng Yongnian, "Can Regime Change Occur in China?" *EAI Bulletin* 5, no. 2 (September 2003): 10.

26. Zheng Yongnian, *Will China Become Democratic? Elite, Class and Regime Transition* (Singapore: Eastern Universities Press, 2004), esp. 318–35.

27. See Minxin Pei, "China's Governance Crisis," *Foreign Affairs* 81, no. 5 (2002): 96–109; and Minxin Pei, *Beijing Drama: China's Governance Crisis and Bush's New Challenge,* Policy Brief 21 (Washington, D.C.: Carnegie Endowment for International Peace, 2002).

28. Pei, "China's Governance Crisis," 99.

29. This was on September 19, 2002.

30. Author's notes.

31. Minxin Pei, *China's Trapped Transition: The Limits of Developmental Autocracy* (Cambridge, Mass.: Harvard University Press, 2006).

32. This list of afflictions is drawn throughout Pei's study.

33. Pei, *China's Trapped Transition,* 212.

34. Ibid., 210–12.

35. See their essays in the *Journal of Democracy* 14, no. 1 (January 2003).

36. See Willy Wo-Lap Lam, *Chinese Politics in the Hu Jintao Era: New Leaders, New Challenges* (Armonk, N.Y.: M. E. Sharpe, 2006), esp. chap. 7.

37. Dali L. Yang, *Remaking the Leviathan: Market Transition and the Politics of Governance in China* (Stanford, Calif.: Stanford University Press, 2004). Also see

Yang's "State Capacity on the Rebound," *Journal of Democracy* 14, no. 1 (January 2003): 43–50.

38. See, e.g., Cheng Li, "The New Bipartisanship within the Chinese Communist Party," *Orbis,* Summer 2005, 387–400; Cheng Li, "China's Next Phase: Hu's New Deal?" *China Business Review,* no. 3 (2003): 48–52; and Cheng Li, "Will China's 'Lost Generation' Find a Path to Democracy?" in *China's Changing Political Landscape: Prospects for Democracy,* ed. Cheng Li (Washington, D.C.: Brookings Institution Press, 2007).

39. David Shambaugh, ed., *Is China Unstable?* (Armonk, N.Y.: M. E. Sharpe, 2001).

40. See, e.g., McCormick and Unger, *China after Socialism.*

41. Yun-han Chu, "Taiwan and China's Democratic Future: Can the Tail Wag the Dog?" in *China's Changing Political Landscape,* ed. Cheng Li.

42. C. Fred Bergsten, Bates Gill, Nicholas R. Lardy, and Derek Mitchell, *China: The Balance Sheet* (New York: Public Affairs, 2006).

43. See Andrew Nathan, "China's Resilient Authoritarianism," *Journal of Democracy* 14, no. 1 (January 2003): 6–17.

44. Alice Miller, "Institutionalization and the Changing Dynamics of Chinese Leadership Politics," in *China's Changing Political Landscape,* ed. Cheng Li; and Jing Huang, "Leadership Transition in China: Progress Towards Institutionalization," in *China's Changing Political Landscape,* ed. Cheng Li.

45. Joseph Fewsmith, "The Communist Party in Evolution," paper presented to the 40th Anniversary Conference of the Universities Service Center, Hong Kong, January 2003.

46. Joseph Fewsmith, "What Kind of Party Is This?" paper presented at the 58th Annual Meeting of the Association for Asian Studies, San Francisco, April 2006, 12.

47. Ibid.

48. Ibid. Fewsmith comes to a similar conclusion in his "What Does the Chinese Communist Party Have to Do to Stay in Power?" in *China's Changing Political Landscape,* ed. Cheng Li.

49. Richard Baum, "The Limits of Consultative Authoritarianism," in *China and Democracy,* ed. Mohr.

50. Bruce Dickson, *Democratization in China and Taiwan: The Adaptability of Leninist Parties* (Oxford: Clarendon Press, 1997).

51. Bruce Dickson, *Red Capitalists in China: The Party, Private Entrepreneurs, and Prospects for Political Change* (Cambridge: Cambridge University Press, 2003).

52. See Andrew G. Walder, "The Party Elite and China's Trajectory of Change," *China: An International Journal* 2, no. 2 (September 2004): 189–209.

53. Bruce Dickson, *Integrating Wealth and Power in China: The Communist Party's Embrace of the Private Sector* (Cambridge: Cambridge University Press, 2008).

54. See Kenneth Jowitt, "Inclusion and Mobilization in European Leninist Regimes," *World Politics* 28, no. 1 (October 1975): 69–97.

55. Kellee S. Tsai, *Capitalism without Democracy: The Politics of Private Sector Development in China* (Ithaca, N.Y.: Cornell University Press, 2007).

56. See Hong Yung Lee, *From Revolutionary Cadres to Party Technocrats in Socialist China* (Berkeley: University of California Press, 1991); Cheng Li, *China's Leaders: The New Generation* (Lanham, Md.: Roman & Littlefield, 2001); Joseph Fewsmith, *Elite Politics in Contemporary China* (Armonk, N.Y.: M. E. Sharpe, 2000).

57. See Melanie Manion, *Retirement of Revolutionaries in China: Public Policies, Social Norms, Private Interests* (Princeton, N.J.: Princeton University Press, 1993).

58. See Lynn T. White III and Cheng Li, "The Sixteenth Central Committee of the Chinese Communist Party: Hu Gets What?" *Asian Survey* 43, no. 4 (July–August 2003): 553–97.

59. For a comparative assessment, see Andrew Walder, "Elite Opportunity in Transitional Societies," *American Sociological Review* 68 (2003): 899–916.

60. Miller's analyses are available at http://www.chinaleadershipmonitor.com. Also see her "Institutionalization and the Changing Dynamics of Chinese Leadership Politics."

61. Nathan, "China's Resilient Authoritarianism," 15.

62. Ibid.

63. His admission is a changed perspective, because Nathan has been one of the harshest critics of the Chinese Communist regime since 1989 and has been a persistent advocate of democracy in the PRC.

64. Bruce Dickson, "Threats to Party Supremacy," *Journal of Democracy* 14, n. 1 (January 2003): 33.

65. Dickson, *Democratization in China and Taiwan.*

66. Bruce Dickson, "Cooptation and Corporatism in China: The Logic of Party Adaptation," *Political Science Quarterly* 115, no. 4 (2000): 517–41.

67. Dickson, "Threats to Party Supremacy," 31.

68. Bruce Dickson, "Populist Authoritarianism: China's Domestic Political Scene," paper presented at the Third American-European Dialogue on China, Washington, May 23, 2005.

69. Kjeld Erik Brødsgaard and Zheng Yongnian, eds., *The Chinese Communist Party in Reform* (London: Routledge, 2006), 2.

70. Personal communication with Kjeld Erik Brødsgaard, August 18, 2006.

71. Larry Diamond, "Authoritarian Learning: Lessons from the Color Revolutions," *Brown Journal of World Affairs* 12, no. 2 (Winter–Spring 2006): 219.

72. Gabriel Almond, "The Record of Soviet Studies," in *Beyond Soviet Studies,* ed. Daniel Orlovsky (Washington, D.C. Woodrow Wilson Center Press, 1995), 194.

73. Comments by Richard Baum at the conference on "The Overseas Study of Contemporary China," Fudan University, Shanghai, November 6, 2005.

Notes to Chapter 4

1. Sections of this chapter will appear in the author's "Leaving from Abroad to Reinvent Itself: External Influences on Internal CCP Reforms," in *China's Changing Political Landscape: Prospects for Democracy,* ed. Cheng Li (Washington, D.C.: Brookings Institution Press, 2008).

2. Gilbert Rozman, *The Chinese Debate about Soviet Socialism, 1978–1985* (Princeton, N.J.: Princeton University Press, 1987).

3. Nina Halpern, "Learning from Abroad: Chinese Views of the East European Economic Experience, January 1977–June 1981," *Modern China* 11, no. 1 (1985): 77–109.

4. Christopher Marsh, *Unparalleled Reforms: China's Rise, Russia's Fall and the Interdependence of Transition* (Lanham, Md.: Lexington Books, 2005).

5. See Minxin Pei, *From Reform to Revolution: The Demise of Communism in China and the Soviet Union* (Cambridge, Mass.: Harvard University Press, 1994); and Peter Nolan, *China's Rise, Russia's Fall: Politics, Economics, and Planning in the Transition from Stalinism* (New York: St. Martin's Press, 1995).

6. Liu Shuchun, "Consider Danger in the Times of Peace: Ring the Warning Bell!" *Makesizhuyi Yanjiu,* October 5, 2006, 16–17, trans. Open Source Center (OSC). Also see OSC Analysis, "China: Lessons from CPSU Demise Reflect CPC Policy Debate," CPF20070615534001, June 15, 2007. The author is in possession of the eight-DVD set.

7. Deng's speech, "Deng Xiaoping tongzhi zai guanjian shoudu jieyan budui jun yishang ganbu shide jianghua" [Comrade Deng Xiaoping's speech to capital martial law troops at the corps level] was first published in *Xuanchuan Dongtai* [Propaganda Trends], no. 20, June 14, 1989, and was republished in *Xuanchuan Dongtai: 1989 Xuanbian Ben* [Edition of Selections from 1989 *Xuanchuan Dongtai*], ed. Central Propaganda Department (Beijing: Renmin ribao chubanshe, 1991), 109–15. Deng's speech and several others from this volume are translated and appear in "The Making of the Big Lie: Content and Process in the CCP Propaganda System," *Chinese Law and Government* 25, no. 1, special issue (Spring 1992).

8. This assessment was published in a series of internal speeches by Politburo members and senior leaders. See CCP Central Committee Propaganda Department, ed., *Xuanchuan Dongtai* (Beijing: Renmin Ribao chubanshe, 1991, *neibu* [internal]).

9. The process of reevaluation and the treatment of Zhao have been well covered in previous scholarship. See, in particular, Richard Baum, *Burying Mao: Chinese Politics in the Age of Deng Xiaoping* (Princeton, N.J.: Princeton University Press, 1994), chaps. 12–14; Joseph Fewsmith, *China since Tiananmen: The Politics of Transition* (Cambridge: Cambridge University Press, 2001), chaps. 1–2.

10. "Yao Yilin tongzhi zai Zhonggong Zhongyang, Guowuyuan zhaokai de ge bumen fuze tongzhi huiyi shang de jianghua" [Comrade Yao Yilin's speech to the meeting of responsible comrades in the Party Central Committee and State Council], in *Xuanchuan Dongtai,* ed. CCP Central Committee Propaganda Department, 125–27.

11. "Wang Renzhi tongzhi zai quanguo xuanchuan buzhang huiyi de jianghua zhaiyao" [Summary of Comrade Wang Renzhi's speech to the national propaganda department heads' meeting], in *Xuanchuan Dongtai,* ed. CCP Central Committee Propaganda Department, 217.

12. "Jiang Zemin tongzhi zai quanguo xuanchuan buzhang huiyi shang de jianghua" [Comrade Jiang Zemin's speech to the national propaganda department heads' meeting], in *Xuanchuan Dongtai,* ed. CCP Central Committee Propaganda Department, 199.

13. For an assessment of these efforts, see David Shambaugh, "China in 1990: The Year of Damage Control," *Asian Survey* 31, no. 1 (January 1991): 36–49.

14. The election was the result of the April 1989 agreement to enfranchise opposition parties and authorize multiparty elections for the National Assembly. Thereafter, Poland established a mixed presidential/parliamentary system.

15. "Quarterly Chronicle and Documentation," *China Quarterly,* December 1989, 912.

16. Deng Xiaoping, "With Stable Policies of Reform and Opening to the Outside World, China Can Have Great Hopes for the Future," excerpted in *Deng Xiaoping Nianpu* [Deng Xiaoping Chronicle], vol. 2 (1975–97), ed. Central Committee Central Literature Research Office (Beijing: Central Literature Publishers, 2004), 1286–88. The full text is at http://english.peopledaily.com.cn/dengxp/vol3/text/d1020.html.

17. The best analysis of the Chinese reactions to events in Eastern Europe is to be found in James Miles, *The Legacy of Tiananmen: China in Disarray* (Ann Arbor: University of Michigan Press, 1996), chap. 2. I am indebted to Miles for his analysis and draw upon it in this section.

18. Ibid., 46.

19. For excellent studies of the collapse of the GDR, see David Childs, *The Fall of the GDR* (Harlow, U.K.: Longman, 2001); Mike Dennis, *The Rise and Fall of the German Democratic Republic, 1945–1990* (Harlow, U.K.: Longman, 2000).

20. Miles, *Legacy of Tiananmen,* 48.

21. See Rudolf Fürst, "The Democratic Transition of Former Czechoslovakia and Its Impact on Czech-Chinese Relations," in *Globalization and Regionalism in East Central Europe and East Asia: A Comparison,* ed. Borivoj Hnizdo (Prague: Charles University Institute of Political Science, 2001), 109–18; Rudolf Fürst, "Supporting Human Rights in the People's Republic of China," *Perspectives: The Central European Review of International Affairs,* Winter 2002–3, 52–76.

22. Miles, *Legacy of Tiananmen,* 48.

23. Jiang Zemin, "Guanyu dang de xinwen gongzuo de jige wenti" [Several problems concerning the party's media work], in *Xuanchuan Dongtai 1990* [Propaganda Trends in 1990], ed. Central Propaganda Department (Beijing: People's Daily Press, 1991, *neibu*), 5.

24. Miles, *Legacy of Tiananmen,* 47.

25. "Quarterly Chronicle and Documentation," *China Quarterly,* March 1990, 179.

26. This is a personal recollection based on a visit to Beijing one week later.

27. This journal changed its name to *Dong-Ou Zhong-Ya Yanjiu* [Research on Eastern Europe and Central Asia], following the collapse of the Soviet Union in 1991.

28. This is according to party documents and reports leaked to the Hong Kong pro-communist media. See Baum, *Burying Mao,* 304, and notes 67–68.

29. Ibid.

30. Central Propaganda Department General Office, eds., *Dang de Xuanchuan Gongzuo Huiyi Gaikuang he Wenzhai* [Survey and Documents of the Party's Propaganda Work and Meetings, 1951–1992] (Beijing: Zhonggong Zhongyang Dangxiao chubanshe, 1994, *neibu*); Central Propaganda Department General Office, ed., *Dang de Xuanchuan Gongzuo Wenxian Xuanbian* [Selected Documents of Party Propaganda Work, 1988–1992] (Beijing: Zhonggong Zhongyang Dangxiao chubanshe, n.d., *neibu*); Central Propaganda Department, ed., *Xuanchuan Dongtai: 1989 & 1990 Xuanbian Ben* [Propaganda Trends: 1989 and 1990 editions] (Beijing: Renmin Ribao chubanshe, 1990 and 1991, respectively, *neibu*).

31. "Zhonggong Zhongyang guanyu jiaqiang he gaijin duiwai xuanchuan gongzuo de tongzhi (Zhongfa [1990] 21 hao" [Central Committee Circular on Central Directive No. 21 (1990) concerning accelerating and improving foreign propaganda work], in *Dang de Xuanchuan Gongzuo Wenjian Xuanbian,* ed. Central Propaganda Department General Office, 1920–29.

32. See "Guowuyuan guanyu jiaqiang waiguo jizhe guanli wenti de tongzhi" [State Council Circular concerning the issue of intensifying management of foreign correspondents], in *Dang de Xuanchuan Gongzuo Wenjian Xuanbian,* ed. Central Propaganda Department General Office, 1941–45.

33. Central Propaganda Department and Central Organization Department, "Guanyu zuzhi geji ganbu shenru xuexi shehuizhuyi lilun de yijian" [Thoughts concerning organizing different level cadres study of socialist theory], *Xuanchuan Dongtai (1990 Xuanbian Ben),* 448–49.

34. "Jianshe Zhongguo tese de shehuizhuyi lilun daode tixi" [Building a system of

socialist ethics with Chinese characteristics]," in *Xuanchuan Dongtai (1990 Xuanbian Ben),* 349–50.

35. See Rozman, *Chinese Debate about Soviet Socialism.*

36. "The Institute of East European, Russian & Central Asian Studies of CASS," institute brochure given to the author, 2003. Though the term "Russian" appears in this foreign-language brochure, it ceased to be part of the institute's formal name after 1991.

37. Interview with the director of the CASS Institute of European Studies, Beijing, June 2004.

38. Bo Tingxiang and Cui Zhiying, "Dong-Ou jubian de lishi jiaoxun: Tan zhizheng-dang yu gongren jieji de guanxi" [Drastic changes in Eastern Europe and their historical lessons: Discussing the relationship between ruling parties and the working class], *Sulian yu Dong-Ou Wenti,* no. 6 (1990): 7–9.

39. Li Jingyu and Ma Shufang, "Liening guanyu zhizhengdang jianshe lilun he Su-Dong ge dang zhizheng shoucuo jiaocun [Lenin's theories regarding party building and the lessons from the mistakes of East European ruling parties], *Sulian yu Dong-Ou Wenti,* no. 2 (1993): 5–11, 26.

40. See, e.g., Jiang Lieqin, "Guanyu minzhushehuiizhuyi sichao yu yuan Sulian he Dong-Ou gonghui de yuanbian" [On the ideological trend of democratic socialism and the evolution of trade unions in the former Soviet Union and East European countries], *Sulian yu Dong-Ou Wenti,* no. 4 (1993): 12–15.

41. "Xifang zai yuan Sulian he Dong-Ou gongyun lingyu ruhe weixing heping yan-bian zhanlue" [Types of peaceful evolution strategies by Western countries in the union movement sphere in the former Soviet Union and Eastern Europe], *Sulian yu Dong-Ou Wenti,* no. 4 (1992): 33–35.

42. Miles, *Legacy of Tiananmen,* 67.

43. See, in particular, Gale Stokes, *The Walls Come Tumbling Down: The Collapse of Communism in Eastern Europe* (Oxford: Oxford University Press, 1993); Renee de Nevers, *Comrades No More: The Seeds of Change in Eastern Europe* (Cambridge, Mass.: MIT Press, 2003); Timothy Garton Ash, *The Magic Lantern: The Revolution of '89 Witnessed in Warsaw, Budapest, Berlin, and Prague* (New York: Random House, 1993); Steven Saxonberg, *The Fall: A Comparative Study of the End of Communism in Czechoslovakia, East Germany, Hungary and Poland* (Amsterdam: Harwood Academic Publishers, 2001).

44. Zhou Xiancheng et al., eds., *Sulian yu Dong-Ou Guojia de Yanbian Jichi Lishi Jiaoxun* [The Historical Lessons of the Collapse of the Soviet Union and East European Countries] (Hefei: Anhui renmin chubanshe, 2000). The following analysis is drawn from chapter 2.

45. Ibid., 119–20.

46. Ibid., 172.

47. See, e.g., the articles throughout 1992 and 1993 in the institute's journal, *Guoji Gongyun Shi Yanjiu* [Research on the History of the International Communist Movement].

48. Yin Xuyi, "Shenhuizhuyi de jiangglai zenmayang de?" [What will be the future of socialism?], *Guoji Gongyun Shi Yanjiu,* no. 3 (1993): 20.

49. The Central Editing and Translation Bureau of the CCP Central Committee is responsible for at least five separate institutes: the Institute for Research on Marx, Engels, Lenin, and Stalin; the Contemporary Marxism Institute; the Documentation Re-

search Institute; the World Socialism Institute; and the International Communist Movement Research Institute. Interview with Wang Xuedong, director of the Institute of World Socialism, Beijing, June 8, 2004.

50. Ibid.

51. See "Luntan: Deng Xiaoping nanxun jianghua yu guoji gongyun" [Forum on Deng Xiaoping's southern tour and the international communist movement], *Guoji Gongyun Shi Yanjiu*, no. 3 (1992): 1–13.

52. See Rozman, *Chinese Debate about Soviet Socialism.*

53. Marsh, *Unparalleled Reforms,* 116.

54. See H. Gordon Skilling and Franklin Griffiths, *Interest Groups in Soviet Politics* (Princeton, N.J.: Princeton University Press, 1970).

55. Comments by Lu Nanquan at the conference "Analyzing the Collapse of the Soviet Union: Chinese & American Perspectives," May 31–June 1, 2004, Beijing.

56. See Jialin Zhang, *China's Response to the Downfall of Communism in Eastern Europe and the Soviet Union* (Stanford, Calif.: Hoover Institution, 1994).

57. See Foreign Broadcast Information Service, *Chinese Views of Soviet Reform* (n.p., April 8, 1987).

58. Liu Keming, "Lun Su Gong ershiqida de xin zouxiang [On the New Orientation of the 27th Congress of the CPSU], *Sulian yu Dong-Ou Wenti,* no. 6 (1986).

59. Ibid.

60. "Beijing bufen zhuanjia xuezhe tan Su Gong ershiqida" [The Beijing segment of expert and scholars discuss the CPSU 27th Congress], *Sulian yu Dong-Ou Wenti,* no. 2 (1986).

61. Li Zhengle, "Sulian shehui de guji jichi zhiyu de kenengxing" [Soviet society's chronic illness and the prospects for a cure], *Sulian yu Dong-Ou Wenti,* no. 2 (1986).

62. Zi Shufang and Du Yejun, "Sulian shehuizhuyi renmin zizhi pouxi," [Soviet socialism and the people's individual expression], *Sulian yu Dong-Ou Wenti,* no. 6 (1986).

63. See, e.g., Gao Rong, "Dui Sulian lilunjie taolun shehuizhuyi shehui maodun he dongli wenti de sandian kanfa" [Three viewpoints on the contradictions of socialist society in soviet theoretical circles], *Sulian yu Dong-Ou Wenti,* no. 5 (1986); Liu Qingjian, "Ge'erbaqiaofu de jingji zhanlue he Sulian de jingji tizhi gaige" [Gorbachev's economic strategy and Soviet economic reforms], *Sulian yu Dong-Ou Wenti,* no. 2 (1986).

64. See Wu Renzhang, "Sulian de dang-zheng guanxi" [Soviet party-government relations], *Sulian yu Dong-Ou Wenti,* no. 1 (1987).

65. Mei Wenbin, "Sulian shehuizhuyi jianshe zhong de zouxiang wenti' [The problem of leftism in Soviet Socialist construction], *Sulian Shehui Kexue Yanjiu,* no. 1 (1987).

66. Tong Baochang, "Ge'erbaqiaofu dui ganbu zhengce de gaige" [Gorbachev's reforms in cadre policy], *Sulian Shehui Kexue Yanjiu,* no. 1 (1988).

67. Ibid.

68. ibid.

69. Zheng Biao, "Sulian jingji gaige shi shang de yici shidai de huiyi" [A far-reaching conference in Soviet economic history], *Sulian Shehui Kexue Yanjiu,* no. 10 (1987).

70. John Garver, "The Chinese Communist Party and the Collapse of Soviet Communism," *China Quarterly,* March 1993.

71. Garver traces General Chi's movements and meetings with Soviet Defense Minister Yazov, as well as Chi's report back to an emergency meeting of the CCP Politburo the day before the coup; ibid.

72. Miles, *Legacy of Tiananmen*, 71.

73. Garver, "Chinese Communist Party," 15.

74. Miles, *Legacy of Tiananmen*, 71–72.

75. See Garver, "Chinese Communist Party," citing Hong Kong media sources.

76. He Boshi, "CCP Issues Successive Emergency Circulars Ordering Entire Party to Guard against Changes," *Dangdai*, September 15, 1991, in FBIS-CHI, September 24, 1991.

77. Zheng Boling, "PLA Reportedly on Alert with Moscow Events," *Hong Kong Standard*, as cited by Garver, "Chinese Communist Party."

78. The text of the speech "Problems Posed by the Soviet Situation" is translated and published in the "Quarterly Chronicle and Documentation" section of *China Quarterly*, no. 130 (June 1992): 482–91. The following descriptions of Gao's speech are all drawn from this verbatim document.

79. Among the many, see the definitive 900-page history of the Soviet Union compiled by the Academy of Social Sciences (but including contributions from authors in other institutions), Lu Nanquan et al., eds., *Sulian Xingwang Shilun* [Historical Essays on the Rise and Fall of the Soviet Union] (Beijing: Renmin chubanshe, 2002, 2004). Also see Yu Sui, *Sulian Jieti Qian Hou* [Before and after the collapse of the Soviet Union] (Nanjing: Jiangsu renmin chubanshe, 1995).

80. Interview with Li Jingjie, Beijing, October 22, 2003.

81. Xu Zhixin, "Lun Sulian shibai de jingji genyuan" [The economic sources of the Soviet Union's defeat], *Dong-Ou Zhong-Ya Yanjiu*, no. 3 (2001): 1–10.

82. Ibid., 4.

83. Wang Luolin, "Sulian Mowu he jingji gaige" [The Soviet model and economic reform], *Dong-Ou Zhong-Ya Yanjiu*, no. 3 (1993): 3–7.

84. Zhou Shangwen, "Sulian jieti de lishi sikao" [Historically pondering the disintegration of the Soviet Union], *Guoji Gongyun Shi Yanjiu*, no. 4 (1993): 24.

85. Huang Zongliang et al., "Su Gong zhizheng sang quanwang lishi jiaoxun zaitan" [Revisited explorations of the historical lessons of the Soviet Communist Party's loss of ruling power] *Guoji Zhengzhi Yanjiu*, no. 3 (2002): 91.

86. Zhang Zhiming, "Personal Views on the Collapse of the Soviet Union," paper presented at the conference "Analyzing the Collapse of the Soviet Union: Chinese & American Perspectives," May 31–June 1, 2004, Beijing.

87. See, e.g., the forum of the CASS Institute of Russian and Eurasian Studies, ed., "Zhongguo xuezhe guanyu Sulian jieti de lunshu [Narrative discussion among Chinese scholars concerning the collapse of the Soviet Union], unpublished internal discussion paper (*neibu*), 2002, 5–7.

88. Lu Nanquan, "Analysis of the Economic Causes of the Drastic Changes in the Former Soviet Union," paper presented at the conference "Analyzing the Collapse of the Soviet Union: Chinese & American Perspectives," May 31–June 1, 2004, Beijing.

89. CASS Institute of Russian and Eurasian Studies, "Zhongguo xuezhe guanyu Sulian jieti de lunshu."

90. See, e.g., Huang Zongliang, "Rang zuotian zhaoshe jintian" [Illuminating the present by reviewing the past], *Guoji Zhengzhi Yanjiu*, no. 1 (2001): 57.

91. Wu Zhenkun, ed., *20 shiji gongchandang zhizheng de jingyan jiaoxun* [Lessons of twentieth-century communist parties' ruling experiences] (Beijing: Zhongyang Dangxiao chubanshe, 2002), 4.

92. Xu Kui, "Guanyu Sulian 74 nian shehuizhuyi shixian he Sulian jubian de lishi

sikao" [Historical reflections on 74 years of practicing socialism and the Soviet severe change], in *Sulian Jubian Xintan,* ed. Gong Dafei (Beijing: Shijie zhishi chubanshe, 1998), 5.

93. Ibid., 12–13.

94. Xiao Guisen, "Zhongyang gaodu jiquan zhidu yu Sulian de yanbian" [The high-level concentration of the power system and Soviet evolution], *Dong-Ou Zhong-Ya Yanjiu,* no. 6 (1992): 27–28.

95. Ibid.

96. Ibid.; and Xu Zhixin, "Muwu de jibi—Sulian zhidu de lishi genyuan [Patterns of long-standing abuse—historical origins of the Soviet system], *Dong-Ou Zhong-Ya Yanjiu,* no. 6 (1992): 23.

97. Xu Zhixin, "Muwu de jibi."

98. Ibid.

99. Xiao Guishu, "Sulian shehuizhuyi jianshe de lishi jingyan yu jiaoxun" [Experiences and lessons from socialist construction in the Soviet Union], in *Zhonggong Zhongyang Dangxiao Jianggaoxuan: Guanyu Dangdai Shijie Zhongda Wenti* [CCP Central Party School teaching texts: Important issues in the world], ed. Yu Yunyao and Yang Changgui (Beijing: Zhonggong Zhongyang Dangxiao chubanshe, 2002), 353–72.

100. Tian Yongxiang, "Features of the Rise and Fall of the Leadership System of the CPSU," paper presented at the conference "Analyzing the Collapse of the Soviet Union: Chinese & American Perspectives," May 31–June 1, 2004, Beijing.

101. Xu Kui, "Guanyu Sulian 74 nian shehuizhuyi shixian he Sulian jubian de lishi sikao."

102. Xiao Guisen, "Zhongyang gaodu jiquan zhidu yu Sulian de yanbian," 27–28.

103. See, e.g., Gao Fang, "Sulian jubian honghuan yanjiu lungang" [A macro-level research essay on the Soviet Union's evolution] in *Sulian Jubian Xintan,* ed. Gong Dafei, 79, 85–86.

104. Ibid., 60.

105. Zheng Yifan, "Sidalin he ruogan lilun wenti" [Stalin and several theoretical problems], in *Sulian Jubian Xintan,* ed. Gong Dafei, 196.

106. Yu Sui, "Sulian jubian yuanyin zongheng duihua" [Free discussion on the causes of the Soviet collapse], in *Sulian Jubian Xintan,* ed. Gong Dafei, 95.

107. Hong Zhaolong, "Sidalin shiqixingcheng de geren jiquanzhi shi Sulian jubian de zhongyao lishi yuanyin" [Stalin's dictatorship as a main historical cause of the collapse of the Soviet Union], in *Sulian Jubian Xintan,* ed. Gong Dafei, 319. Also see Li Wanshu, "Sulian Zhengdang zhidu de jubian" [The collapse of the Soviet party system], *Sulian yu Dong-Ou Wenti,* no. 1 (1990): 1–8, 16.

108. Hong Zhaolong, "Sidalin shiqixingcheng," 334–35.

109. See Rong Zhi, "Sulian duiwai zhengce de cuowu jichi jiaoxun" [The mistakes and other lessons of Soviet foreign policy], in *Sulian Jubian Xintan,* ed. Gong Dafei, 431–45; and Luo Zhaohong, "Sidalin duiwaibu shijie renshi de wuqu" [Stalin's misconceptions of the external world], in *Sulian Jubian Xintan,* ed. Gong Dafei, 446–73.

110. Lu, "Analysis of the Economic Causes of the Drastic Changes in the Former Soviet Union."

111. Hu Yanxin, "Ideological Reasons for the Collapse of the Soviet Union," paper presented at the conference "Analyzing the Collapse of the Soviet Union: Chinese & American Perspectives," May 31–June 1, 2004, Beijing.

112. One volume was devoted entirely to cataloguing and critiquing these ideological errors. See Cao Changsheng et al., *Sulian yanbian jinchengzhong de yishi xingtai yanjiu* [Research on the ideological aspects of the Soviet Union's evolution] (Beijing: Renmin chubanshe, 2004).

113. See Pan Guang, "Zhizheng dang de lingdao sixiang guanxi dao guojia de xingwang" [Impact of a ruling party's guiding ideology on the rise and fall of a state], *Dong-Ou Zhong-Ya Yanjiu*, no. 6 (2001): 9–14; Pan Deli, "Sulian Xinjinxing de sangfu yu Sulian jubian [The CPSU's Loss of Progressiveness and Soviet Disintegration], *Dong-Ou Zhong-Ya Yanjiu*, no. 6 (2001): 1–8; Xiang Zuwen, "Xuexi 'Sange Daibiao' sixiang, zonghe Sugong lishi jiaoxun yantaohui jiyao" [Summary of the conference "Learning from the 'Three Represents' and the Historical Lessons of the CPSU"], *Dong-Ou Zhong-Ya Yanjiu*, no. 1 (2002): 82–84; "Luntan: Deng Xiaoping de nanxun tanhua yu guoji gongyun luntan" [Forum on Deng Xiaoping's southern tour and the international communist movement], *Guoji Gongyun Shi Yanjiu*, no. 3 (1992): 1–16.

114. See Xin Jiping, " 'Rendao de minzhu de shehuizhuyi' lilun de yanbian" [The theoretical evolution of the theory of "humanistic and democratic socialism"], *Guoji Gongyun Shi Yanjiu*, no. 2 (1992): 7–13.

115. Ibid.

116. Ding Weiling, Li Dongyu, and Zhao Lianzhang, *Sulian Dong-Ou Jubian Qishi Lu* [Revelations from the dramatic changes in the Soviet Union and Eastern Europe] (Changchun: Jilin renmin chubanshe, 1992), 300–1.

117. Ji Jun, "Dong-Ou Jubian de shenke jiaoxun: lingdaoceng sangshile shehuizhuyi xinnian" [Lessons of the drastic changes in Eastern Europe: Loss of the leadership's socialist ideology], *Dangjian Yanjiu Neican*, no. 5 (2001, *neibu*): 13–14.

118. See CCP Organization Department Party Building Research Institute, ed., *Dangjian Yanjiu Zong-Heng Tan (2000–2001)* [A broad-gauged discussion of party building] (Beijing: Dangjian duwu chubanshe, 2002, *neibu*), 237.

119. Ibid.

120. Among others arguing this point, see Tong Baochang, "Sulian zhibian de jiaoxun" [Lessons of the Soviet systemic change], *Dong-Ou Zong-Ya Yanjiu*, no. 3 (1993): 8–12.

121. Xu Xin et al., eds., *Chaoji Daguo de bengkui: Sulian Jieti Yuanyin Fenxi* [Collapse of a superpower: Analysis of the causes of the Soviet Union's disintegration] (Beijing: Shehui kexue wenzhai chubanshe, 2001), 202.

122. Zhao Yao, "20 shiji lai Sulian Jubian yuanyin de shencengce fenxi" [Further analysis of the causes of the sudden change in the Soviet Union in the late twentieth century], *Zhonggong Zhongyang Dangxiao Xuebao*, no. 7 (2003): 10.

123. Wang Changjiang, "Sugongdang de jianshe de lishi jiaoxun [Historical lessons of party building from the Soviet Communist Party], in *Zhonggong Zhongyang Dangxiao Jianggaoxuan*, ed. Yu and Yang, 351–52.

124. Xu et al., *Chaoji Daguo de bengkui*, chap. 2.

125. Zhang Yuliang, "Ge'erbaqiaofu de beiju" [The tragedy of Gorbachev], *Guoji Gongyun Shi Yanjiu*, no. 4 (1993): 30–34.

126. Party Building Research Institute of the CCP Organization Department, *Dangjian Yanjiu Zong-Heng Tan (1994)* [A broad-gauged discussion of party building] (Beijing: Dangjian duwu chubanshe, 1995, *neibu*), 250–51.

127. Ibid.

128. Xu et al., *Chaoji Daguo de bengkui,* chap. 7.

129. Party Building Research Institute of the CCP Organization Department, *Dangjian Yanjiu Zong-Heng Tan (2000–2001),* 234.

130. Zhao Yao, "Ershishijimo Sulian jubian yuanyin de shencengci fenxi" [A deep analysis of the causes of the radical change in the Soviet Union at the end of the 21st century], *Zhonggong Zhongyang Dangxiao Xuebao* 7, no. 3 (2003): 4–11.

131. Yang Zheng, "Gorbachev Has Regrets—After Having Seriously Reflected on the Past 'Reform,' He Spoke to a Reporter from the Bottom of his Heart," *Beijing Huanqiu Renwu,* May 1, 2006, 16–19, trans. OSC.

132. National Party Building Association's Investigation Group to Russia and Cuba, "Sugong kuatai he Sulian jieti de zhuyao yuanyin jiaoxun" [Major reasons and lessons from the collapse of the Soviet Communist Party and the dissolution of the Soviet Union], *Dangjian Yanjiu Neican,* no. 5 (2004) (*neibu kanwu, zhuyi baocun*): 3–4.

133. Ibid.

134. Zhao, ""Ershishijimo Sulian jubian yuanyin de shencengci fenxi.".

135. Ye Shuzhong in "Zhongguo xuezhe guanyu Sulian jieti de lunshu," ed. CASS Institute of Russian and Eurasian Studies, 11.

136. Wang, "Sugongdang de jianshe de lishi jiaoxun," 347–50.

137. Milovan Djilas, *The New Class: An Analysis of the Communist System* (New York: Frederick A. Praeger, 1957).

138. Huang Zongliang, "Jian lun Sulian jubian de yuanyin he jiaoxunzhong de liu-da guanxi" [A brief discussion of the six major relationships concerning the causes and lessons of the abrupt change in the Soviet Union], *Dong-Ou Zhong-Ya Yanjiu,* no. 1 (1993): 42–43.

139. Huang Zongliang, "The Vested Interest Group and the Collapse of the Soviet Union," paper presented at the conference "Analyzing the Collapse of the Soviet Union: Chinese & American Perspectives," May 31–June 1, 2004, Beijing.

140. Huang Zongliang, comments made at conference "Analyzing the Collapse of the Soviet Union: Chinese & American Perspectives," May 31–June 1, 2004, Beijing.

141. Huang, "Rang zuotian zhaoshe jintian," 64.

142. Huang Weiding, *Su Gong Wang Dang Shinian Lu* [The tenth anniversary of the death of the Soviet Union] (Nanchang: Jiangxi gaoxiao chubanshe, 2002), 321–23.

143. He Qiugang, "Cong Su-Gong zhizheng qijian de fubai wenti yinchu de sikao" [Some thoughts on the corruption problem during the CPSU's rule], *Dangjian Yanjiu Neican,* no. 9 (2001): 14.

144. See Jiang Changbin, "Su Gong zai dang de zhongda zuzhi yuanze he shixian fangmian de shibai jiaoxun" [The lessons of failure of the CPSU regarding important organizational principles and practices], *Dong-Ou Zhong-Ya Yanjiu,* no. 1 (1993): 49–50.

145. See Xiang Zuwen, "Xuexi 'Sange Daibiao' sixiang, zonghe Su-Gong lishi jiaoxun yantaohui jiyao" [Circular from the research meeting on studying the thought of the "Three Represents" and the comprehensive historical lessons of the CPSU], *Dong-Ou Zhong-Ya Yanjiu,* no. 1 (2002): 83.

146. See Editing Group, *Xingshuai Zhilu* [The Road of Rise and Decline] (Beijing: Dangdai shijie chubanshe he Zhonggong Zhongyang dangxiao chubanshe, 2002), 173–78.

147. Ibid., 18.

148. Ibid.

149. See Xu, "Muwu de jibi"; and Liu Dexi, *Sulian Jieti Hou de Zhong-E Guanxi*

[China-Russia Relations after the Collapse of the Soviet Union] (Harbin: Heilongjiang jiaoyu chubanshe, 1996), 59–63.

150. Editing Group, *Xingshuai Zhilu*, 18.

151. Zhen Yifan, "Suweiai shehuizhuyi gongheguo lianmeng: Cong chengwei dao jieti" [The USSR: From establishment to disintegration], *Guoji Gongyun Shi Yanjiu*, no. 1 (1992): 1–7.

152. Xin Guangcheng, "Sulian jieti hou geguo guanxi poxi" [An investigation of relations with various countries after the disintegration of the Soviet Union], *Dong-Ou Zhong-Ya Yanjiu*, no. 2 (1992): 53–60.

153. Zuo Fengrong, "Historical and Ethnic Causes for the Collapse of the Soviet Union," paper presented at the conference "Analyzing the Collapse of the Soviet Union: Chinese & American Perspectives," May 31–June 1, 2004, Beijing.

154. See, e.g., Xu Zhixin, "Historical Causes of the Drastic Changes in the Soviet Union," *Sulian yu Dong-Ou Wenti*, no. 6 (1992): 19–26.

155. See, e.g., Li Jingjie, "Historical Lessons of the Failure of the CPSU," *Sulian yu Dong-Ou Wenti*, no. 6 (1992): 1–12.

156. Ibid.; and Huang et al., "Su Gong zhizheng sang quanwang lishi jiaoxun zaitan."

157. Pan Deli, "Gaige de cuowu—Sulian jubian de zhixu yuanyin" [Errors in Reform—the Direct Causes of the Soviet Collapse], *Dong-Ou Zhong-Ya Yanjiu*, no. 6 (1992): 16.

158. Editing Group, *Xingshuai Zhilu*, 18.

159. These themes are stressed in a number of assessments but are systematically assessed in Zuo Fengrong, *Zhiming de cuowu: Sulian duiwai zhanlue de yanbian yu yingxiang* [Fatal mistakes: The evolution and influence of Soviet external strategy] (Beijing: Shijie zhishi chubanshe, 2001); and Yu Sui, "Diplomatic Perspectives on the Collapse of the Soviet Union," paper presented at the conference "Analyzing the Collapse of the Soviet Union: Chinese & American Perspectives," May 31–June 1, 2004, Beijing.

160. Zheng Bijian, "Peacefully Rising China, Firm Defender of World Peace," speech at the conference "East Asia Cooperation and U.S.-China Relations," convened by the China Foreign Affairs University and China Policy Program of George Washington University, Beijing, November 2–3, 2005. The quotation is from an original speech delivered at the conference, although it was published with slightly different wording by the Xinhua News Agency on November 22, 2005.

161. See, e.g., Zhang, "Ge'erbaqiaofu de beiju."

162. Ibid.; and Xu et al., *Chaoji Daguo de bengkui*, chap. 11.

163. See Wang Chaowen et al., *Meiguo heping yanbian zhanlue* [America's strategy of peaceful evolution] (Changchun: Jilin renmin chubanshe, 1992), esp. chap. 5; and Ding, Li, and Zhao, *Sulian Dong-Ou Jubian Qishi Lu*, chap. 13.

164. Ibid.

165. Li Jingjie, "The Historical Lessons of the Failure of the CPSU."

166. Interview with Li Jingjie, Institute of East European, Russian, and Central Asian Studies, CASS, Beijing, October 22, 2003.

167. Ibid.

168. Ibid.

169. Comments by Li Jingjie at the conference "Analyzing the Collapse of the Soviet Union: Chinese & American Perspectives," May 31–June 1, 2004, Beijing.

170. Ma Shufang and Li Jingyu, "Su-Gong sangshi zhizheng dang diwei jiaoxun

lunxi" [An analysis of the lessons of the CPSU in losing its status as a ruling party], *Dong-Ou Zhong-Ya Yanjiu,* no. 3 (1994): 3–11.

171. Lu Nanchuan, Jiang Changbin, Xu Kui, and Li Jingjie, *Sulian Xing Wang Shilun* [Historical analysis of the rise and fall of the Soviet Union] (Beijing: Renmin chubanshe, 2002), 859–81.

172. Li Zhengju, "Sulian Gongchandang xingshuai chengbai de shige jingyan jiaoxun [Ten experiences and lessons from the rise and decline of the Soviet Communist Party], *Dangdai Shijie yu Shehuizhuyi,* no. 1 (2004): 10–16.

173. Zhong Lian Bu Ketizu [International Department's Specialized Topics Research Group], "Su-Gong kuatai he Sulian jieti jie zhizheng Gongchandang ren de jingshi" [The CPSU's fall from power and the Soviet Union's disintegration serve as a warning to ruling Communist Party members], *Dangjian Yanjiu Neican,* no. 4 (2001): 13–15.

174. Xu et al., *Chaoji Daguo de bengkui.*

175. Huang, *Su Gong Wang Dang Shinian Lu,* appendix.

176. Ibid., 271.

177. He, "Cong Su-Gong zhizheng qijian de fubai wenti yinchu de sikao."

178. CCP Central Organization Department Party Building Research Institute, *Dangjian Yanjiu Zong-Heng Tan (2000–2001),* 238.

179. National Party Building Association's Investigation Group to Russia and Cuba, "Sugong kuatai he Sulian jieti de zhuyao yuanyin jiaoxun," 5.

180. See, e.g., Xiao, "Zhongyang gaodu jiquan zhidu yu Sulian de yanbian," 31.

181. See Jiang Changbin, "Su-Gong zai dang de zhongda zuzhi yuanze he shixian fangmian de sangshi jiaoxun" [Lessons of the failure of the CPSU regarding its important organizational principles and practices], *Dong-Ou Zhong-Ya Yanjiu,* no. 1 (1993): 50.

182. Editing Group, *Xingshuai Zhilu,* 159–68.

183. Ibid.

184. Wang Renzhi, Zhichi zhengque fangzhen" [Upholding the correct line], in *Dang de Xuanchuan Gongzuo Huiyi Gaikuang he Wenzhai (1951–1992)* [Survey and Documents from Party Propaganda Department Work Conferences], ed. Central Propaganda Department General Office (Beijing: Zhonggong Zhongyang Dangxiao chubanshe, 1994, *neibu*).

185. See, e.g., Wu, *20 shiji gongchandang zhizheng de jingyan jiaoxun,* 460–93.

186. Shan Bianji, "21 shiji shijie shehuizhuyi qianjing zhanwang" [The outlook for socialism in the 21st century], *Dangjian Yanjiu Neican (neibu),* nos. 1–2 (2000): 33.

187. See Li Jian, *Tianqian Tongtu: Zhongguo Gongchandang Duiwai Jiaozhu Jishi* [A Natural Moat and Thoroughfare: Recollections of the Chinese Communist Party's Foreign Exchanges] (Beijing: Dangdai shijie chubanshe, 2001), 867–77.

188. See, e.g., Party Building Research Institute of the CCP Central Organization Department, ed., *Zhongguo Gongchandang Zhizheng Guilu Yanjiu* [Research on the CCP's Ruling Laws and Regulations] (Beijing: Dangjian duwu chubanshe, 2004), 396–98.

189. Ibid.; and Editing Group, *Xingshuai Zhilu,* 20–21.

190. These impressions have been gained from personal interviews with staff members of the Shanghai Academy of Social Sciences, China Institute of International Studies, and China Institute of Contemporary International Relations during the period 2000–3. For further analysis of China's views of North Korea, see David Shambaugh, "China and the Korean Peninsula: Playing for the Long Term," *Washington Quarterly* 26, no. 2 (Spring 2003): 43–56.

191. Philip Pan, "In China, Kim Vows Commitment to Talks," *Washington Post,* January 19, 2006; Joseph Kahn, "The Secret's Out: North Korea's Leader Did Visit China," *New York Times,* January 19, 2006.

192. Quotation from North Korean News Agency, as reported in Kahn, "Secret's Out."

193. The following analysis is drawn from the Party Building Research Institute of the CCP Organization Department, *Zhongguo Gongchandang Zhizheng Guilu Yanjiu,* 372–74.

194. Party Building Institute of the CCP Central Organization Department, *Dangjian Yanjiu Zong-Heng Tan (1999)* (Beijing: Dangjian duwu chubanshe, 2000), 344–48.

195. Ibid.

196. See Chen Yanhua, "Yuenan de gaige kaifang de chenggong he wenti" [Successes and problems in Vietnam's reform and opening], *Guoji Gongyun Shi Yanjiu,* no. 1 (1993): 11–13.

197. Yue Gang and Wang Zongxian, *Guba Shehuizhuyi* [Cuban Socialism] (Beijing: Renmin chubanshe, 2004); Mao Xianglin, *Guba Shehuizhuyi Yanjiu* [Research on Cuban Socialism] (Beijing: Shehui kexue wenzhai chubanshe, 2005)

198. Yue and Wang, *Guba Shehuizhuyi,* in particular.

199. See Mao Xianglin, "Guba gaige kaifang de neirong jichi tedian" [The content and characteristics of Cuba's reform and open door policy], *Dangjian Yanjiu Neican,* no. 5 (2002): 11–13.

200. See Yinghong Cheng, "Castro and 'China's Lesson for Cuba': A Chinese Perspective," *China Quarterly,* March 2007, 24–42.

201. Party Building Research Institute of the CCP Organization Department, *Zhongguo Gongchandang Zhizheng Guilu Yanjiu,* 380–87.

202. Li Jianhua, "Guba Gongchandang shi ruhe shixian dang de jianshe" [How does the Cuban Communist Party carry out party building?], *Dangjian Yanjiu Neican,* no. 6 (2000): 15–17.

203. Mao, *Guba Shehuizhuyi Yanjiu,* chaps. 3–4.

204. Editing Group, *Xingshuai Zhilu,* 60–70.

205. See, e.g., "Castro, Other Cuban Officials Hold Official Talks with China's Luo Gan," *Granma,* December 21, 2005, trans. OSC; and "CPC, PRC Government Attach Great Importance to Sino-Cuban Ties," Xinhua News Agency, December 22, 2005, trans. OSC.

206. Willy Wo-Lap Lam, "Hu Jintao and Wen Jiabao Draw Inspiration from Castro," *Pingguo Shibao* (Hong Kong), October 24, 2005, trans. OSC.

207. "Wu Guanzheng Meets Castro," Xinhua News Agency, April 22, 2007.

Notes to Chapter 5

1. Hu Jintao, "Helpful Practices of Foreign Political Parties Should Be Studied, Borrowed," Xinhua News Agency, December 30, 2005, in OCS, December 30, 2005.

2. Sections of this chapter will appear in the author's "Leaving from Abroad to Reinvent Itself: External Influences on Internal CCP Reforms," in *China's Changing Political Landscape: Prospects for Democracy,* ed. Cheng Li (Washington, D.C.: Brookings Institution Press, 2008).

3. "Forum on 'Color Revolutions' and Beyond" (including contributions by individual authors, as noted below), *Contemporary International Relations* 15, no. 6 (June 2005): 1–32.

4. Ji Zhiye, contribution in ibid., 7.

5. Ding Xiaoxing, contribution in ibid., 9.

6. Liu Jianfei, *Meiguo yu Fangongzhuyi* [America and Anti-Communism] (Beijing: Zhongguo shehui kexue chubanshe, 2001); Wang Chaowen et al., *Meiguo Heping Yanbian Zhanlue* [America's Strategy of Peaceful Evolution] (Changchun: Jilin renmin chubanshe, 1992).

7. Chen Xiangyang, contribution in "Forum on 'Color Revolutions,'" 26.

8. Jiang Li, contribution in ibid., 27.

9. Qi Zhi, "What a Warning Signal Given by 'Color Revolution'!" *International Strategic Studies,* no. 3 (2005): 30.

10. Liu Jianfei, "The U.S. Strategy of Promoting Democracy as Viewed from 'Color Revolutions,'" *Zhongguo Dangzheng Ganbu Luntan,* August 1, 2005, in FBIS-CHI, August 1, 2005.

11. Ibid.

12. E.g., Qi, "What a Warning Signal," 31; and Ding Xiaoxing, contribution in "Forum on 'Color Revolutions,'" 17.

13. Qi, "What a Warning Signal."

14. Ibid., 32.

15. Ding, contribution in "Forum on 'Color Revolutions,'" 17.

16. Xu Tao, contribution in "Forum on 'Color Revolutions,'" 18–19.

17. Ibid., 18; Qi, "What a Warning Signal," 30.

18. Feng Yujun, "'Color Revolutions' and CIS Trends," *Contemporary International Relations* 15, no. 10 (October 2005): 15.

19. Ibid., 23.

20. Jiang Li, contribution in "Forum on 'Color Revolutions,'" 29.

21. See, e.g., Peter Finn, "Revised Russian Bill Governing NGOs Fails to Mollify Critics," *Washington Post,* December 22, 2005.

22. Joel Brinkley, "Rice Criticizes Russia's Plan to Curb Private Rights Groups," *New York Times,* December 8, 2005.

23. Personal discussions with analysts at the CICIR and the Central Party School, November 2005.

24. This is as quoted by Mure Dickie and Richard McGregor, "Beijing Concerned about 'Color Revolution,'" *Financial Times,* November 18, 2005.

25. Ibid.

26. Personal communication from a member of Soros's delegation.

27. Interview with a Chinese Foreign Ministry official, Beijing, November 5, 2005.

28. Ibid.

29. Liu Jianfei, "U.S. Strategy of Promoting Democracy."

30. Ibid.

31. Ibid.

32. See Li Luyou, *Dangdai Ya-Tai Zhengdang Zhengzhi de Fazhan* [Development of Contemporary Political Parties in East Asia] (Shanghai: Xueshu chubanshe, 2005); Sun Shulin, *Dangdai Ya-Tai Zhengzhi* (Beijing: Shijie zhishi chubanshe, 2002).

33. For an evaluation of these schools of thought and debates between them, see Joseph Fewsmith, *China since Tiananmen* (Cambridge: Cambridge University Press, 2001), esp. 86–93; Richard Baum, *Burying Mao: Chinese Politics in the Age of Deng Xiaoping* (Princeton, N.J.: Princeton University Press, 1994), chaps. 9–10; Yan Sun, *The Chinese Reassessment of Socialism, 1976–1992* (Princeton, N.J.: Princeton University

Press, 1995); and Kalpana Misra, *From Post-Maoism to Post-Marxism: The Erosion of Official Ideology in Deng's China* (London: Routledge, 1998).

34. See David Shambaugh, *The Modern Chinese State* (Cambridge: Cambridge University Press, 2000).

35. Fewsmith, *China since Tiananmen,* chap. 4.

36. Editing Group, *Xingshuai Zhilu* [The Road of Rise and Decline] (Beijing: Dangdai shijie chubanshe he Zhonggong Zhongyang dangxiao chubanshe, 2002), 224–29.

37. Interview with Lee Kuan Yew, Singapore, April 13, 2005.

38. Editing Group, *Xingshuai Zhilu,* 225.

39. Ibid., 224–29.

40. Party Building Research Institute of the CCP Central Organization Department, ed., *Zhongguo Gongchandang Zhizheng Guilu Yanjiu* [Research on the CCP's Ruling Laws and Regulations] (Beijing: Dangjian duwu chubanshe, 2004), 431–32.

41. Chen Feng, "*Xinjiapo renmin xindongdang minzhu shehuizhuyi de ruogan lilun*" [Some theoretical viewpoints on the PAP's social democracy], *Guoji Gongyun Shi Yanjiu,* no. 1 (1993): 5–10.

42. Editing Group, *Xingshuai Zhilu,* 227.

43. Li Wen, "Xinjiapo renmin xingdongdang de zhizheng mowu jichi jiejian yiyi" [Singapore's People's Action Party's Ruling Methods and Enlightenment], *Dangdai Yatai,* no. 5 (2005): 3–8.

44. See Cai Dingjian, "What Should We Learn from Singapore?" *Zhongguo Qingnian Bao,* November 9, 2005, in FBIS-CHI, August 1, 2005. Cai is a professor of constitutional studies at the China University of Politics and Law (*Zhengfa Daxue*) in Beijing. All the following quotations are taken from this work.

45. Editing Group, *Xingshuai Zhilu,* 230–37.

46. Wang Changjiang and Jiang Yao, *Xiandai Zhengdang Zhizheng Fangzhen Bijiao Yanjiu* [Comparative Research on the Ruling Methods of Modern Political Parties] (Shanghai: Shanghai renmin chubanshe, 2002), 105–50.

47. Ibid.

48. Ibid., chap. 16.

49. Ibid., chap. 14.

50. Ibid., chap 15.

51. Ibid., chap. 16; also Li, *Dangdai Ya-Tai Zhengdang Zhengzhi de Fazhan,* chap. 3.

52. See *Qiushi* Editing Group, *Jiaqiang Dang de Zhizheng Nengli Jianshe Da Cankao* [Main Reference Materials on Intensifying the Building of the Party's Ruling Capacity] (Beijing: Hongqi chubanshe, 2004), 199–201.

53. Editing Group, *Xingshuai Zhilu,* 253–62.

54. Party Building Research Institute of the CCP Organization Department, *Zhongguo Gongchandang Zhizheng Guilu Yanjiu,* 418–19.

55. Wang and Jiang, *Xiandai Zhengdang Zhizheng Fangzhen Bijiao Yanjiu,* chap. 13; Liu Zicheng, "Moxige geming zhidudang xiatai de yuanyin" [Causes of the fall from power of Mexico's Institutional Revolutionary Party], *Dangjian Yanjiu Neican,* no. 6 (2002): 11–14.

56. See the annual volume cataloguing such exchanges, *Zhongguo Gongchandang Duiwai Gongzuo Gaikuang* [Survey of the Chinese Communist Party's External Work] (Beijing: Dangdai shijie chubanshe, 1992–). For a broader survey of the CCP International Department's work, see David Shambaugh, "China's 'Quiet Diplomacy': The International Department of the Chinese Communist Party," *China: An International Journal* 5, no. 1 (March 2007): 26–54.

57. See "Chinese Envoy to Venezuela: Business Interests Prevail over Political Concerns," *Caracas El Universal,* August 29, 2005, in FBIS-CHI, August 1, 2005.

58. "Impressive Achievements in Pragmatic and Innovative Foreign Contacts of the Communist Party of China," http://www.idcpc.org.cn/english/article/20021028.htm.

59. Latin America Research Group, "Report on China's Latin America Policy," *Contemporary International Relations* 14, no. 4 (April 2004): 14.

60. For surveys of the historical evolution of these parties, see Gu Junli, ed., *Ouzhou Zhengdang Zhizheng Jingyan Yanjiu* [Research on European Political Parties Ruling Experiences] (Beijing: Jingji guanli chubanshe, 2005); and Han Ling, *Zhanhou Xi Ou Shehuidang yu Gongchandang Bijiao Yanjiu* [Comparative Research on West European Social Democratic Parties and Communist Parties] (Beijing: Zhongyang bianyi chubanshe, 2006).

61. For a good survey of what Chinese have studied and learned about European social models, see Zhou Hong, "EU Social Policy Studies in China," *Asia Europe Journal,* no. 1 (2004): 1–13.

62. For an interesting Chinese critique of the errors of the Second International and rejection of democratic socialism, see Cao Changsheng, "Makesizhuyi zhengdang yu shehuiminzhudang de genbenchubie" [The basic differences between Marxist parties and social democratic parties], *Dangjian Yanjiu Neican,* no. 6 (2002): 1–4. Cao is a professor at Beijing University.

63. See Li Jian, *Tianqian Tongtu: Zhongguo Gongchandang Duiwai Jiaozhu Jishi* [A Natural Moat and Thoroughfare: Recollections of the Chinese Communist Party's Foreign Exchanges] (Beijing: Dangdai shijie chubanshe, 2001); and Shambaugh, "China's 'Quiet Diplomacy.'"

64. In the case of the United Kingdom, a number of these delegations came under the auspices of the British Academy (I was a member of the academy's committee overseeing such exchanges).

65. Hua Qing, "Wulun minzhushehuizhuyi de lilun jichu" [On the theoretical basis of democratic socialism], *Guoji Gongyun Shi Yanjiu,* no. 3 (1992): 38–44.

66. Editing Group, *Xingshuai Zhilu,* 311–21.

67. See ibid., 357–63; and Chen Lin and Lin Deshan, eds., *Disantiao Daolu* [The Third Way] (Beijing: Dangdai shijie chubanshe, 2001).

68. Cao Changsheng, "Ouzhou shehuizhuyidang lilun he shixian de xin tiaozheng" [On the adjustment of theory and practice by social democratic parties in Europe], *Guoji Zhengzhi Yanjiu,* no. 1 (2002): 119–23; Shen Yihuai, "Ouzhou zhengdang zhengzhi xin bianhua jichi xiangxiang" [The political evolution and direction of European parties], *Xiandai Guoji Guanxi,* no. 4 (2002): 24–28.

69. Editing Group, *Xingshuai Zhilu,* 321.

70. See, e.g., Party Building Institute of the CCP Central Organization Department, *Dangjian Yanjiu Zong-Heng Tan (1999)* (Beijing: Dangjian duwu chubanshe, 2000), 350–51; Party Building Institute of the CCP Central Organization Department, *Dangjian Yanjiu Zong-Heng Tan (2002)* (Beijing: Dangjian duwu chubanshe, 2003), 328–30; Jiang Jun, "Fenxi Ouzhou fada guojia gongchandang gaikuang zhuyao de sange wenti" [Analyzing three main problems with communist parties in West European countries], *Dangjian Yanjiu Neican,* no. 2 (2003): 15–17.

71. See, e.g., Gu Junli, *Ouzhou Zhengdang Zhizheng Jingyan Yanjiu* [Research on European Political Parties' Ruling Experiences] (Beijing: Jingji guanli chubanshe, 2005).

72. Li Liangdong, "Dangdai Xifang de Minzhu Lilun" [Contemporary Western Democratic Theories], in *Zhonggong Zhongyang Dangxiao Jianggaoxuan: Guanyu Shijie Zhongda Wenti* [Central Party School Teaching Texts: Important Issues in the World], ed. Yu Yunyao and Yang Chungui (Beijing: Zhonggong Zhongyang Dangxiao chubanshe, 2002), 314–26.

73. China Academy of Social Sciences Institute of European Studies and China Association of European Studies, *Ouzhou Fazhan Baogao (2003–2004): Ouzhou Mowu yu Ou-Mei Guanxi* [The 2003–2004 Europe Yearbook: The European Model and European-American Relations] (Beijing: Zhongguo shehui kexue chubanshe, 2004), 4.

74. See David Shambaugh, "Introduction: The Evolving and Eclectic Modern Chinese State," in *Modern Chinese State,* ed. Shambaugh, 1–14.

Notes to Chapter 6

1. Samuel P. Huntington, "Social and Institutional Dynamics of One-Party Systems," in *Authoritarian Politics in Modern Society: The Dynamics of Established One-Party Systems,* ed. Samuel P. Huntington and Clement H. Moore (New York: Basic Books, 1970), 23–40; and Samuel Huntington, "Adaptability of Party Systems," in *Political Order in Changing Societies* (New Haven, Conn.: Yale University Press, 1968), 420–33.

2. For a classic example of such reasoning, see Joseph Khan, "In China, Talk of Democracy Is Simply That," *New York Times,* April 14, 2007. For a contrasting view, see David Shambaugh, "Chinese Communism: Let a Thousand Democracies Bloom," *International Herald Tribune,* July 7–8, 2007.

3. Interview, Beijing, June 8, 2004.

4. For the best analysis of these phenomena, see Kalpana Misra, *From Post-Maoism to Post Marxism* (London: Routledge, 1998); and Daniel C. Lynch, *After the Propaganda State: Media, Politics, and "Thought Work" in Reformed China* (Stanford, Calif.: Stanford University Press, 1999).

5. See David Shambaugh, "China's Propaganda System: Institutions, Process, and Efficacy," *China Journal,* No. 57 (January 2007): 25–60. The discussion in this section is adapted from this article.

6. *Zhongguo Gongchandang Jianshe Dazidian 1921–1991* [An Encyclopedia on the Building of the CCP 1921–1991] (Chengdu: Sichuan renmin chubanshe, 1992), 676.

7. National Bureau of Statistics of China, *China Statistical Yearbook 2004* (Beijing: China Statistics Press, 2004), 844–46, 853. There is some discrepancy in the number of operating television stations. The figure provided in the text is taken from the *China Statistical Yearbook,* but the 2004 *Xinwen Nianjian* lists only 358. This probably reflects the elimination of all county-level stations as content producers on July 1, 2002. I am grateful to Ashley Esarey for this distinction. In an interview with Vice-Minister Tian Jin of the State Council Agency of Film, Radio, and Television, he indicated that China had 3,800 radio and television broadcasters altogether. Interview, Beijing, June 26, 2007.

8. Estimates provided by Xiao Qiang, director of China Internet Project, Graduate School of Journalism, University of California, Berkeley, "Prepared Statement" for "Proceedings of Hearings on 'China's State Control Mechanisms and Methods,' Con-

vened by the U.S.-China Economic and Security Review Commission," April 14, 2005, 83.

9. See John G. Palfrey Jr., executive director of Berkman Center for Internet and Society, Harvard Law School, "Prepared Statement" and testimony.

10. Examples of newspaper closures include the Guangzhou newspaper *21 Shiji de Shijie Huanqiu Daobao* [21st Century World Global Herald] in 2003, and the Beijing periodical *Zhanlue yu Guanli* [Strategy & Management] in 2004. Previous closures included *Shijie Jingji Daobao* [World Economic Herald] and a number of other publications in 1989; *Qingnian Baokan Shijie* [Youth Press World] in 1996; *Lingnan Wenhua Shibao* [Lingnan Cultural Times] in 1998; *Fangfa* [Method] in 1999; *Dongfang* [Eastern] in 1999; *Guangxi Shangbao* [Guangxi Business Daily] and *Jingji Zaobao* [Morning Economic News] in 2001. More recently, in 2006, *Bing Dian* [Freezing Point] was shut down. See Philip Pan, "Leading Publication Shut Down in China: Party's Move Is Part of Wider Crackdown," *Washington Post,* January 25, 2006; and Joseph Kahn, "China Shuts Down Influential Weekly Newspaper in Crackdown on Media," *New York Times,* January 25, 2006.

11. He Qinglian, "Media Control in China," *China Rights Forum,* no. 4 (2004): 1–25.

12. See, e.g., Perry Link, "China: The Anaconda in the Chandelier," *New York Review of Books,* April 11, 2002.

13. For an excellent assessment of the propaganda campaign associated with the SARS epidemic and cover-up, see Ashley Esarey, "Caught between State and Society: The Commercial News Media in China," Ph.D. dissertation, Department of Political Science, Columbia University, 2006; and Ashley Esarey, "Cornering the Market: State Strategies for Controlling China's Commercial Media," *Asian Perspective* 29, no. 4 (2005): 37–83.

14. Jiao Guobiao, "Dui Wo Zhong Xuan Bu" [Concerning Our Propaganda Department], March 28, 2004. Available in Chinese at http://www.chinesenewsnet.com and in English at http://www.chinadigitalnews.org.

15. See Joseph Kahn, "Beijing Censors Taken to Task in Party Circles," *New York Times,* February 15, 2006.

16. See Chin-chuan Lee, ed., *Power, Money, and the Media: Communications Patterns and Bureaucratic Control in Cultural China* (Evanston, Ill.: Northwestern University Press, 2000); He Qinglian, "Media Control in China," *China Rights Forum,* no. 4 (2004); Esarey, "Caught between State and Society"; and Lynch, *After the Propaganda State.*

17. See Esarey, "Caught between State and Society," 129.

18. Quoted by Mure Dickie, "Market the New Master," *Financial Times,* December 7, 2004.

19. Ibid.

20. Ibid.

21. See Philip Pan, "In China, an Editor Triumphs, and Fails," *Washington Post,* August 1, 2004.

22. Anne-Marie Brady, "Guiding Hand: The Role of the CCP Central Propaganda Department in the Current Era," *Westminster Papers in Communication and Culture* 3, no. 1 (Spring 2006): 66.

23. Ashley Esarey, *Speak No Evil: Mass Media Control in Contemporary China* (Washington, D.C.: Freedom House, 2006).

24. "Statement of Frank Smyth, Washington Representative of the Committee to

Protect Journalists," in "Proceedings of Hearings on 'China's State Control Mechanisms and Methods,' " 93.

25. See "Proceedings of Hearings on 'China's State Control Mechanisms and Methods.' " Other useful surveys are Christopher R. Hughes and Gudrun Wacker, eds., *China and the Internet: Politics of the Digital Leap Forward* (London: Routledge, 2003); and Michelle W. Lau, *Internet Development and Information Control in the People's Republic of China* (Washington, D.C.: Congressional Research Service, 2005).

26. As cited by Tom Zeller Jr., "Beijing Loves the Web Until the Web Talks Back," *New York Times,* December 6, 2004; and Richard Cohen, "Business, and Repression, as Usual, *Washington Post,* January 19, 2006.

27. Howard French, "Chinese Censors and Web Users Match Wits," *New York Times,* March 4, 2005.

28. Frida Ghitis, "Google, We Hardly Knew You," *International Herald Tribune,* January 27, 2006.

29. Jiang Zemin, "Zai Qingzhu Zhongguo Gongchandang Chengwei Bashi Zhounian Dahui shangde Jianghua" [Speech on the Occasion of Celebrating the 80th Anniversary of the Founding of the Chinese Communist Party] in *Lun "Sange Daibiao"* [The Theory of the "Three Represents"], by Jiang Zemin (Beijing: Zhongyang Wenzhai chubanshe, 2001), 143–85.

30. Interview with Liu Ji, Madrid, November 7, 2006,.

31. Interview with a CCP member, Beijing, October 10, 2003.

32. "Investigating Work in Jiangsu, Zhejiang, and Shanghai, Jiang Zemin Stresses Going Deep into the Grass Roots, Summing Up Practice, Actively Exploring, Clearing the Way to Forge Ahead, and Building the Party in Line with the Demands of the 'Three Represents,' " Xinhua News Agency, Domestic Service, May 15, 2000, trans. Open Source Center (OSC).

33. Interview with CCP member, Beijing, October 10, 2003.

34. Interview with Zheng Bijian, Washington, November 12, 2003.

35. Sun Chengbin and Wang Lili, "The 'Three Represents'—the CPC's Party Building Program for the New Period," Xinhua News Agency, Hong Kong Service, July 2, 2000, trans. in FBIS-CHI, July 2, 2000.

36. I am grateful to Akio Takahara of Tokyo University for these distinctions. See his "The Political Economy of the Advent of the Important Thought of the 'Three Represents,' " paper presented at the Fortieth Anniversary Conference of the Universities Service Center, Hong Kong, January 6–7, 2004.

37. Central Party School, ed., *"Sange Daibiao" Zhongyao Sixiang Yanjiu* [Research on the Important Thought of the "Three Represents"] (Beijing: Zhonggong Zhongyang Dangxiao chubanshe, 2003).

38. See Editorial Department, *Xin Shiji Dang de Jianshe de Weida Gangling: Xuexi Jiang Zemin Zongshuji "Qi Yi" Jianghua Zhidao* [The Great Cause of Party Building in the New Century: Directive on Studying General Secretary Jiang Zemin's "July 1" Speech] (Beijing: Central Party School Press, 2001).

39. The main study guide was Central Propaganda Department, *"Sange Daibiao" Zhongyao Sixiang Xuexi Gangyao* [Study Circular on the Important Thought of the "Three Represents"] (Beijing: Xuexi chubanshe, 2003.). Also see Central Party School Scientific Socialism Department, ed., *Dangyuan Ganbu "Sange Daibiao" Zhongyao Sixiang Xuexi Jiben* [Party Cadres Study Guide on the Important Thought of the "Three Represents"] (Beijing: Hongqi chubanshe, 2003).

40. See Bruce Dickson, *Red Capitalists: The Party, Private Entrepreneurs, and Prospects for Political Change in China* (Cambridge: Cambridge University Press, 2003).

41. Jane Duckett, *The Entrepreneurial State* (London: Routledge, 1998).

42. Dickson's subsequent research illustrates this difficulty. See Bruce Dickson, "The Political Impact of Privatization in China: Rethinking the Influence of 'Red Capitalists,'" paper presented at Association for Asian Studies Annual Meeting, San Francisco, 2006.

43. Bruce Dickson, "Beijing's Ambivalent Reformers," *Current History,* September 2004, 249–55.

44. This statistic was provided by Li Jingtian, deputy head of the Central Leading Group for the Educational Campaign for Maintaining CCP Members' Advanced Nature, at a news conference on July 8, 2005. See Cui Shixin, "Answers to Reporters' Questions by the Central Leading Group for the Educational Campaign for Maintaining CPC Members' Advanced Nature," *Renmin Ribao* (Internet edition), July 8, 2005, trans. OSC. This was the first press conference ever held by the CCP Organization Department.

45. As reported in Richard McGregor, "Business and Party Members in 'Joint Venture,'" *Financial Times,* July 14, 2006.

46. Bruce Dickson, *Integrating Wealth and Power in China: The Communist Party's Embrace of the Private Sector* (Cambridge: Cambridge University Press, 2008).

47. Hu Jintao, *Zai "Sange Daibiao" Zhongyao Sixiang Lilun Yantaohui shangde Jianghua* [Speech at the Theoretical Discussion Meeting on the Important Thought of the "Three Represents"] (Beijing: Renimin Ribao chubanshe, 2003).

48. "Hu Jintao Emphasizes the Necessity of Gaining a Thorough Understanding of the Great Importance of Building a Socialist Harmonious Society and Earnestly Doing a Good Job in Vigorously Promoting Social Harmony and Unity, at the Opening Session of a Seminar for Provincial and Ministerial Principal Leading Cadres on the Special Topic of Increasing the Ability to Build a Socialist Harmonious Society," Xinhua News Agency, Domestic Service, February 19, 2005, trans. OSC.

49. Ibid.

50. "Hu Jintao Addresses Provincial Leaders on Building Society with Harmony," Xinhua News Agency, Domestic Service, February 19, 2005, trans. OSC.

51. Wang Weiguang, "Under the Premise of Giving Priority to Efficiency, Give Consideration to Fairness in a Better Way, and Build a Harmonious Socialist Society," *Xuexi Shibao,* August 15, 2005, trans. OSC.

52. Richard McGregor, "Data Show Social Unrest on the Rise in China," *Financial Times,* January 19, 2006; Joseph Kahn, "Pace and Scope of Protest in China Accelerated in '05," *New York Times,* January 20, 2006.

53. These and other cases are discussed in C. Fred Bergsten, Bates Gill, Nicholas R. Lardy, and Derek Mitchell, *China: The Balance Sheet* (New York: PublicAffairs, 2006), 41–42. I am grateful to Bates Gill for his tabulation.

54. "Energetically Push Forward Income Distribution System Reform, Promote Building of Harmonious Socialist Society," Xinhua News Agency, Domestic Service, July 6, 2006, trans. OSC.

55. See "CCP Central Committee Proposal on Formulating the 11th Five-Year Program for National Economic and Social Development," Xinhua News Agency, October 21, 2005. I am also indebted to Kjeld Erik Brødsgaard for identifying these priorities.

See his "The Fifth Plenary Session: A Note on Recent Policy Initiatives and China's 11th Five-Year Plan," *Copenhagen Journal of Asian Studies,* no. 22 (2005): 92–99.

56. "11th Five-Year Program: Pushing Forward the Building of a Socialist Harmonious Society," Xinhua News Agency, March 6, 2006, trans. OSC.

57. Ibid.

58. "Communiqué of the Sixth Plenum of the 16th CPC Central Committee," Xinhua News Agency, October 11, 2006, http://www.chinadaily.com.cn/china/2006-10/11/content_706239.htm. Also see Maureen Fan, "China's Party Leadership Declares New Priority: 'Harmonious Society,'" *Washington Post,* October 12, 2006; and Joseph Kahn, "China Makes a Commitment to Achieving Social Harmony," *New York Times,* October 11, 2006.

59. Joseph Fewsmith, "Promoting the Scientific Development Concept," *China Leadership Monitor,* no. 11 (2004).

60. Interview at the Central Party School, Beijing, October 21, 2003. Many of the components to emerge over the next two years are contained in a volume developed by Central Party School researchers and published in February 2004. See Pang Yuanzheng, ed., *Dangdai Zhongguo Kexue Fazhanguan* [Contemporary China's Scientific Development Concept] (Beijing: Zhonggong Zhongyang Dangxiao chubanshe, 2004).

61. Hu Jintao, "Comprehensively Implement and Fulfill the Scientific Development Concept," *Qiushi,* no. 1 (2006), trans. OSC.

62. Hu Jintao, "Implement the Strategy of Human Resources and a Strong Country, Firmly Uphold the Principle of the Party Managing Human Resources," Xinhua News Agency, December 20, 2003, trans. OSC.

63. Central Party School Research Center for Deng Xiaoping Thought, "Closely Uniting the Establishment and Implementation of the Concept of Scientific Development with Strengthening Construction of the Ability to Govern," *Qiushi,* no. 21 (2005), November 1, 2005, trans. OSC.

64. "Hu Jintao's Speech at the June 30 Rally to mark the 85th CPC Founding Anniversary and to Sum Up the Results of the Educational Drive Launched for Maintaining Communist Party Members' Advanced Nature," Xinhua News Agency, Domestic Service, June 30, 2006, trans. OSC.

65. "Full Text of Premier Wen Jiabao's News Conference with Chinese and Foreign Reporters at the Great Hall of the People in Beijing," March 16, 2007, trans. OSC.

66. Wen Jiabao, "A Number of Issues Regarding the Historical Tasks in the Initial Stage of Socialism and China's Foreign Policy," Xinhua News Agency, Domestic Service, February 26, 2007, trans. OSC.

67. "Hu Jintao zai Zhongyang Dangxiao Fabiao Zhongyao Jianghua" [Hu Jintao Gives Important Speech at the Central Party School], *Renmin Ribao,* June 26, 2007.

68. Interview with Liu Ji, Madrid, November 7, 2006.

69. Yu Keping, "The Change of Political Ideology and Development of Incremental Democracy in Reform China," in *China's Changing Political Landscape: Prospects for Democracy,* ed. Cheng Li (Washington, D.C.: Brookings Institution Press, 2008). Yu's original ideas are put forward in his book *Incremental Democracy and Good Governance* (Beijing: Social Science and Compilation Press, 2005).

70. Ibid.

71. Discussion with Yu Keping, Washington, April 12, 2007.

72. Yu Keping, "A Few Theoretical Issues Concerning Citizens' Participation," *Xuexi Shibao,* December 18, 2006, trans. OSC.

73. Much of the following discussion of Li Junru's thinking derives from personal interviews with him in Shanghai, September 17, 2006, and at the Central Party School, Beijing, June 27, 2007.

74. Ibid.

75. Wen, "Number of Issues Regarding the Historical Tasks."

76. Ibid.

77. "Full Text of Premier Wen Jiabao's News Conference."

78. See, e.g., Khan, "In China, Talk of Democracy Is Simply That."

79. This document is found in *Dang de Shiliu ju Sizhing Quanhui "Jueding"* [The Decision of the 16th Party Congress Fourth Plenary Session], ed. Central Propaganda Department (Beijing: Xuexi chubanshe and Dangjian Duwu chubanshe, 2004).

80. "Chinese Communist Party Publishes Key Policy Document on Governance Capability," http://www.english.peopledaily.com.cn/200409/26/eng20040926_158378 .html.

81. See http://www.idcpc.org.cn/english/events/040926.htm.

82. Ibid.

83. Zeng Qinghong, "Jiaqiang Dang de Zhizheng Nengli Jianshe de Ganglingxing wenzhai" [Programmatic Materials for Strengthening the Party's Ability to Govern], in *Dang de Shiliu ju Sizhong Quanhui "Jueding,"* ed. Central Propaganda Department, 31–63.

84. Ibid., 36.

85. Ibid., 40.

86. See, e.g., Chen Daichang, *Jiaqiang Dang de Zhizheng Nengli Jianshe de Diaocha yu Yanjiu* [Investigation and Research on Enhancing the Party's Governing Ability Construction] (Beijing: Zhonggong Zhongyang Dangxiao chubanshe, 2004).

Notes to Chapter 7

1. Interview with Qi Yu, director of the Central Organization Department Party Building Research Institute, Beijing, June 29, 2007.

2. See, e.g., Commentator, "Adopting Ways and Methods That Suit the Reality of Rural Areas: Commentary for Promoting the Educational Campaign to Maintain the Advanced Nature of Party Members among the Third Group of Work Units," *Renmin Ribao,* December 27, 2005, trans. Open Source Center (OSC).

3. Joseph Fewsmith, "CCP Launches Campaign to Maintain the Advanced Nature of Party Members," *China Leadership Monitor,* no. 13 (Winter 2005): 1–10.

4. Interview with CCP member, Beijing, June 13, 2005.

5. Ibid.

6. Interview with CCP members, Shanghai, November 6–7, 2005.

7. Ibid.

8. Yu Jinghua et al., *Baochi Gongchandangyuan Xianjianxing Jiaoyu: Yaodian 20 Jin* [Ensuring the Advanced Nature Education of Communist Party Members: 20 Key Points] (Beijing: Zhongguo Fangzhen chubanshe, 2005); Central Party School Party Building Research Department, eds., *Baochi Gongchandangyuan Xianjianxing Jiaoyu: Xuexi WenjianTedu* [Ensuring Party Members Advanced Nature Education: Special Study Documents] (Beijing: Zhonggong Zhongyang dangxiao chubanshe, 2005); Edi-

tors, *Baochi Gongchandangyuan Xianjianxing Jiaoyu* [Ensuring Party Members Advanced Nature Education] (Beijing: Zhonggong Zhongyang Dangxiao chubanshe, 2004); Ye Mali et al., eds., *Xinbian Gongchandangyuan Xianjianxing Jiaoyu Duben* [The New Edition Communist Party Members Advanced Nature Education Reader] (Beijing: Hongqi chubanshe, 2003).

9. See, e.g., Central State Organs Work Committee Research Office, *Dang de Xianjianxing Jianshe yu Jiguan Dang de Jianshe* [The Party's Building Its Advanced Nature and Party Construction in Work Organs] (Beijing: Zhonggong Zhongyang Dang-xiao chubanshe, 2005); Shen Zhishao, ed., *Dang de Xianjianxing Yanjiu* [Research on the Party's Advanced Nature] (Beijing: Dangjian duwu chubanshe, 2004); and Shen Chendong et al., *Dang de Xianjianxing Jianshelun* [The Theory of Building the Party's Advanced Nature] (Beijing: Zhonggong Zhongyang Dangxiao chubanshe, 2006).

10. Interview with CPP member, Shanghai, March 24, 2007.

11. "Official in Charge of the Central Leading Group for Advanced Nature Education Activity Fields Reporters' Questions," Xinhua News Agency, Domestic Service, July 13, 2006, trans. OSC; "CPC Official Briefs Media on Education Campaign to Preserve Advanced Nature," Beijing Zhongguo Wang, July 13, 2006, trans. OSC; "CPC Official Gives Statistics on Advanced Nature," Xinhua News Agency, July 13, 2006, trans. OSC; "Communist Party of China Expels Nearly 45,000 Party Members Last Year," Xinhua News Agency, July 13, 2006, trans. OSC. Data in this paragraph are drawn from these reports.

12. Interview with Qi Yu, Central Organization Department Party Building Research Institute, Beijing, June 29, 2007.

13. Interview with the director of the Rural Economy Department, State Council Development Research Center, Beijing, June 28, 2007.

14. "Number of CPC Members Reaches 69.6 Million," Xinhua News Agency, May 23, 2005, trans. OSC.

15. Interview with Wang Tingda, director of the Organization Department's Party Building Research Institute, Beijing, October 21, 2003.

16. Interview at CDIC, Beijing, October 21, 2003.

17. For a survey and brief history of the CDIC, see Jeffrey Becker, "The Evolution of CCP Control Organizations: The Central Discipline Inspection Commission," unpublished paper, September 2005.

18. "Hu Jintao's Speech at June 30 Beijing Rally to Mark CPC Founding Anniversary," *China Daily,* July 1, 2004.

19. "Zhonggong Zhongyang Jiwei Jianchabu Guanyu Zhongyang Jiwei Jianchabu Jiguan Heshu Bangong he Jigou Shizhi Youguan Wenti de Qingshi" [Central Discipline Inspection Commission—Ministry of Supervision Instructions Regarding the Questions on the Establishment of Joint Management and Organizations for the CDIC-MoS Work], in *Jijian Jiancha Ganbu Gongzuo Shouce* [Discipline Inspection Cadre Work handbook] (Beijing: Zhongguo Fangzheng chubanshe, 2002), 164–65.

20. Interview with CDIC staff, Beijing, October 21, 2003.

21. *A Brief Introduction to the Ministry of Supervision* (n.d.), received at the ministry on June 28, 2007.

22. See Zou Yingyi, ed., *Jundui Jilu Jiancha Gongzuo Gailun* (Beijing: Zhangzheng chubanshe, 1988).

23. *Hongqi* Political Editing Office, *Dang de Jilu Jiancha Gongzuo Zhishi Shouce* [Knowledge Handbook of the Party's Discipline Inspection Work] (Beijing: Jingji Kexue chubanshe, 1997), 369–74.

24. Interview, CDIC, Beijing, June 28, 2007.

25. Ibid.

26. "CPC Punished 115,143 Members Last Year," Xinhua News Agency, February 14, 2006, as reported by *China Daily:* http://www.chinadaily.com.cn/english/doc/2006-02/14/content_519914.htm. The data in this paragraph draw on this report. Also see Edward Cody, "China Cracks Down on Corruption," *Washington Post,* February 15, 2006.

27. Interview at CDIC, Beijing, June 28, 2007.

28. Ibid.

29. Ibid.

30. Interview at CDIC, Beijing, October 21, 2003.

31. Ibid.

32. Chen received a sixteen-year prison sentence, of which he served half. Chen was removed in September 2006 and awaits sentencing. See Geoff Dyer, "Shanghai Party Chief Sacked as Hu Bolsters Power," *Financial Times,* September 26, 2006; and Joseph Kahn, "Shanghai's Party Leader, Mistrusted by Hu, Is Purged," *New York Times,* September 26, 2006.

33. Li Yonggang, "Analyzing Party Spirit Is a Lifelong Required Course for Party Members: Interview with Yu Yunyao," *Xuexi Shibao* (Internet edition), December 24, 2004, trans. OSC. Yu retired from his position at the CPS in July 2006.

34. "Communiqué of the Sixth Plenum of the CPC Central Commission for Discipline Inspection," Xinhua News Agency, Domestic Service, January 7, 2006, trans. OSC.

35. Interview, CDIC, Beijing, October 21, 2003.

36. "Hotline Established to Allow Public Supervision of Party Official Selection," Xinhua News Agency, March 30, 2004, trans. OSC.

37. "Number of CCP Members Increases by 6.4 Million," Xinhua News Agency, October 8, 2007.

38. See the candid discussion in the annual "Blue Book" investigation conducted by the Academy of Social Sciences: Huang Weiping and Wang Yongcheng, eds., *Dangdai Zhongguo Zhengzhi Yanjiu Baogao III* [Research Report on Contemporary Chinese Politics] (Beijing: Shehui kexue chubanshe, 2004), 197–201, 339–41.

39. "Statistics of Civic Organizations in 2005," available at Ministry of Civil Affairs Web site, http://www.mca.gov.cn/. Cited by Yu Keping, "The Change of Political Ideology and Development of Incremental Democracy in Reform China," in *China's Changing Political Landscape,* ed. Cheng Li (Washington, D.C.: Brookings Institution Press, 2008).

40. See CCP Organization Department Training Center, ed., *Dang de Zuzhi Gongzuo Rumen* [The Rudiments of Party Organizational Work] (Beijing: Dangjian duwu chubanshe, 2004).

41. Party Building Institute of the CCP Central Organization Department, ed., *Dangjian Yanjiu Zengheng Tan 2000–2001* [Comprehensive Research on Party Building 2000–2001] (Beijing: Dangjian Duwu chubanshe, 2001), 307–9.

42. Ibid.

43. Ibid., 378–91.

44. Special Research Section of the Central Organization Department Party Building Research Institute, *2001–2002 Xin Xingshixia Dangjian Gongzuo Redian Nandian Wenti Yanjiu* [2001–2002 Research on Hot and Troublesome Problems in Party Building Work on New Conditions] (Beijing: Dangjian Duwu chubanshe, 2002, *neibu*), chap. 1. All data come from this chapter.

45. Special Research Section of the Central Organization Department Party Build-

ing Institute, *Xin Shiqi Dangjian Gongzuo Redian Nandian Wenti Diaocha Baogao (3)* [Investigative Report on Hot and Troublesome Problems in New Era Party Building Work, Vol. 3] (Beijing: Dangjian Duwu chubanshe, 2003, *neibu*), chap. 1.

46. See Yang Shaohua, "Strengthening Party Conduct and Ethical Governance Construction among Grassroots Work Units in Rural Areas, Reinforcing the Basis for the Party's Governance in Rural Areas: An Interview with He Yong, Member of the CPC Secretariat and Secretary of the Discipline Inspection Commission," *Qiushi* (Internet edition), November 15, 2005, trans. OSC. Also see Stig Thøgersen, "Parasites or Civilizers: The Legitimacy of the Chinese Communist Party in Rural Areas," *China: An International Journal,* no. 2 (September 2003): 200–23.

47. Interview with Zheng Bijian, executive director, China Reform Forum, Beijing, September 18, 2006.

48. "CPC Issues Document on System of Multi-Party Cooperation and Political Consultation," March 20, 2005, http://www.idcpc.org.cn/english/events/050320.htm.

49. Interview, United Front Work Department, Beijing, June 25, 2007.

50. Interview at CPPCC, Beijing, June 28, 2007.

51. Interview with member of the CPPCC, Shanghai, June 19, 2005. Also see "Chinese President Refers to Multi-Party Advisory Body as Key for Socialist Democracy," September 21, 2004, http://www.idcpc.org.cn/english/events/040921.htm.

52. Interview with CPPCC member, near Shanghai, June 25, 2005.

53. State Council Information Office, *Building of Political Democracy in China,* http://www.china.org.cn/english/2005/Oct/145718.htm.

54. Interview, United Front Work Department, Beijing, June 25, 2007.

55. See Wu Meihua, *Dangdai Zhongguo de Duo-Dang Hezuo Zhidu* [Contemporary China's System of Multi-Party Cooperation] (Beijing: Zhonggong dangshi chubanshe, 2005), 251–52.

56. *Shiliu Da Fudao Duben* (Beijing: Renmin chubanshe, 2002), 417–30.

57. See, e.g., "Hu Jintao Chairs 32nd Collective Study Session of the CPC Central Committee Political Bureau on July 3, and Stresses Need to Govern Through Science, Democracy, and the Rule of Law," Xinhua News Agency, July 3, 2006, trans. OSC.

58. See, e.g., Deng Changzong, *Zhongguo Gongchandang Dangnei Minzhu Zhidu Fenxi* [Analysis of the CCP's Inner-Party Democracy System] (Tianjin: Tianjin renmin chubanshe, 2005); Xu Danmei, *Zhongguo Gongchandang Dangnei Minzhu Yanjiu* [Research on the CCP's Inner-Party Democracy] (Beijing: Danjian Duwu chubanshe, 2004); Zeng Jun and Mei Lihong, *Zhongguo Gongchandang yu Dangdai Zhongguo Minzhu: Lishi yu Jiangyan* [The Chinese Communist Party and Contemporary Chinese Democracy: History and Experiences] (Shanghai: Shanghai renmin chubanshe, 2004); and Zhonggong Zhongyang Zuzhibu Dangjian Yanjiusuo Ketizu, *Difang Dangwei Zhizheng Nengli Jianshe Diaocha* [Investigation into Building a Ruling Party in Local Party Committees] (Beijing: Dangjian duwu chubanshe, 2004, *neibu*).

59. See Wu Zhenkun et al., *20 Shiji Gongchandang Zhizheng de Jingyan Jiaoxun* [Study Materials on the Governing Experiences of Twentieth-Century Communist Parties] (Beijing: Zhonggong Zhongyang Dangxiao chubanshe, 2002), 268–300.

60. See, e.g., the discussion by CPS professor Hong Shaowen, "Jianshe you Zhongguo Tese Shehuizhuyi Minzhu Zhengzhi yu Wo Guo Zhengzhi Tizhi Gaige" [Building Socialism with Chinese Characteristics: Democratic Politics and Our Country's Political System Reform], in *Zhonggong Zhongyang Dangxiao Jinaggaoxuan Guanyu Makesizhuyi Jiben Wenti* [Central Party School Selected Lectures Concerning Fundamental

Problems in Marxism], ed. Yu Yunyao and Yang Chungui (Beijing: Zhonggong Zhongyang Dangxiao chubanshe, 2002), 397–406.

61. See, e.g., "Zhuanjia xuezhe tan dangnei minzhu jianshe wenti" [Specialists and scholars discuss the issue of building intra-party democracy], *Dangjian Yanjiu Neican,* no. 7 (2003): 15–17.

62. See *Dang Zuzhi Xuanbian Gongzuo Shouce* [Party Organizations Electoral Work Manual] (Taiyuan: Shanxi renmin chubanshe, 2001).

63. Interview with Central Committee member, Beijing, April 12, 2007.

64. Interview with Zheng Bijian, Beijing, September 18, 2006.

65. See Joseph Fewsmith, "Pressures for Expanding Local-Level Democracy," *China Leadership Monitor,* no. 12 (Fall 2004): 1–10.

66. See, e.g., John Pomfret, "Delegates Take on One-Party Rule in China's Heartland: Communists Spurned in Local Elections," *Washington Post,* March 4, 2003.

67. Cited by Joseph Kahn, "For China, One Party Is Enough, Leader Says," *New York Times,* September 16, 2004.

68. See Melanie Manion, "Official Candidate Losses and Communist Party Gains? Congress Delegates and Party Committee Selectorates in Mainland China," paper presented at 58th Annual Meeting of Association for Asian Studies, San Francisco, April 6–9, 2006.

69. Zhou Tianyong, *Zhongguo Zhengzhi Tizhi Gaige* [China's Political System Reform] (Beijing: Zhonggong Zhongyang Dangxiao chubanshe, 2004), chap. 1.

70. Zeng Qinghong, "Diligently Improve the Quality and Ability of Leading Cadres," *Xuexi Shibao* (Internet edition), September 26, 2005, trans. OSC.

71. Ibid.

72. These figures apply to the 1998 *nomenklatura* list. See John P. Burns, "The Chinese Communist Party's *Nomenklatura* System as a Leadership Selection Mechanism," in *The Chinese Communist Party in Reform,* ed. Kjeld Erik Brødsgaard and Zheng Yongnian (London: Routledge, 2006), 34.

73. Interview with Wang Tingda.

74. Kjeld Erik Brødsgaard, "*Bianzhi* and Cadre Management in China," in *Chinese Communist Party in Reform,* ed. Brødsgaard and Zheng, 104. Also see Brødsgaard, "Institutional Reform and the *Bianzhi* System in China," *China Quarterly,* no. 170 (June 2002): 361–86.

75. This information is from *2004 China Statistical Yearbook,* as cited in *Chinese Communist Party in Reform,* ed. Brødsgaard and Zheng, 105.

76. These figures were current as of June 2002. See General Office of the CCP Central Organization Department, ed., *Shisanju Sizhong Quanhui Yilai Dang de Zuzhi Gongzuo Chengjiu Gaishu* [Narrative of the Party's Organization Work Achievements since the Fourth Plenum of the Thirteenth Party Congress] (Beijing: Dangjian Duwu chubanshe, 2002), 98.

77. *Zhonggong Zhongyang "2001–2005 Quanguo Ganbu Jiaoyu Peixun Guihua" Zhidao* [Central Committee Directive on 2001–2005 National Cadre Education & Training Plan] in *Zhongguo Sixiang Zhengzhi Gongzuo Nianjian* [Yearbook China's Ideological Political Work 2001] (Beijing: Zhonggong Zhongyang dangxiao chubanshe, 2002), 50–54.

78. See Cui Shixin, "A General Description of New Reform Measures to Further Realize Cadre Personnel Reform," *People's Daily* (Internet edition), January 8, 2005, http://politics.people.com.cn/GB/1026/3105420.html. Another excellent source detail-

ing these measures is Wang Yang, *Xin Shiqi Dang de Ganbu Zhidu Jianshe* [Building the Party Cadre System in the New Era] (Beijing: Zhonggong dangshi chubanshe, 2006).

79. "Central Organization Department of CPC Central Committee Issues Circular Enforcement of Regulations on the Selection and Appointment of Party and Government Leading Cadres," Xinhua News Agency, Domestic Service, July 28, 2003, trans. OSC.

80. Interview with Wang Tingda.

81. Ibid.

82. Ibid.

83. See Central Organization Department party Building Research Institute, ed., *Dangjian Yanjiu Zongheng Tan 2002* [Broadgauged Research on Party Building in 2002] (Beijing: Dangjian Duwu chubanshe, 2003, *neibu*), 101–9.

84. *Zhongguo Gongchandang Dangnei Fagui Xinbian 2005* [New Edition the CCP's Internal Party Regulations] (Beijing: Falu chubanshe, 2005).

85. "Hu Jintao zai Quanguo Dangxiao Gongzuo Huiyi shang Qiangdiao wuli ba Dangxiao jiaoyu shiye tigao dao Xin Shuiping" [At National Party School work conference, Hu Jintao stresses need to take Party School education to a new level], in *Xin Shiqi Dangxiao Gongzuo Lun* [Theory of Party School Work in the New Era], by Li Xintiao (Beijing: Zhonggong Zhongyang Dangxiao chubanshe, 2002), 8.

86. Interview with CCP Organization Department personnel, Shanghai, September 22, 2006.

87. General Office of the Central Organization Department, *Shisanju Sizhong Quanhui Yilai Dang de Zuzhi Gongzuo Chengjiu Gaishu,* 98–104.

88. Ibid.

89. Wang Fuyi, ed., *Zhongguo Gongchandang Jianshe da Cidian* [Encyclopedia on Chinese Communist Party Construction] (Jinan: Shandong renmin chubanshe, 2001), 292.

90. "Zhongyang Dangxiao Jieshao" [Introduction to the Central Party School], http://www.ccps.gov.cn/dxjj/index.jsp.

91. Yang Chungui, *Dangxiao Jiaoxue Lun* [Theory of Party School Teaching] (Beijing: Zhonggong Zhongyang Dangxiao chubanshe, 2002), 299.

92. Wang Yang, *Xin Shiqi Dang de Ganbu Zhidu Jianshe,* 310. Though 2,700 Party Schools may seem like a lot (and it is), this source states (p. 316) that in 1985 there were 11,000 cadres training schools of all kinds in China (including Party Schools)!

93. "2001–2005 Nian Quanguo Ganbu Jiaoyu Peixun Guilu," in *Zhongguo Sixiang Zhengzhi Gongzuo Nianjian* [Yearbook on National Ideological Political Work], ed. Editors (Beijing: Zhonggong Zhongyang Dangxiao chubanshe, 2002), 52–53.

94. Each of the 2,600 Party schools is listed in *Quanguo Dangxiao Gaikuang* [Survey of National Party Schools], ed. Editorial Committee (Beijing: Hongqi chubanshe, 1996). A more recent source lists the total as 2,700. See Wang Yang, *Xin Shiqi Dang de Ganbu Zhidu Jianshe,* 310.

95. These are all listed in the *Quanguo Dangxiao Galilan* [Survey of National Party Schools] (Beijing: Hongqi chubanshe, 1996).

96. For a description of party schools at these subprovincial levels, see Liu Jiaqi, Tie Jin, and Shen Huiqing, *Dangxiao Jiaoyu Yuanli Gailun* [Survey of Basic Principles of Party School Education] (Beijing: Zhonggong Zhongyang Dangxiao chubanshe, 1989), 114–24.

97. Huang Yong, "Shengdangxiao Weigui fa Wenping, Hainan Chachu Wenping Pifa Da'an" [Provincial Party School Confers Diplomas Illegally, Hainan Investigates Diploma Sales Case], *Zhongguo Qingnian Bao* [China Youth Daily], June 16, 2004.

98. Benjamin Kang Lim, "China Vice-Principal Demoted for Bible Study Session," Reuters, March 1, 2007.

99. Huang Haixia et al., "Probing the Secrets of China's Three Cadre Academies," *Liaowang Xinwen Zhoukan,* November 7, 2005.

100. Ibid.

101. Interview at the Pudong Cadre Academy, Pudong, September 22, 2006.

102. Ibid.

103. See Jason Leow, "Leadership Training College Opens in Shanghai," *Straits Times,* March 24, 2005.

104. This account is based primarily on a visit and interviews with administrators at CELAP, September 22, 2006.

105. Ibid.

106. The data in this paragraph are derived primarily from an interview with CPS vice president Wang Weiguang and other staff, Beijing, October 21, 2003, but also from other published sources and the CPS Web site, http://www.ccps.gov.cn. For another overview of the CPS, see Ignatius Wibowo and Lye Liang Fook, "China's Central Party School: A Unique Institution Adapting to Changes," in *Chinese Communist Party in Reform,* ed. Brødsgaard and Zheng.

107. The vast majority of country-level party secretaries are trained in provincial-level Party Schools.

108. "Zhonggong Zhongyang Dangxiao Jieshao" [Introduction to the Central Party School], http://www.ccps.gov.cn/dxjj/index.jsp.

109. See, e.g., Li Weiping, "Shanghai Private Entrepreneurs Participate in Study Program at Central Party School in Beijing," *Wen Wei Po,* January 10, 2003, in FBIS-CHI.

110. He Huifeng, "Taking Care of Business at Central Party School," *South China Morning Post,* April 24, 2006.

111. Ibid.

112. See Bruce Dickson, *Red Capitalists in China: The Party, Private Entrepreneurs, and Prospects for Political Change* (Cambridge: Cambridge University Press, 2003).

113. See Charles Hutzler, "China's New Generation of Leaders Keep a Low Profile as They Push for Reforms," *Wall Street Journal,* January 3, 2002.

114. Interview, Beijing, October 21, 2003.

115. Jiang Zemin, "Zai Qingzhu Zhongguo Gongchandang Chengwei Bashizhounian Dahui shang de Jianghua" [Jiang Zemin's Speech Celebrating the 80th Anniversary of the Founding of the Chinese Communist Party] in *Zhongguo Sixiang Zhengzhi Gongzuo Nianjian 2001* [2001 Yearbook on China's Ideological Political Work], ed. Editors (Beijing: Zhonggong Zhongyang Dangxiao chubanshe, 2002), 7–17.

116. Yu elaborates these concepts in "The Scientific Development Concept Is a World Outlook and Methodology for Seeking Faster and Better Development," *Jingji Ribao,* October 31, 2005, trans. OSC.

117. See *China's Peaceful Rise: Speeches of Zheng Bijian, 1997–2005* (Washington, D.C. Brookings Institution Press, 2006). A more extended collection of Zheng's speeches has been published by the CPS-affiliated China Reform Forum (2 vols.), of which he is chairman.

118. See Melanie Manion, *Retirement of Revolutionaries in China* (Princeton, N.J.: Princeton University Press, 1993).

119. See David Shambaugh, "The CCP's Fifteenth Congress: Technocrats in Command," *Issues & Studies,* January 1998, 1–37.

120. For excellent analyses of each meeting and the turnover of party elite personnel, see Li Cheng and Lynn White III, "The Sixteenth Central Committee of the Chinese Communist Party: Hu Gets What?" *Asian Survey,* 43, no. 4 (July–August 2003): 553–97; and H. Lyman Miller, "The 10th National People's Congress and China's Leadership Transition," *China Leadership Monitor,* no. 7 (Summer 2003): 1–8.

121. I am grateful to Alice Lyman Miller for these tabulations.

122. See Li and White, "Sixteenth Central Committee"; H. Lyman Miller, "The Sixteenth Party Congress and China's Political Processes," in *The Sixteenth CCP Congress and Leadership Transition in China,* Asia Program Special Report 105, ed. Gang Lin and Susan Shirk (Washington, D.C.: Woodrow Wilson International Center for Scholars, 2002); David M. Finkelstein and Maryanne Kivlehan, eds., *Chinese Leadership in the Twenty-First Century: The Rise of the Fourth Generation* (Armonk, N.Y.: M. E. Sharpe, 2002); and Joseph Fewsmith, "Generational Transition in China," *Washington Quarterly* 25, no. 4 (Autumn 2002): 23–36.

123. See David Shambaugh, "The Changing of the Guard: China's New Military Leadership," in *The New Chinese Leadership: Challenges and Opportunities After the 16th Party Congress,* ed. Yun-han Chu, Chih-cheng Lo, and Ramon H. Myers (Cambridge: Cambridge University Press, 2004).

124. See the discussion in Li and White, "Sixteenth Central Committee," 557.

125. Biography of Liu Yunshan, available at http://www.xinhuanet.com.

126. Gao Xin, *Lingdao Zhongguo de Xin Renwu: Zhonggong Shiliuju Zhengzhiju Weiyuan* [New Personalities Leading China: Members of the 16th CCP Politburo] (Hong Kong: Mingjing chubanshe, 2003), 492–95.

127. See Cheng Li, "Hu's Policy Shift and the *Tuanpai's* Coming of Age," *China Leadership Monitor,* no. 15 (Summer 2005): 1–16.

128. See Cheng Li, "One Party, Two Factions: Chinese Bipartisanship in the Making?" speech delivered at Carnegie Endowment conference "Behind the Bamboo Curtain: Chinese Leadership, Politics, and Policy, Washington, November 2, 2005; and Cheng Li, "China's Next Phase: Hu's New Deal?" *China Business Review,* May–June 2003, 48–52.

129. Ibid.

130. See Li Cheng, *China's Leaders: The New Generation* (Lanham, Md.: Roman & Littlefield, 2001).

131. On this subject, see Joseph Kahn, "China's Leader, Ex-Rival at Side, Solidifies Power," *New York Times,* September 25, 2005.

132. See Richard McGregor, "Cultivating the Countryside: Hu Takes Pains to Keep China Free from a Peasants' Revolt," *Financial Times,* September 8, 2005.

133. See Philip Pan, "Hu Tightens Party Grip on Power: Chinese Leader Seen as Limiting Freedoms," *Washington Post,* April 24, 2005.

134. See "Hu's in Charge," *The Economist,* August 18, 2005.

135. See "A New Push to Enforce the Unwritten Rules," *Financial Times,* September 8, 2005.

136. See, e.g., Hu Jintao, "Zai Quanguo Disanci 'San Jiang' Jiaoyu Gongzuo Huiyi shang de jianghua" [Hu Jintao's Speech at the Third National "Three Stresses" Education Work Conference], in *Xin Shiqi Dangde Jianshe de Chenggong Tansuo* [Explorations on the Successes of Party Construction in the New Era] (Beijing: Dangjian Duwu chubanjshe, 2000, *neibu ziliao, zhuyi baocun*).

137. This is also the observation of Willy Lam. See Willy Wo-Lap Lam, *Chinese Politics in the Hu Jintao Era: New Leaders, New Challenges* (Armonk, N.Y.: M. E. Sharpe, 2006), 249.

138. Interview with CCP member, Beijing, March 2005.

139. See Philip Pan, "China Plans to Honor a Reformer," *Washington Post,* September 9, 2005.

Notes to Chapter 8

1. See Andrew Walder, "The Party Elite and China's Trajectory of Change," *China: An International Journal* 2, no. 2 (September 2004): 189–209.

2. For elaboration, see David Shambaugh, *Modernizing China's Military: Progress, Problems, and Prospects* (Berkeley: University of California Press, 2003), chap. 2.

3. Ibid., chap. 4.

4. Lu Xiaobo, *Cadres and Corruption: The Organizational Involution of the Chinese Communist Party* (Stanford, Calif.: Stanford University Press, 2000); Melanie Manion, *Corruption by Design: Building Clean Government in Mainland China and Hong Kong* (Cambridge, Mass.: Harvard University Press, 2004).

5. See Andrew Walder, *Communist Neo-Traditionalism: Work and Authority in Chinese Industry* (Berkeley: University of California Press, 1986).

6. See David Shambaugh, "China's Propaganda System: Structure, Process, and Efficacy," *China Journal,* January 2006, 25–60.

7. Organization for Economic Cooperation and Development, *Governance in China* (Paris: Organization for Economic Cooperation and Development, 2005).

8. "Government Work Report Delivered by Wen Jiabao at NPC Session," trans. Open Source Center, March 5, 2007.

9. For more on this distinction, see James MacGregor Burns, *Leadership* (New York: Harper & Row, 1978); and James MacGregor Burns, *Transforming Leadership* (New York: Atlantic Monthly Press, 2003).

10. Bruce Dickson, "Populist Authoritarianism: The Future of the Chinese Communist Party," presentation to Carnegie Endowment for International Peace conference "Behind the Bamboo Curtain: Chinese Leadership, Politics, and Policy, Washington, November 2, 2005.

11. Robert Scalapino, "China in the Late Leninist Era," *China Quarterly,* December 1993, 949–71. This essay draws on Scalapino's earlier study, *The Last Leninists: The Uncertain Future of Asia's Communist States* (Washington, D.C.: Center for Strategic and International Studies, 1992).

12. Scalapino, "China in the Late Leninist Era," 963.

13. Ibid., 964.

14. Ibid., 965.

15. Richard Baum, "China after Deng: Ten Scenarios in Search of Reality," *China Quarterly,* March 1996, 153–75.

16. Ibid., 174.

17. Walder, "Party Elite," 205–6.

18. Ibid., 209.

19. Anthony Saich, "Political Change in China," *U.S.-China Relations* (Aspen Institute) 20, no. 3 (2005): 25–29.

20. Bruce Dickson, "The Future of the Chinese Communist Party: Strategies for Survival and Prospects for Change," in *Charting China's Future: Political, Social, and international Dimensions,* ed. Jae Ho Chung (Lanham, Md.: Roman & Littlefield, 2006).

21. Ibid.

22. Cheng Li, "China in the Year 2020: Three Political Scenarios," *Asia Policy,* no. 4 (2007): 20.

23. See Shambaugh, *Modernizing China's Military.*

24. See Kenneth Lieberthal, *U.S. Policy Towards China,* Brookings Policy Brief 72 (Washington, D.C.: Brookings Institution, 2001).

25. I am indebted to my graduate student, Daniel Melleby, for some of these suggestions; see his "Glaring Anachronism: The Communist Party's Search for Relevance in Modern China," seminar paper, Fall 2004.

26. See "Introduction," in *The Modern Chinese State,* ed. David Shambaugh (Cambridge: Cambridge University Press, 2000).

Index

accountability, 30, 180
adaptation: atrophy plus adaptation
    scenario, 177; biological metaphor, 5;
    four possible problems, 178; measures
    recommended, 38; optimists on,
    37–38; party reform, 103; political, 9;
    predictions of outcome, 5; propaganda
    system, 106; recruitment initiative, 35;
    reforms and readjustment, 4; relative
    balance with atrophy assessed,
    161–70; summarized, 39–40
adaptation phase, per Huntington, 34,
    167
adaptational reforms, 103
administrative management schools, 143
administrative state, 93
advanced forces in society, Three
    Represents, 111, 112
advanced nature of the party, 128–31,
    136, 151, 167
Afghanistan, Soviet occupation, 22, 72
agriculture, 64, 158; rural sector, 116;
    Vietnam, 84
alienation, 21, 27, 30
Andropov, Yuri, 67
armed forces,
Armenia, 91
arms race, 22, 77
Asian economies, lessons of, 77
Asian political parties, 92

atrophy issue, 3–4; atrophy as
    incremental, 39; atrophy plus
    adaptation scenario, 177; China
    specialists on, 24–25; comparison with
    former communist states' collapse,
    164; implosion, 17; party
    organizations, 7–8, 131; propaganda
    system, 106, 110; relative balance with
    adaptation assessed, 161–70;
    summarized, 39–40; symptoms, 5;
    tools of rule restrengthened, 175
authoritarian pluralism, 171
authoritarian regimes: dangers to, 17;
    from totalitarian to, 15;
    neoauthoritarianism, 29, 92, 172;
    resilience, 36, 38, 174, 176, 178;
    Singapore, 95; soft authoritarianism
    scenario, 173; transition as sui generis,
    39
authority, erosion of state, 28

Baltic states, 20
Beijing Youth Daily, 109
Belarus, 91
bianzhi system, 141
Bible study sessions, 146–47
Blair, Tony, 99
Bolivia, 98
borrowing culture, China as, 6
bourgeois liberalization, 44, 55, 158

Brezhnev Doctrine, 22
bribery, 80, 133
Brzczinski, Zbignicw, 12, 14–15, 185n21
Bulgaria, 47, 52
bureaucratism: criticisms of Soviet, 56; routinization in Soviet bloc, 21; stages, 14–15
Bush, George W., 90

cadre management schools, 143
cadre management system, 80; evaluation norms, 142–43; improving cadre competence, 140–43; midcareer training, 136, 141, 143, 149–51, 165; Party School system, 143–48; qualities preferred, 140; regulations, 141–42; Scientific Development System, 120
cadre training academies, 148–49
Cai Dingjian, 93–95, 203n42
campaign financing, 100
capitalism with a human face, 98
Castro, Fidel, 84, 85–86
CCP Propaganda Department (CCPPD), 107, 108, 167. See also propaganda system
CCP. See Chinese Communist Party
CDIC. See Central Discipline Inspection Commission of the Central Committee
Ceauşescu, Nicholas and Elena, 47
CELAP. See China Executive Leadership Academy Pudong
censorship, 107
Central Asian republics, 87–92
Central Directive No. 21 of 1990, 48
Central Discipline Inspection Commission of the Central Committee (CDIC), 131–34; dual leadership system, 133
Central Editing and Translation Bureau, 52, 193–94n48
Central Leading Group for Advanced Nature Education, 130
Central Military Commission (CMC), 155
Central Party School (CPS): cadres

served, 149; cadre training academies, 148; curriculum, 149; described, 149 51; entrepreneurs and business-people, 150; fields of instruction, 144; ideological indoctrination, 144; Institute of Strategic Studies, 89, 90; midcareer cadre training, 149–51; on people's sovereignty, 100; personnel training, 143; researchers, 53, 68, 70, 78, 81, 96, 111, 122, 123, 139, 140; role, 144; Scientific Development Concept, 119; think tank for reform policies, 144, 150. See also Party School system
Chávez, Hugo, 98
checks and balances, 179
Cheng Li, 156, 174
Cheng Su, 151
Chen Liangyu, 154
Chen Xiangyang, 89
Chen Yun, 48
Chi Haotian, 57, 194n70
Chile, 98
China, as remaining communist party-state, xiii
China Central Television (CCTV), 57, 109
China Executive Leadership Academy Pudong (CELAP), 148–49
China Institute of Contemporary International Relations (CICIR), 88, 89
China Institute of International Strategic Studies, 89
China Reform Forum, 139, 141
Chinese Academy of Sciences, 93
Chinese Academy of Social Sciences, 100
Chinese Communist Party (CCP): in 1989, 42–45; advanced nature of, 128–31; Chang's midterm assessment, 27; competing agendas/factions, 156–57; corruption, 80; as focus of this study, 1; general line, 53; as hollow institution, 25; impact of color revolutions, 92; as institution, 1, 3;

Kuomintang compared, 33, 34; predictions, 174; principal challenges, 102; real challenge to, 169; reinvention, 104; Singapore party compared, 94–95; specific lessons from Soviet collapse, 80–81; three main problems, 29; triad of power, 165; use of term, 183n1; value of being adaptable and flexible, 104. *See also* noncommunist parties in China; party reform

Chinese culture, new concepts in ideology, 105. *See also* Confucian political culture

Chinese People's Political Consultative Congress (CPPCC), 137–38, 180

Chinese solution, 46

Christians, 146–47

CIA: analyses, 12, 184n5; espionage training and NGOs, 90

CICIR. *See* China Institute of Contemporary International Relations

citizen empowerment, 180

citizen participation, benefits of, 122

civil society: control strategies, 36–37, 168; GDR, 20; not analyzed, 50; rise of, 20

clans, 27

coercion: civil society, 168; Hu-Wen era, 158; as insufficient, 5; legitimacy issues, 3, 7; longevity and, 40; party monopoly of, 175–76

coercive factors in implosion, 16, 18t–19t, 65–73; China in comparison, 163t–64t; summarized, 62t–63t

Cold War, scholarly focus, 11

collapse of Chinese system: Chang on disintegration, 26–27; failure to, 23–24; implosion potential, 26; potential analyzed, 32; predictions, 26

collapse of communist states (1989–91): causes of, 12–13; China's failure to, 23–24; CIA on, 12; confluence of factors, 22; "period of shock" after, 82; scholarly views, 12–13, 15

collapse of other party-states, systematic assessments after, 2

collapse of the USSR. *See* USSR collapse/implosion

Colleges of Socialism, 144, 145

color revolutions, 87–92

command economies, 17, 64

Committee to Protect Journalists, 110

Commonwealth of Independent States (CIS), 89, 91

communist fascism, 52

communist parties, Western European, 100

Communist Party of China. *See* Chinese Communist Party (CCP)

Communist Party of the Soviet Union (CPSU): collapse, 77; democracy discourse, 121; emphasis on weaknesses, 54; failures in "propaganda work," 67; Gorbachev erosion (steps), 69–70; ideological dogmatism, 67, 77; lessons from collapse, 79; membership composition, 71; need for reform of, 69; perquisites, 72; Twenty-Seventh Congress, 56; undermining political hegemony of, 68–69

communist party-state, Chinese: buffers, 32–33; challenges to, 32; debates over control exercised, 38

communist party-states: causes of implosion, 15–22; criticized, 50; evolution, 13–15; learning from, 9, 13; organized dependence, 20; popular cynicism and alienation, 21; problems in, 20

communist-type political systems, functions, xi

Communist Youth League (CYL), 154, 155, 159

Community of Democracies, 91–92

comparative communist studies: American Council of Learned Societies, 183n1; Cold War era, 11; collapse of, xiii; described, 11; remaining party-states, xiii; usefulness of paradigm, 13

comparative perspective, 23–25
competition, political, 179
competitive initiatives, 179–81
Confucian political culture, 6, 116;
    personnel system, 142. *See also*
    Chinese culture
Congress Party (India), 96
consultation with the public, 139
consultative democracy, 122–23
consultative Leninism, 33–34, 175, 180
control by CCP: decline considered, 3–4;
    erosion, 32
co-optation strategies, 35, 37, 150, 155,
    156; civil society, 168. *See also* Hu
    Jintao, political alignments
corporatism, 37, 97
corruption: assessed, 166; causes, 8;
    CDIC, 132; collusion of local officials,
    30; CPSU critiqued, 72; dangers, 134;
    dangers of, 80; implosion predictions,
    26; as "life and death" issue, 131–32,
    166; market reforms, 17; mechanisms
    of supervision, 132; new measures,
    134; officials removed, 134, 212n32;
    party building, 131–34; party
    dynamics, 29; ruling capacity related,
    125; three systemic flaws, 166
coup d'état scenario, 176
CPPCC. *See* Chinese People's Political
    Consultative Congress
CPS. *See* Central Party School
criminal activity, 133
Cuba, 82, 84–86; Chinese research, 71;
    as remaining communist party-state,
    xiii
Cuban Communist Party, 84–86
cultural factors in implosion, 16, 18t–19t,
    73–74; China in comparison, 163t;
    summarized, 62t–63t
Cultural Revolution generation, 154
cultures, diversity of, 101
Czechoslovakia, 20, 45, 47, 52

decay, as a progressive condition, 39
decentralized state predation, 30–31
Decision of the CPC Central Committee

*on Enhancing the Party's Ruling
    Capacity* (2004), 60
*Decision on the Enhancement of the
    Party's Governing Capacity,* 124–27,
    128
delegation diplomacy, 57
democracy: with Chinese characteristics,
    120–24; Chinese opinion, 37; consul-
    tative, 122–23; electoral, 122–23;
    electoral accountability, 95; Hu on,
    115–16; incremental, 121–22;
    intraparty, 121; long wait for, 123;
    orderly, 122; predictions, 172, 174–75;
    role in Singapore, 93–95; socialism
    related, 123–24; use of term, 121; Wen
    on, 123–24; Western assumptions
    about reform, 2–3
democracy promotion, 89–90, 92
democratic breakthrough, 28, 40
democratic centralism, 66, 139
Democratic People's Republic of Korea.
    See North Korea
"democratic space," 178
democratization: Gorbachev on, 70–71;
    predictions, 28, 173, 174–75; response
    to notion, 37
demonstrations in 1989: explaining
    causes, 43–44; goals of demon-
    strators, 43; martial law, 45; use of
    force, 59
demonstrations, in Eastern Europe, 51
Deng Xiaoping: challenges in 1989,
    42–43, 47; democracy discourse, 121;
    on events in Eastern Europe, 45–46;
    on failed Soviet coup, 57–58; on
    Gorbachev, 48; intellectuals
    reclassified, 112; leadership turnover,
    152; leftist thinking critiques, 53;
    party-to-party relations, 98–99;
    reforms and ideology, 105; Southern
    Tour, 53; theory in provincial party
    schools, 146
deterioration, pace of, 39
Ding Xiaoxing, 88
diploma-for-fee schemes, 146
direct democracy, 122

discipline inspection officers, 133. *See also* party discipline
disintegration, signs of, 26–27
Djilas, Milovan, 71
Dong Deguang, 151
DVD set, eight-volume, on historical lessons, 42
dynamic stability, 177–78

East Asia, 33, 97
Eastern Europe, collapse of: changes analyzed, 49–50; Gorbachev's "New Thinking Diplomacy," 68; immediate assessment, 48; impact assessed, 49; interpreting, 45–53; later set of analyses, 52–53; learning from, 126; party line, 48; repetitive pattern seen, 52
Eastern Europe, Russia, and Central Asia Institute (CASS), 64, 77
eclectic state, 6, 101–2, 181
economic determinism thesis, 55
economic factors: China in comparison, 162t; China and Soviet bloc compared, 33; corporatism and cooptation, 37; in implosion, 16, 18t–19t, 62t–63t, 64–65; Scientific Development Concept, 119–20; Three Represents, 112
economic growth: rising expectations, 7; as source of legitimacy, 3, 103; stagnation, 29; three stages, 14
economic reform: governance reforms, 32; key components, 83; North Korea, 82, 83; political reform related, 30; social democracy, 99–100; Vietnam, 83–84
economic reform diplomacy, 83
elections, local, 139
electoral democracy, 122–23
Eleventh Five-Year Program, 117–18
elites, 35–36; circulation of, 35–36; elite-based party, 29, 112, 157; fractured, 28; predictions, 175
émigré scholars, 26–31
end of history paradigm, 12, 36

Enlightenment tradition, 92
entrepreneurial class. *See* private-sector entrepreneurs
environmental issues, 117
ethnicity issue, former Soviet bloc, 20, 76
executions, 133–34
external posture, China specialists on, 24, 187n4
extraparty consultation and supervision, 137–38

factional alignments: elite factions, 157, 165; Hu Jintao, 154, 155–56
fascist-type scenarios, 173, 176–77
Feng Yujun, 91
five-year programs, 117–18
focus of this study, 1
foreign journalists, 48–49
foreign policy, U.S. and European compared, 101
fragile regime thesis, 25
freedom, meaning viewed, 44
freedom of press, meaning viewed, 44

G-7 nations, 45
gangs, 27
Gao Di, 58–60
Gao Fang, 66
GDP index, 142
GDR. *See* German Democratic Republic
general line, 53; research on collapse of other party-states, 2
Geng Sude, 146–47
George Soros Foundation, 50
German Democratic Republic (GDR, East Germany), 20, 21, 45, 46; collapse analyzed, 51–52
Germany, 99
glasnost, 51, 58, 59, 67, 180; "eight negations" and, 68
globalization: CCP control, 3–4; media control, 107, 108; Mexico's PRI, 97; propaganda system and, 106, 107, 108; regime change, 29; Three Represents, 113

Golkar Party (Indonesia), 96–97
Gorbachev, Mikhail: Beijing visit, 56, 57; China's political climate, 55; controls on government and military, 165; criticisms, 48, 59; early praise for, 56; East Germany, 20; economic reforms, 65; "humanistic and democratic socialism," 67, 81; ideological deviation, 67–68, 105; implosion causes, 16, 55; inner-party reforms, 138–39; media reforms, 81; openings too rapid, 180; reforms misguided, 70; steps usurping CPSU rule, 69–70; warning by, 70–71; Western analyses on, 2
governance challenges, 6–7
governance crisis thesis, 29–32
governing capacity, 124–27., *See also* ruling capacity
grassroots party building, 71
grassroots party cells, 80; rebuilding local party apparatus, 134–37; rectification campaign, 130; ruling capacity related, 125
Great Harmony concept, 116
Guangdong province, 83
guanxi (connections), culture of, 80, 166
guided democracy, 93

Havel, Václav, 47
hegemony, 28
He Guoquiang, 148, 156
He Qinglian, 107
He Quigang, 80
Honecker, Erich, 46
Hong Kong-like model, 173, 179
Hong Zhaolong, 66
household responsibility system, 84
Hou Shaowen, 151
Huang Ju, 154
Huang Weiding, 80
Huang Zongliang, 71–72
Hua Qing, 99
Hu Jintao: accommodationist approach, 180; background, 153, 154–56; cadre training, 143; consultation reforms, 180; consultative mechanisms, 34; core themes, 169; on Cuba, 85; on democracy, 121; "democratic space," 178; factional alignments, 154, 155–56; Hu-Wen leadership characterized, 157–60, 169; inner-party democracy, 138; on inner-party supervision, 132; media crackdown, 107, 158; on multiparty systems, 139; "New Deal," 32; noncommunist parties, 137–38; on noncommunist party-states, 87; organizational reforms, 131; party turnover, 153; on personnel policy, 120; Putin warning on NGOs, 91; reinstitutionalization under, 33; on ruling capacity, 115; Scientific Development Concept, 115, 119–20; Socialist Harmonious Society, 115–19, 150–51; social policy, 118–19; Three Represents, 114–15; Zeng and party ruling capacity, 125
Hungary, 20, 43, 46; collapse analyzed, 51
Huntington, Samuel, 34, 167
Hu Yanxin, 67
Hu Yaobang, 55, 98, 121, 152, 159
hybrid party, 6, 178

identity crisis, 29
ideological campaigns, recent, summarized, 106
ideological terminology (*tifa*), 105
ideology: alternative approaches, 105; crisis of, 104; as post hoc rationalization, 105; reforms, 104–6; role in policy process, 105
implosion of communist party-states: categories of factors, 15–16, 18t–19t; causes, 15–22; clusters of factors (listed), 16; states listed, 185–86n22; tables summarizing factors, 18t–19t, 62t–63t
income disparity/distribution, 116, 117
incremental democracy, 121–22
incumbency, power of, 94

India, 77, 96
Indonesia, 96–97
industrialization/industries, 6, 7, 13, 51, 62t, 64, 84, 113
inner-party corruption: as indiscipline, 131; Soviet bloc, 20
inner-party democracy: bipartisanship scenario, 174; Cuba, 85; Gorbachev critiqued, 68–69, 71; improving, 81; reforms to improve, 138–40, 151
Institute of East European and Central Asian Studies, 49
Institute of the History of the International Communist Movement, 53
Institute of International Studies, 79
Institute of Russian and Central Asian Studies (CASS), 53, 193n35
Institute of Soviet and East European Studies, 49
Institute of World Socialism, 52, 53, 66, 78, 104, 194n48
institutionalization, 36
Institutional Revolutionary Party (PRI, Mexico), 76, 97
intellectual property rights, 158
intellectuals: in East Europe, 50; private-sector, 112; reclassifying, 112; self-censorship, 107 8
intelligence: on Eastern Europe, 51; functions of think tanks, 49; U.S., 90
interest articulation, 168
internal discourse, 54
internal scene, China specialists on, 24, 187n4
International Communist Movement Research Institute, 52, 194n48
International Department (CCP), 53, 79, 82, 83, 85, 98; on social democratic parties, 100
international factors in implosion, 16, 18t–19t; China in comparison, 164t; summarized, 62t
Internet users, 107; monitoring, 107, 110, 158
intraparty democracy, 121

intraparty reforms, assessments triggering, 2
issue politics, 151

Japan, 96
Jia Guobiao, 108
Jiang Changbin, 81
Jiang Li, 89
Jiang Qinglin, 154
Jiang Zemin: on 1989 demonstrations, 44, 47; factional alignments, 154–55; on failed Soviet coup, 57; on Gorbachev, 48; growth emphasis, 118; organizational reforms, 131; on party membership, 34; reinstitutionalization under, 33; in retirement, 157–58; suppression of demands, 180; third generation, 152; Three Represents policy, 111–15, 150; well-off society, 115
Jingganshan Academy, 148
journalism, 110; newspaper closures, 206n10
journals, comparative communism, 11, 12, 183n2

Khrushchev, Nikita, 35, 60–61, 66, 67
Kim Jong Il, 82–83
Krenz, Egon, 45, 46
Kuomintang: failure of, 96; present-day CCP compared, 33, 34
Kyrgyzstan, 88

Labor Party (Britain), 99
laissez-faire liberalism, 92
language studies, 11
Laos, 82
Latin American corporatist systems, 97
Latin Americanization, 7
leadership: critique of USSR, 152; Deng's reforms, 152; party committees, 141; ruling capacity related, 125; split in 1989, 42; tension after Romanian coup, 47–48; view of future, 169; Zhao on succession, 57

leadership succession: assessed, 164–65; Cultural Revolution generation, 154; Deng's role, 152; fifth generation, 165, 169; fourth generation, 35, 153, 154, 169; Hu-Wen era, 159–60; one-party states, 8; retirement norms, 35–36, 152; Soviet, 70; third generation, 152, 164–65; turnover, 35–36, 152–53, 153t, 164–65; Zhao on, 57

Lee Kuan Yew, 93

leftist thinking critiques, 53

legitimacy: CCP's operation, 8; coercion, 3; crisis seen, 28; justifying control, 28; political reform, 33; rising expectations, 7; sources of, 3; staying in power and, 102

Leninism: atrophy, 167; cadre training, 144; changes to, 103; civil society, 36–37; as comparative lens, 13; Confucian political culture, 6; consultative, 33–34; corporatism, 28; in CPPCC, 137; discipline, 131; essence of party, 127; governance challenges, 6–7; Hu's approach, 158–59; local level, 134; reinstitutionalization, 33; Singapore, 94; transitions, 39

lessons for China from Soviet collapse, 38, 41, 54, 76–77, 125, 126; in *Decision...on Party's Ruling Capacity,* 60, 125–26; longevity, 1–3; party organization atrophied, 7–8, 131; postmortem, 59; third phase analysis, 55

Liao Xilong, 155

Liberal Democratic Party (LDP, Japan), 96

liberalism, political, 28

liberalization, political, 29

Li Changchun, 155

Li Cheng, 157

Li Jingjie, 61, 76–77

Li Jingyu, 77

Li Junru, 122–23, 151

Li Keqiang, 155

Li Liangdong, 151

Li Peng, 47, 152

Liu Binjie, 109

Liu Fengyan, 132

Liu Ji, 111, 121

Liu Jianfei, 89, 90, 91 92

Liu Shaoqi, 121

Liu Yandong, 156

Liu Yunshan, 155, 156

living standards, 5, 6, 60, 62t, 74, 76, 77, 79, 118, 159; assessed, 167–68

Li Wen, 93

Li Xueju, 156

Li Yuanchao, 155

Li Zhengju, 78

Li Zhilun, 156

lobbyists, 100–101

local party apparatus, 134–37. *See also* grassroots party cells

local party committees, 135, 166

longevity of CCP: author's perspective, 174–81; Cuba, 84–85; hybrid party, 6; Japan's LDP, 96; lessons for, 1–3; Mexico's PRI, 97; one-party states, 4–5; predictions, 170–74; Singapore, 93; Soviet bloc examples, 4–5

Lu Nanquan, 55, 64, 66

Mahathir bin Mohammad, 95–96

Malaysia, 95–96

malfeasance: party support and, 26; provincial parties schools, 146–47

Maoism: predictions, 177; propaganda system, 106; provincial parties schools, 146

Mao Xianglin, 85

Mao Zedong, 61, 129; lack of comparisons to era, 67; North Korea compared, 83

market economy: economic reform impact, 20; Eleventh Five-Year Program, 117; Gorbachev reforms, 56; Hu-Wen reforms, 158; incentives compared, 114; legitimacy crises, 8; media impact, 108–9, 110–11; predictions, 171, 176; regime change, 29; rent-seeking, 17, 19t; Soviet failures, 64; Three Represents, 113

martial law, 45

Marxist-Leninist doctrine: alternatives to, 168–69; Cuba, 85; dilution of, 26; evolution of, 17; nationalism replacing, 167; new concepts, 105; in provincial party schools, 146; reform related, 104; Stalinism, 66

Ma Shufang, 77

masses' accusation centers, 134

media: advanced nature of party campaign, 129; conglomerates, 109; control compared to Gorbachev, 81; control under Hu-Wen, 158; control in U.S., 101; on failed Soviet coup, 57–58; foreign investment in, 109; investigative journalism, 110; outline of propaganda system, 106–7; silent on East Germany and Hungary, 46; Soviet control, 81; U.S. in Central Asia, 90–91

Mexico, 76, 97

midcareer training of party cadres, 136, 141, 143, 149–51, 165

migrant population, 130

Miles, James, 50

military, Chinese, 165. *See also* People's Liberation Army

military, Soviet bloc, 21, 72

military-industrial complex: in China, 64; in Soviet bloc, 17, 72; U.S., 92

military intervention scenario, 172, 173

military rule, one-party states, 97

Ministry of Supervision (MOS), 132–33

mobile telephone users, 107

modernization: lessons for Chinese, 77; predictions, 170; problems associated, 8; rising expectations, 7

muddling through scenario, 172, 173

"multiparty cooperation," 137–38

multiparty system, as option, 139

Nathan, Andrew, 190n63

National Bureau of Corruption Prevention, 133

National Defense Law (1997), 165

National Defense University, 69

National Democratic Institute (U.S.), 50

National Endowment for Democracy (NED, U.S.), 50

nationalism: replacing Marxism, 167; as source of legitimacy, 3, 103; Soviet bloc, 20

National People's Congress (NPC), 179

neoauthoritarianism, 29, 92, 172

neocolonialism, 22

neoconservatism, 92, 172, 177

neo-Maoist revival scenario, 172

New Labor, 99

newly industrialized countries, 13, 168, 169, 171, 180

nomenklatura system: China, 141; USSR, 56, 71–72

noncommunist parties in China, 137–38, 175, 178–79, 179–80

noncommunist party states: color revolutions, 87–92; Hu on, 87; lessons summarized, 6; reasons to study, 102; views of, 92–101

nongovernmental organizations (NGOs), 88, 90, 91

nonideological authoritarianism, 15

North Korea, 81–83; as remaining communist party-state, xiii

one-party states: Asia and military, 97; Asian political parties, 92; China as wonder, 27; competitive constituencies, 174–75; Huntington typology, 34; inner-party reforms, 139; intrinsic problems, 8; leadership succession, 8; longevity, 4–5; military rule, 97; noncommunist party states, 87; predictions, 175; Taiwan and Mexico, 76

Open Door policy, 98

Open the West campaign, 158

optimists, about CCP as political system, 25, 32–38

orange revolution, 88

orderly democracy, 122

organizational reforms: advanced nature of, 128, 136; assessed, 165–66; lessons from USSR, 131

organization of the book, 9–10
Organization Department (CCP), 53,
    114, 128, 130, 140; assessed, 167;
    cadre approval, 141; cadre training,
    144; cadre training academies, 148;
    described, 141; hotline complaints
    number, 134; local party cells, 135,
    136; Party Building Institute, 130;
    party personnel assignments, 141–43;
    trips to Russia and Cuba, 71
organized dependence, 20
Ostpolitik, 20, 21, 22
Ouyang Song, 130

Pang Yuanzheng, 151
PAP. *See* People's Action Party
    (Singapore)
parliamentary systems, 100
party cell formation, 71
party discipline, 131–34; Central
    Discipline Inspection Commission of
    the Central Committee, 131–32
party membership: assessed, 165–66;
    party survivability, 35; rectification
    campaign, 129–30; tactics, 35;
    "unqualified," 130
party organizations, atrophy, 7–8, 131
party privileges, Soviet, 72
party reform: adaptation, 103; assess-
    ments triggering, 2; dynamic stability,
    178; Three Represents, 112–13
party rule, instruments of, 106
Party School system: 143–48, 215n91;
    cadre midcareer training, 141;
    categories of cadres targeted, 145;
    Five Contemporaries, 146; provincial
    level, 145–46, 216n106;
    subprovincial-level party schools, 145;
    think tank and incubator of reform
    ideas, 144, 150; Three Basics, 146. *See
    also* Central Party School (CPS)
party of the whole people concept, 61
patronage systems, 29
"peaceful evolution" efforts by Western
    countries, 50, 55, 59; as cause of
    collapse, 77; Central Asia, 88–91;

Gorbachev's "humanitarianism," 68;
    three aspects, 88–91
People's Action Party (PAP, Singapore),
    93–95, 140, 178
People's Congress, 151
People's Daily, 58, 109, 129
People's Liberation Army (PLA), 53, 69,
    152, 165, 176
People's University, 99
perestroika, 67
personality, cult of, 82–83
personnel policy: meritocratic, 151; party
    monopoly, 175; Scientific
    Development Concept (Hu), 120
Peru, 98
pessimists, about CCP as political
    system, 25–32, 39
Philippines, 97
"playing line balls," 109–10
pluralistic politics, 15, 68, 171, 178
Poland: 20, 43, 45, 50, 191n13; collapse
    analyzed, 51
political change, possible scenarios,
    170–74
political culture, skeptical, 21
political determinism thesis, 55
political factors in implosion, 16,
    18t–19t, 65–73; China in comparison,
    162t–63t, 164; summarized, 62t–63t
political fission scenario, 172
political protection racket, 114; CPS
    seminars as, 150
political reform: debates over, 38, 151;
    described, 37; economic reform
    related, 30; Hu-Wen era, 159;
    incremental, 181; Soviet bloc, 20;
    status of CCP, 33; Vietnam, 84
popular cynicism and alienation, 21, 108,
    166
populism, 95, 156, 158, 169–70, 174
post-communist authoritarianism, 15
post-communist pluralism, 15
post-mobilization regimes, 14
postsecondary education, 147, 147f
post-totalitarian transition, 14
power, nature of, 101

pragmatism, 101
predatory autocracy, 30–31
presidents compared, 100
prime ministers, 100
private-sector entrepreneurs, 34–35, 112;
    CPS seminars and courses, 150; party
    cells, 135, 136
privatizations, 114
professional groups, 134
proletarian political party, 126
propaganda system: adaptation amid
    atrophy, 106–11; atrophied, 110; CCP
    Propaganda Department (CCPPD),
    107, 108, 167; loosening/tightening,
    106; party rule, 106; scope of
    oversight, 106
provincial-level party schools, 145–46,
    216n106
public administration school system, 144
public feedback, 136
public goods, 6, 7, 20, 30, 180
publishing industry, 108–9
Pudong Academy, 148–49
Putin, Vladimir, 91

Qian Qichen, 58
Qiao Shi, 47, 165
Qi Yu, 128
Qi Zhi, 89
questions raised in this book, 1–2

rationalism, 101
recruitment initiative: adaptation, 35;
    advanced productive forces, 112;
    opening up, 113; private-sector
    entrepreneurs, 34–35, 112, 114, 136;
    recent results, 114
rectification campaign, 129–30
Reddaway, Peter, 184n9
redistribution, 7
reform: efficacy, 2–3; goal of, 3; liberal,
    98; proactive, 2
reform policies: reasons summarized, 41;
    scholarly focus on, 41–42
reform-readjust-reform-readjust cycles,
    104

regime change, four pathways, 28–29
*Regulations on the Selection and
    Appointment of Party and Government
    Leading Cadres* (2002), 142
reinstitutionalization, 33–34
renewal process, 38
Renmin (People's) University, 79
rent-seeking: local party committees,
    135; market economy, 17, 19t; reasons
    for, 166
Reporters without Borders, 110
resilient authoritarianism, 36
retirement norms for party leaders,
    35–36, 152
revitalization process, 38
revolutionary party, ruling party and, 33
revolution of rising expectations, 7,
    167–68, 169
Romania, 21, 22, 47, 52
rose revolution, 88
rule of law, Hu on, 115–16
ruling capacity: assessed, 166–67, 168;
    cadre training academies, 148;
    Decision..., 60, 127–7, 128; Hu on,
    115; legitimacy and staying in power,
    102; pressures rising, 180; Scientific
    Development Concept, 120;
    strengthening party's governing
    capacity, 124–27, 151
ruling party: CCP as, 103; CCP as party
    of elites, 112; core themes, 169;
    Europe, 100; India, 96; Indonesia,
    96–97; revolutionary party evolving,
    33; in Singapore, 94
Russia, 71, 89, 91
Russian Federal Security Bureau, 91

SARS crisis (2003), 108, 156, 158
Scientific Development Concept, 115,
    119–20, 151, 156
secret police/security services, 21
self-censorship, 107–8
Self-Strengtheners (1870s), 169
separating party and state principle, 69,
    165
Seventeenth Party Congress, 36

Shanghai bang (clique), 152, 154
Shevardnadze, Eduard, 88
Shi Taifeng, 151
Shi Zhongyun, 91
Singapore, 92–95, 140
Singaporean Model, 93–95
Sino-Soviet schism, 61, 153
Sixteenth Party Congress, political
    initiatives, 33
skeptical political cultures, 21
smuggling cases, 133
social democratic parties, 52, 68, 98–100
Social Democratic Party (Germany), 99
social factors in implosion, 16, 18t–19t;
    China in comparison, 163t;
    summarized, 62t–63t
social groups, 134, 136
social inequities: Hu's vision, 116; im-
    plosion predictions, 27; modernization
    and, 7; regional differences, 114–15;
    resentment, 114; social goals, 117–19
Socialist Harmonious Society, 115–19,
    151, 156, 168–69
Socialist Unity Party (GDR), 20
social stratification, 116
social unrest: in April and June 1989,
    42–45; Deng on, 46; implosion
    predictions, 27; inequities and,
    116–17; popular support, 37; Soviet
    bloc, 22; stable unrest, 32
socioeconomic weaknesses: capacity to
    manage, 27; threat considered, 3
soft authoritarianism scenario, 173
Solidarity trade union movement, 50
Solovyev, N. N., 58
Soros, George, 50, 91
South Korea, 97
Soviet bloc: Eastern Europe, collapse of,
    45–53; failure of reforms, 42; learning
    from failure of, 126; stages, 36;
    terminal symptoms, 39
Soviet and East European Studies, 48,
    192n26
special interests, 80
stability issues, 177–78
stage theories, 13–14, 36

stagnation scenario, 176
stagnation thesis, 26, 31
Stalinist model/legacy, 52, 61; foreign
    policy, 66; totalitarianism, 65–66
Stalin-Soviet Socialist model, 66
State Council, 132–33, 137, 141, 165
state incapacitation, 30
state incapacity thesis, 29–32
state-owned industrial sector, 113
State Press and Publications Committee,
    91
static stability, 177–78
status quo continuance scenario, 170–71,
    173
strong China paradigm, 24
subprovincial-level party schools, 145
Sweden, 50
Syria, 97
systemic collapse scenario, 175–76

Taiwan, 76, 96; diplomatic recognition in
    Latin America, 98. *See also*
    Kuomintang
Taiwan issue, 92
Tajikistan, 91
technocracy, 71
technocrats, 152, 153
television, 57, 109, 205n7
Thailand, 97
Third Way, 99
Three Represents policy, 34, 111–15,
    136, 151, 156, 167, 168–69
Tiananmen demonstrations: assessments
    changing, 57; impact, 45. *See also*
    demonstrations in 1989
tipping point scenario, 175
totalitarian bureaucratic phase, 14
totalitarianism, Soviet, 65–67
transition, democratic, 139–40
transparency of decision making, 136,
    168, 180
trapped transition thesis, 31

Ukraine, 88
United Front Department, 144, 145,
    155–56

united front tools, 138
United Kingdom, 50, 99
United Malays National Organization (UNMO), 95–96, 178
United Nations, China's role, 92
United States: analyzing USSR, 54; democracy promotion, 89–90, 92; European parties compared, 100–101; European worldview compared, 101; multiparty democracy advocated, 122; neoconservatives, 92; role in color revolutions, 88; subversive intentions (1989), 44
USSR: economic reforms, 56; media control, 81; U.S. foreign policy analyses, 54
USSR collapse/implosion: agreement over factors, 54; cause analyzed, 53–60; CCP inner-party reforms, 138; CCP postmortems, 2, 4, 58–63, 125, 151; Chinese analysis (timeline), 55f; comparison with China, 161, 162t–64t, 164–68; economic factors, 16, 18t–19t, 62t–63t, 64–65; eight-volume DVD set on, 42; failed coup d'état, 57–58, 73; four categories of factors, 60–61, 62t–63t; imperial overstretch, 21–22; internal causes, 77; international factors, 16, 18t–19t, 62t, 74–75; lessons, 38, 41, 54, 76–79, 125, 126; more postmortems, 60–63; most important factor, 104; phases of discourse on, 55; political and coercive factors, 16, 18t–19t, 62t–63t, 67–73; predictions, 184n9; problems, 20–21; radical critiques, 56; role of ideology, 105; social and cultural factors, 16, 18t–19t, 62t–63t, 73–74; specific lessons for CCP, 80–81, 125, 126; systemic causes, 60; Three Represents, 113; unforeseen, 4–5. *See also* collapse of communist states (1989–91)

Velvet Revolution, 50
Venezuela, 98

Vietnam, 82, 83–84; as remaining communist party-state, xiii
Vietnamese Communist Party (VCP), 83–84
vulnerabilities of system, debates, 38

Wang Changjiang, 68–69, 151
Wang Huanchao, 151
Wang Huning, 111
Wang Ruoshui, 67
Wang Tingda, 130
Wang Weiguang, 150, 151
Wang Xuedong, 52, 104
Wang Zhen, 48
Wen Jiabao, 32, 114–15, 119–20, 123–24, 151; background, 153; consultation reforms, 180; core themes, 169; "democratic space," 178; Hu relationship, 155, 156; Hu-Wen leadership characterized, 157–60, 169; social services, 169
Western countries: causes for Soviet collapse, 60; fall of Eastern Europe, 48; Hu on, 158; "peaceful evolution" efforts, 50; social democracy to be avoided, 81; subversive intentions (1989), 44
Western Europe: social democratic parties, 52, 68, 98–100; U.S. parties compared, 100–101; U.S. worldview compared, 101
World Trade Organization, 158
Wu Bangguo, 154
Wu Guanzheng, 85, 155
Wu Zhongmin, 151

xianjianxing campaign, 140–41
Xie Chuntao, 151
Xie Zhiqiang, 151
Xinhua News Agency, 57, 129
Xu Kui, 65
Xu Zhixin, 64

Yan'an Academy, 148
Yang brothers, 165
Yang Shangkun, 47

Yan Shuhan, 151
Yao Yiln, 43–44, 46
yellow (tulip) revolution, 87
Yeltsin, Boris, 57, 58, 59
Yugoslavia, 20, 22
Yu Keping, 121–22
Yu Yanyao, 134, 151

Zeng Peiyan, 154
Zeng Qinghong, 125–26, 140, 148, 151, 154, 156, 157, 159
Zhang Baoshun, 155
Zhang Jialin, 55

Zhang Xixian, 151
Zhao Yao, 70
Zhao Ziyang, 55, 98, 152; "humanism" advocated, 67; memorial at death, 159; party-state separation, 165; purged, 42, 43; reform debates, 56–57
Zheng Bijian, 113, 139, 151
Zheng Yifan, 66
Zhongnanhai, 47
Zhou Tianyong, 139–40, 151
Zhuang Congsheng, 151
Zhu Fu'en, 151